Torrington Uncovered

A guide and brief history

Moira Brewer

Moira Brewer .

Creedy Publishing
DEVON

First published 2013
Creedy Publishing
Creedy House
Warren Lane
Torrington
Devon EX38 8DP

ISBN 978-0-9528446-8-6

© Moira Brewer

Reprinted November 2013

Torrington Uncovered

A guide and brief history

Moira Brewer

Cover photograph by Thomas Andrews
courtesy of Linda Downing

Typeset, printed and bound by
Lazarus Press
Caddsdown Business Park
Bideford
Devon
EX39 3DX
www.lazaruspress.com

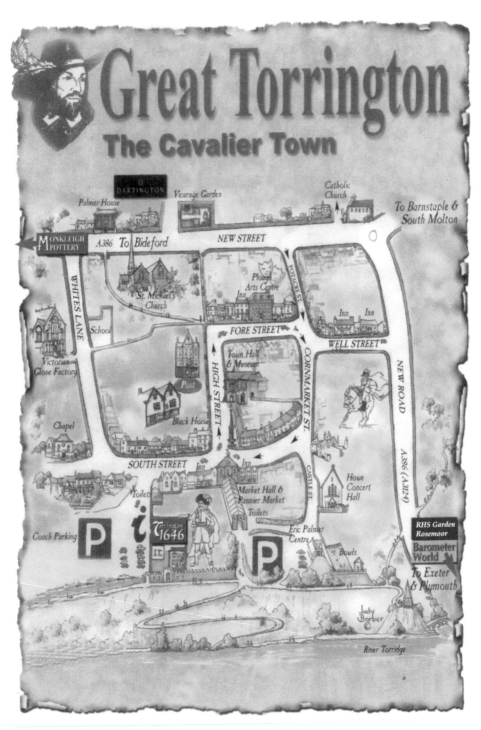

Map by Judy Barber courtesy of Graeme Barber

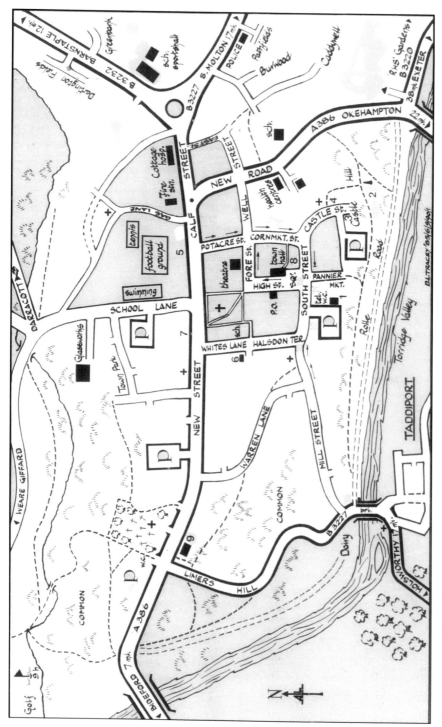

Pictorial map of Great Torrington based on an original by Denis Tracey.

Key: 1. Library, 1646, TIC. • 2. Waterloo Monument. • 3. Eric Palmer Centre. • 4. Castle House Nursing Home. 5. Vicarage. • 6. Old Glove Factory. • 7. Palmer House. • 8. Shambles. • 9. Woodland Vale

For my mother
Eileen Mary Miller
a relative newcomer to Torrington
and for all the people of this town

Moira Anne Brewer is the author of 'Torrington Burning',
'Take me Home to Torrington', 'Daughter of Lundy'
and 'Sweet Singing in the Choir' and lives in Torrington

Acknowledgements

Many people have helped me in the production of this book and I hope I have managed to thank them all in individual chapters.

In particular, I would like to thank my husband, Bob, for his practical help and his moral support. He has scanned hundreds of photos into the computer for me and, after reading my manuscript, assured me I had a book worth publishing which gave my confidence a boost. He also helped me organise the order of the different chapters. He has put up with my almost constant preoccupation with this project over many months. It was his appointment as Deputy Head at Great Torrington School in the 1980s that brought our family to Torrington and we have enjoyed very much living in this friendly town.

I would like to thank Keith Hughes, an active member of the local community, who first suggested this project to me. I don't suppose the book has turned out quite as he envisaged but I hope he will enjoy it nevertheless. The title was also his idea.

I would like to thank my daughter, Hannah, who came up with the format in which I finally decided to write the book. I had spent years, literally, wondering how to go about writing about Torrington's history, daunted by the enormity of the task, and her suggestion finally got me going. I hope the question and answer style makes the book clear and easy to use and enjoy.

My thanks go also to my son, Daniel, for getting my manuscript ready for printing and performing various tasks on the computer for me that were beyond my technical expertise.

I would like to thank all the other local authors from whose books I have borrowed heavily and I must acknowledge my debt to the late Alexander and Hooper whose 'History of Great Torrington' has been my constant reference book.

I am grateful to those who have been willing to share with me their old photos of Torrington, especially Linda Downing, who has a collection of Thomas Andrews postcards, John and Tilly Kimber, Dave Kelly, Roy Beer and Margaret Trounson. I'd also like to thank Ron Andrews, Bill Brook, Roger and Sally Cole, Philip Dixon, John Down, David Eadie, Hilary Green, Sue Scrutton, Jean Shorters, Graham Truepenny, Kerry Jordan, Elaine Weeks and Torrington Bowling Club.

In addition to them and all the people who have provided me with information, there are others who have helped me with reference books, pictures, photocopying and all kinds of advice. These include Pauline Baker, Graeme Barber, Ken Egan, John Hayes, Adam Walter, Jan Welch, Roger Hickman, Ruth Ward, Suzanne Fawcitt, Sarah Chesters, Pauline Crawley-Tweed, the staff at Webbers, Tanya and Ian Kevern, Bob Hutchings and Kate, Lisa and Becky at Torrington library.

Lastly, I would like to thank Edward Gaskell of Lazarus Press for making a professional job of producing this book.

MAB

Contents

Introduction

Five years ago former Community Tutor, Keith Hughes, suggested to me that it was time for a new history of Torrington. He was thinking of a community project, which I would oversee, similar to the one he helped organise in Weare Giffard. I felt there were other people in Torrington more qualified than I to attempt such a task but, as time wore on, the idea of writing about Torrington and its history increasingly appealed to me and I decided to try and write something myself.

I wondered what the best way would be to approach such an enormous subject. Who would I be writing for, visitors or inhabitants – who probably knew more about the town than I did? Kate Greaves in the library and Roger Hickman in the book shop told me they were frequently asked for a book about Torrington and, although there are a number of books and pamphlets about different aspects of the town, there has been no general history since 'The History of Great Torrington' by Alexander and Hooper written in the 1940s.

My daughter, Hannah, came up with the idea of writing the book as a series of questions that newcomers are likely to ask about Torrington and its surroundings and the answers, of varying length and detail, to those questions. I liked this idea and it got me started on what has been a lengthy but fascinating project. I hope that, as well as providing a guide for visitors, this book will contain material that is of interest to townspeople. Although I have written this book myself, it has been a community project in that I have had help from a lot of people who have provided me with facts, stories and photographs. Everyone has shown an interest in what I am doing and I have enjoyed talking to them all.

I am sure there are people, places and events that should have been included in this book but in a work of this kind you can only write about what you have seen, heard or read and you have to stop somewhere! I hope readers will treat it as a starting point for their own research. I have tried to make sure the facts are correct but, if there are any errors, I take full responsibility for them. In a community, things are always changing – pubs and shops are closing or moving or reopening, people are coming and going or, sadly, dying – but I have tried my best to make my information as up to date as possible.

Finally, I hope everyone will enjoy the book.

1   Where is Torrington?

Torrington enjoys a superb hilltop position in North Devon overlooking the River Torridge, after which it is named. This impressive situation has led to the town being referred to as 'the English Jerusalem'[1] and it must have been valued for its strategic importance during the Middle Ages.

The town is on the A386 Okehampton to Bideford road which links Dartmoor to the North Devon coast. It is also on the main route from Bideford to Exeter, following the A386, B3124 and A377, and is situated 36 miles to the north-west of Exeter. Torrington is 7 miles to the south-east of Bideford, 12 miles to the south-west of Barnstaple and 10 miles from the nearest coast at Westward Ho! When approached from the direction of Exeter, the town appears high up ahead perched on its hill whereas coming from Barnstaple it is laid out below you with higher hills around. There are commanding viewpoints at Castle Hill, facing south – on a clear day the northern granite tors of Dartmoor can be seen in the distance beyond Rosemoor – and at Furzebeam Hill, facing north.

Castle Hill

Photo by the author

2   Is the town called Torrington or Great Torrington?

Officially called Great Torrington, to distinguish it from nearby Little Torrington and Black Torrington, the town is more generally known simply as Torrington. This can sometimes lead to confusion when searching for the town in a list – whether to look under G or T!

Before the middle of the 8th century, there were probably three farms or estates on the bank of the 'Toric' (the Old English name for the River Torridge meaning 'violent, rough stream') which each had the name Toricton or, later, Toritun. After the Norman Conquest this name varied between Toriton, Torinton and Torintone.[1] To avoid confusion, the three places were later distinguished by the prefixes 'Chepyng' (Market) or 'Magna' (Great) for the town and 'Little' and 'Black' for the villages.

Little Torrington lies about a mile and a half away from the town over the hill to the south, out of sight except for the top of the church tower. Black Torrington is some 9 miles away, as the crow flies, higher up the River Torridge and it has been suggested that the village derives its special title from the black colour of the water[2] or perhaps from the dense woods which surrounded it in ancient times.[3]

Torrington town square   Photo courtesy of Ron Andrews

3   How old is the town?

The first mention of Torrington is found in the 'Domesday Book' but evidence has been discovered of settlement in the locality long before that date. Flint tools from the Neolithic age have been excavated at Weare Giffard and Bronze Age artefacts and human remains have been found in ancient burial mounds (tumuli) near Torrington. Stones of the Saxon period were found on the site of the old castle when the foundations of the new bowling club pavilion were being prepared in 1987.

Britain was under Roman domination from 43 AD but their presence was minimal in North Devon, merely passing through, although some people believe they may have had camps at Clovelly Dykes and in and about Countisbury.[1] After they withdrew in 407 AD Germanic Angles and Saxons overran the whole of England except for Cornwall, Wales and Cumberland. The West Saxons had annexed most of east and central Devon, including Exeter and Crediton, by 685 and were in the north of the county by 710. Gradually, the area was settled but even as late as the Norman Conquest (1066) some parts of North Devon were fairly empty. Most of the original settlers tilled the soil or kept flocks and herds.

Invading Danes were beaten off in North Devon in the late 9th century[2] and some of the lesser landholders, fearful of raids, had placed themselves under the protection of the more wealthy landowners who thus became owners of large estates consisting of a number of farms and smallholdings. Great Torrington seems to have passed under the control of a family claiming to be descended from Alfred the Great. The head of this family during the reign of Edward the Confessor (1042-1066) was Beorhtric.

Beorhtric was stripped of his lands and manors (he had about 40 of them in Devon) and his manor of Great Torrington fell to Odo, son of Gamelin. William the Conqueror reached Devon early in 1068 and occupied the whole county within a year. He distributed the forfeited estates among his Norman followers, reserving some for his own use. His 'Domesday Book', completed in 1086, included a record of Torrington lands and of the early barons. Odo (c1040-1105) was the Domesday holder of Great Torrington and may be regarded as the first baron of Torrington. His descendants and heirs took the surname 'De Toriton'.

The section of the 'Domesday Book' concerning Torrington reads:

'Land of Odo son of Gamelin
  Odo holds (Great) Torrington himself. Brictric held
        "TORITONE"
  it before 1066. It paid tax for 3½ hides. Land for
  40 ploughs. In lordship 4 ploughs; 7 slaves; 3 virgates.
    45 villagers and 10 smallholders with 26 ploughs and 2 hides.
    Meadow, 20 acres; woodland, 300 acres; pasture
      2 leagues long and 1 league wide. 12 cattle;
      10 pigs; 146 sheep.
    25 pigmen who pay 110 pigs.
  Formerly £24; value now £20.
    Three Frenchmen hold 3 virgates also of this land.
    Value 45s.'[3]

The 12th and 13th centuries were the great age of colonisation which took the form of the spread of settlement and the cultivation of the countryside. The other aspect of the colonisation movement was the creation of 'boroughs' by lords of rural manors. All of them had a weekly market, many of them an annual fair. There were nearly 70 places in Devon which had the attributes of a 'borough'. Some of them were created in the 12th century (e.g. Ashburton, Plympton, Tavistock, South Molton, Torrington) and many more in the 13th and 14th centuries. By the 13th century Torrington was known as 'Villata de Chepyng Toriton' (Town of Market Torrington). These 'boroughs' must be regarded 'as hopeful speculations by the lords of rural manors who hoped to see a town grow, through markets and fairs and daily road traffic, and to reap substantial benefits from tolls and burgage rents in place of a modest income from agricultural land.'[4]

Torrington was in and out of the hands of a succession of barons who were related to, or in favour with, the current king and then fell out of favour. When Richard III was killed at Bosworth in 1485, Henry VII took possession of the baronies of Barnstaple and Torrington but two years later handed them over to his mother, the Lady Margaret, Countess of Richmond and Derby (c1442-1509), through whom his claim descended.

'She outlived her son, Henry VII, by ten weeks, and much of her property, including Torrington, passed to her grandson in June 1509. That grandson was Henry VIII, and by the fact of his inheritance the "honour" of Torrington became once more a possession of the Crown, just about four centuries after its recognition as a feudal barony in the days of the Norman kings.'[5]

The lordship of the borough belonged to King Henry VIII but in about 1525 he granted it, with other North Devon properties, to his illegitimate son, Henry Fitz Roy, Duke of Richmond and Somerset (1519-36) who died suddenly. It is thought he may have been poisoned by Anne Boleyn and her brother who were both beheaded in May of that year.

In 1537 Henry VIII granted the manor of Torrington to his childhood friend, William Fitz William (c1490-1542). It was during Fitz William's tenure that John Leland came to Torrington and wrote:

> 'Torington is a great large Toune, and stondith on the brow of an Hill, and hath 3 fair Streates yn it, and a good Market every weke, and ons a Yere upon S. Michael's day the best Fayr in al those Quarters.'[6]

After the death of Fitz William the manor of Torrington seems to have reverted to the Crown and no other lord is recorded until about twelve years later when Queen Mary bestowed it by a royal grant in 1554 on James Basset (1523-58), a member of her Privy Council. He was a son of Sir John Basset of Umberleigh and his wife, Honora, daughter of Thomas Grenville of Bideford. It may have been through James Basset's influence that the charter of incorporation was conferred in 1554. Torrington was one of the earliest towns in Devon to receive a charter of incorporation, coming fourth after Plymouth (1439), Totnes (1505) and Exeter (1537). (Barnstaple achieved corporation in 1557, Bideford in 1573 and South Molton in 1590).

James Basset left the manor of Torrington to his son, Philip Basset, who sold it to Sir John Fortescue (c1531-1607) of Ponsbourne near Hatfield, Herts, who left it to his younger son, Sir William Fortescue, from whom it was purchased by the Rolle family.

Lady Margaret Beaufort, Countess of Richmond and Derby   Photo courtesy of the Guardian

George Rolle (c1485-1552), who had acquired the property of Stevenstone in the adjoining parish of St Giles-in-the-Wood during Henry VIII's time, was the founder of the Rolle dynasty which came to an end after more than 350 years with the death of Mark Rolle in 1907. Mark Rolle left no male heir so his estates passed to his nephew, Charles John Robert Hepburn-Stuart-Forbes-Trefusis, the 21st Baron Clinton (1863-1957). The 22nd Baron is Gerald Neville Mark Fane-Trefusis, born in 1934, and the heir apparent is the present holder's son, the Hon. Charles Patrick Rolle Fane-Trefusis, born in 1962.

4   What is the Population of Torrington?

In 2011 the population of Great Torrington parish was 5,815. The population hasn't changed a great deal over the years.

1547	1,500	('houselyng people' i.e. communicants)
1645	2,270	approx.[1]
1801	2,044	
1811	2,151	
1821	2,538	
1831	3,093	
1851	3,308	
1861	3,298	
1871	3,529	
1881	3,445	
1891	3,436	
1901	3,241	(48 inmates in workhouse)
1911	3,041	
1921	2,931	
1931	2,913	
1951	2,873	

In his book, 'Devon', W. G. Hoskins describes North Devon in 1939 as 'a land of static or decaying towns in an abandoned countryside' but by 1951 this decay had been arrested to a large degree. Barnstaple and Bideford had grown at about the same pace as the rest of the county but Torrington's population had fallen between 1931 and 1951 by nearly 7% and was continuing to decline. Hoskins feels that Torrington's decay was due to its proximity with Barnstaple and Bideford which had more to offer in the way of shopping and entertainment. He says that Torrington had fewer people in the 1950s than in the 1820s.

Between 1961 and 1981 the town grew considerably with a 41% increase in population:

1961	2,920	
1971	3,531	
1981	4,107	(parish population increased steadily by 9.4% from 1981-1991)
1991	4,493	(Torrington's population twice what it was in 1646 while nationally [England and Wales] the population was nearly 10 times bigger)[2]
1999	4,905	(Torridge District Council estimate which indicated a higher average annual rate of growth since 1991)
2001	5,150/5,278	(slightly differing figures from two different sources)
2004	5,337	
2009	5,400	
2011	5,815	

There has been a good deal of new building in Torrington during the last few years and people moving into the town, though one wonders where they find work. One local man reckons that if building had been allowed on the commons Torrington would be a city by now. If this had happened, the town would almost certainly have lost its individual character and sense of identity that it retains to this day.

With thanks to:
Kate Greaves
Ron Juniper
Colin MacDonald, North Devon Record Office
Sandy Wildash, North Devon Record Office

5   Where was the Medieval Castle situated?

The castle was on the south side of the town near the edge of the high, steep precipice overlooking the River Torridge, now called Castle Hill. Its commanding position, with strong natural defences to the south and far-reaching views of the surrounding countryside, can still be appreciated.

'In the Middle Ages it was an important site occupied for about four centuries. As the heavily fortified property of the lords of Torrington it was the most imposing secular residence in the locality, as well as being the administrative centre of numerous rural estates. The borough of Torrington grew under its influence, eventually becoming more important than the castle itself.'[1]

Castle Street leads to the old castle site where there is now a bowling green, car park and the castle mound which is all that remains of the old fortification and is sometimes referred to as the 'tump'.

The original castle was built in the 12th century and the site is first mentioned in 1139 when it was attacked in the civil war waged in the reign of King Stephen (1135-54). Henry de Tracy, a supporter of King Stephen who had received Barnstaple castle and lands in North Devon, took the castle from its lord, William de Toriton, but

William's family later regained control and kept the castle until 1227 when its estates were divided among various families. It is understood that the first castle was built without royal licence and in 1228 the Sheriff of Devon ordered it to be pulled down and the ditches around it to be filled up level with the ground. A second castle was built, with permission, by Richard de Merton in 1338 on the same site.

In their study, Higham and Goddard state that various parts of the castle are mentioned in contemporary documents. The castle of 1139 had a tower which was possibly situated on the earthwork to the west of the bowling green. There is later reference to a bailey and the site may have been of the well-known motte (mound) and bailey (courtyard) pattern. (The name of the Barley Grove car park could well be a corruption of 'bailey'). Although there was extensive destruction of the site in 1228 when its ditches were mentioned, this mainly affected its defences for in the 14th and 15th centuries several domestic buildings were said to be still in use. The chambers, hall, kitchen, grange and cowshed were mentioned in 1343 and the chapel still survived in the 16th century.

By the time of John Leland's visit in around 1538 'nothing remainith stonding but a neglect Chapelle' which had been used as a school house since 1485. Tristram Risdon in his 'Survey of Devon' in the 1630s states,

'Towards the south the ruins of an old castle hath for many years hovered, which, by extreme age, is almost brought to its period, whereof there only remaineth a chapel within the scite, now converted into a schoolhouse.'

This was eventually demolished in 1780. Another school house was built on the same site which, in later years, became the Blue Coat School, then the Eric Palmer Community Centre. This closed in 2010 and the building is now (2012) being used as a health and fitness centre.

Torrington Acrostic

Photo courtesy of Linda Downing

The east end of the castle site, said to be the location of the castle keep, is now occupied by the bowling green. The castellated walls together with the arrow slits seen here were, however, constructed by Lord Rolle in around 1846 and he built Town Mills (by New Bridge on the A386) in the same flamboyant style. When the old bowling pavilion was pulled down in 1987 to make way for a new clubhouse, an archaeological study was made and the masonry foundations of part of a domestic building were discovered, the tail of a rampart of clay and stone was located and considerable quantities of medieval pottery were recovered.[2]

6   Are the crenellated walls on the top of Castle Hill the old town walls?

Torrington was originally a walled town with a castle in an excellent defensive position (where the bowling green is now) looking out across the Torridge valley and over the land to the south. Taddiport was outside the town walls and members of its leper colony who tilled the strip fields down in the valley weren't allowed up into the town.

The present walls are not the original town walls although parts of them may have been built with stones from the old ruined castle. They were constructed in around 1846, when the Rolle family were lords of the manor, as an added attraction to the town and built in the same flamboyant style as Town Mills down by the New Bridge on the A386. The bridge was built in 1843. Town Mills, now called Orford Mill, was a former grist mill using water power for grinding corn. The castellated appearance of the building was also at the instigation of Lord Rolle to create a romantic riverside feature that could be seen from the town.

Town walls at Castle Hill   Photo by the author

7   What happens at May Fair?

A fair was said to have been held in Torrington from at least 1220 and the right to hold fairs in the town was confirmed by Royal Charter in 1554. It was not until after 1873 that the first Thursday in May was set as the opening day of the fair and by this time traditions were long-established. In Victorian times it was the custom for young girls to get up early on May Day and wash their faces in pools, believing this would make them beautiful. A favourite place for this ritual was Lady Wash, a stream that runs down Castle Hill.

In the early days there was also a cattle market with animals penned in New Street. Men, women and children came into town from the surrounding villages on horseback and on foot. The main streets were lined with stalls selling a variety of wares. On Barley Grove the pleasure fair offered peep shows, boxing booths, shooting galleries and a variety of entertainments. At night, with flaring lights and a din from gongs, drums and trumpets, the excitement reached its climax.

The fair continued for a further two days. There were sporting contests, wrestling matches, sack racing, climbing the greasy pole, a marathon cross-country run, 'cock-cubbitting' where a live cockerel was trapped under an earthenware pot and sticks were thrown at the pot until it broke and the cockerel chased until it was caught by the winner. There was bull-baiting at the Bull Ring Tannery just off the square and the bull was eventually released into the streets causing great concern.

The fair almost disappeared in the late 1880s, although the proclamation was still read from the window of the Town Hall. In 1924 an effort was made to revive the May Fair and an article in the *North Devon Journal* on 8th May states:

> 'The ancient May Fair, the glories of which had of recent years been allowed to lapse, was revived with old-time pomp and circumstance, and with joyous ringing of bells and a gay floral dance in the square, in which the townsfolk and their children (the latter to the number of several hundreds), and visitors participated. Old inhabitants of the town state that the crowds who filled the borough in the course of the happy proceedings had never been equalled for fifty years.'[1]

In local vernacular, the exhortation to take part was:

> 'Come, Goody, stop your humdrum wheel,
> Sweep up your orts*, and get your hat;
> Old joys reviv'd once more I feel,
> 'Tis Fair Day.'

As well as a wish to preserve the past, the Town Council and Chamber of Commerce were at least as concerned for the future. Under the banner of 'Uz be plaised to zee 'ee' it was hoped to gain both publicity and custom for the town. After fair proclamations outside the Town Hall, near Vaughan's glove factory in Whites Lane and at Cornmarket Street, the festivities began in the square with folk and floral dancing. The choral society gave its performance and school children danced around the maypole. In the afternoon there was a marathon race followed by a clay

(*orts = crumbs, scraps)

Butchers and children at May Fair   Photo courtesy of John and Tilly Kimber

pigeon shoot on Castle Hill, skittles on Castle Green and a bowling tournament. The finale was a grand carnival. Cattle and sheep were auctioned and the funfair was in full swing at Barley Grove.

Pat Wilks and Dulcie Leate remember how excited they were about May Fair as children in the 1920s and 30s. At a time before there was television and a wide variety of activities and entertainments, May Fair was a great event in their lives. The May Queen was chosen from one of the two Torrington schools (the Board School in Halsdon Road and the Blue Coat School at Barley Grove) on alternate years. Pat says, 'She wasn't chosen entirely for her attractiveness, but was expected to show helpfulness as well as charm.' The first May Queen in 1925 was Mary Heywood from the top class (aged 14) of the Halsdon Road school. Pat says she loved taking part in the floral dance and you had to organise a group of four soon after Christmas or you wouldn't be able to take part. These days maypole dancing is practised for many months down at the junior school. The floral dancers would start out from the pannier market led by four local butchers in their best butchers' apparel and their wives who wore elaborate dresses and wonderful hats. Dulcie remembers everyone buying a balloon and the boys would prick them all before you started! In those days the dancers would go up South Street, along Whites Lane, down New Street and back along Potacre Street and Cornmarket Street to the square. This dance took place twice, once in the morning and again in the afternoon. Dulcie remembers the children from Sydney House taking part in the afternoon, all wearing sun bonnets and lifting their knees up high as they danced. They were frail children and exhausted by the time they had finished. Dulcie also remembers a group of foreign women taking part in the dancing one year – Swiss or Dutch or Austrian – wearing their own national costume. They had a wonderful time but did their own version of the dances. Eventually, Miss Mortlock, who was headmistress of the Board School, went over to them and said, 'Do you mind?' as they were completely dominating the whole event! The May Queen and her attendants used to ride in a horse and cart decorated mostly with gorse and they followed the route of the floral dance. Tommy Hearn used to look after the horse.

Pat remembers the excitement of the fair:

'We were thrilled by all the rides, the colourful lights and the music. The fair was owned by "Granny Lock" and all the local lasses were smitten by her handsome, gypsy-like sons. "Go 'ome and leave my boys alone!" Granny Lock used to shout, while her sons just looked amused.'

By 1939 the programme had expanded considerably. The crowning of the May Queen became the main feature of the Thursday opening ceremony. The church bells rang to announce the start of the day's festivities, the fair was formally opened by the Mayor and there was floral and maypole dancing.

'In the afternoon there was a new departure – the staging of an open-air boxing tournament at the Vicarage Field. In the evening the final for the Torridge Association Football Cup between Ilfracombe and Holsworthy was staged. The Royal Naval Barracks Blue Jacket Band was in attendance throughout the day.'[2]

On the Saturday there was a cross-country race over Castle Hill (the forerunner of the present-day 'Round the Tree Race' which goes down the commons paths to Taddiport Bridge whereas, previously, runners plunged straight down the hill and through the river!) and a river boat race from Town Mills to Taddiport. In the evening a carnival brought the celebrations to an end and the funfair continued into the night.

The Bishop of Exeter attended the 1939 May Fair and, contrasting what was happening at Torrington that day with what was going on in several other countries, the Bishop said no doubt the times were serious, but to be serious did not necessarily mean to be solemn, and they would probably go back to the serious business of life all the better for having forgotten for a day at least what was going on elsewhere.

The May Queen that year was Beryl Guard who was crowned by Muriel Bryant. Eight little girl attendants wore dresses in Elizabethan style with net bonnets and the two heralds, George Lake and Harold Sing, were in red and white Elizabethan costumes.

In 1940 the May Queen was chosen from the new senior school in Calvesford Road but the war situation led to the cancellation of the May Fair ceremony. The proclamation was read to an empty square but after the war the festivities were started up again and in 1946 the senior school tried to elect a May Queen from amongst its pupils once again but the head teacher of the Blue Coat School, Mrs Blair-Williams, declared 1946 was an 'even' date year and so it was her school's turn to provide the queen. From then on the Board and Blue Coat schools continued to alternate in providing the queen and court until Great Torrington junior school opened in September 1978. (After 1946 the age of the Queen was 11 rather than 14).

May Fair 2010   Photo courtesy of Jayne Poole

In 1965 the Town Council took over the running of May Fair from the Chamber of Commerce who had organised it since 1924.

The May Fair costumes always have a theme commemorating a national event. When my daughter, Hannah, was crowner in 1990 it was the 50th anniversary of the Battle of Britain. The May Queen, Katey Svensson, and crowner were dressed in white with light and dark blue sashes while the attendants had either pale blue or royal blue dresses and the two heralds, Tom Wittram and Julian Lynch, wore specially made RAF dress uniforms, including hats with pale blue feathers. It was hot and sunny that year and the boys were boiling in their heavy serge suits!

Gladys Sing told me in January 2011 that she was the second oldest surviving May Queen – she was Queen in 1934 – the oldest being Doreen Darch who was queen in 1933. (Sadly, Doreen passed away the following month aged 91 so Gladys is now the oldest surviving May Queen – April 2012). 2011 was thought to be the first time the May Queen's mother had also been queen. In fact, Molly Magarotto was the third generation in her family to be May Queen. Her mother, Andrea, had that honour in 1981 and her grandmother, Gwen, was May Queen 50 years before in 1961. Three sets of sisters have been queen: Squires in the 1950s, Giles in 1969 and 1971, and Downs, Joanna in 2000 and Kimberly in 2002. In 1972 Jennifer Cramp was queen, her sister Abigail was crowner and a third sister, Annette, was one of the attendants. The heralds that year were twin brothers, Tony and Terry Gilbert. The other pair of twins who were heralds were Austin and Brian Mitchell in 1936. There was a reunion of May Queens in 2001 when the queens of 1931, 1933 and 1934 were all present.

Gladys Sing, May Queen 1934   Photo courtesy of Gladys and Jack Sing

May Fair continues to be an important annual event for the people of Torrington. When a former headmistress of the senior school announced one year that she wished all pupils to be in school on the Thursday of May Fair, there was an outcry from local people. Eventually, a compromise was reached and just those pupils taking SATs had to go into school and were able to leave once they had finished their exams.

A report of a 'Brilliant May Fair at Torrington' from May 1960 captures perfectly the spirit of the event:

'Into the sunlit square at Torrington yesterday went the smiling May Queen – a symbol of country pageantry and of the steadfast refusal of country people to make the slightest break with tradition.

'Torrington May Fair was never more crowded and never more colourful. May Fair inevitably means a new spring dress, and the square was a riot of colour as the queen – 10-year-old Gwendoline Copp – walked slowly under the banner "Us be plaised to zee 'ee" to the dais beneath the maypole where she was to be crowned.

'Vivid yellow broom and other spring flowers decorated the tips of each of the two may-poles, and small children in frilly dresses of every imaginable colour curtseyed to the May Queen as she passed between their ranks. The little girls clutched posies of spring flowers; each of the boys carried his posy on a long stick.

Maypole dancing   Photo courtesy of Bob Brewer

'Softly the band played "Early one morning" as the children, with measured and stately tread, went through the ritual they have been practising since February. Chosen by her own school fellows at Barley Grove School, Torrington, Gwendoline was crowned by 10-year-old Alison Finnamore.

'Alan Gould and John Copp were the two heralds, and the queen had eight attendants – Janet Copp, Gillian Hopkins, Lindsay Faulkner, Amanda Wheeler, Kathryn Symons, Dorothy Dymond, Jacqueline Vanstone, and Susan Finnamore.

'The scorching sun which flooded the square was reflected from the gilt chains and medallions worn by civic heads from all parts of Devon. Like the people of Torrington, the visitors were caught up in the emotion of the moment as the queen in a full-length dress of cream brocade was solemnly invested with her crown of lilies of the valley, for-get-me-nots, and geraniums.

'The two heralds wore knee breeches, suits of green taffeta, and white wigs, while of the eight small attendants four were in green chintz and four in pink. Their cream straw hats were tied with black ribbon, and the whole of the queen's retinue wore costumes based on 18th century design.

'Then the queen watched as the children of the two primary schools at Torrington weaved an intricate pattern of contrasting colours as they danced round the two may-poles.

'Earlier there had been floral dancing in the square, and after the civic ceremony in the town hall, the Mayor, Col. J. E. Palmer, in his rich red robes, escorted by Sergeants of Mace, Police and Beadles, was followed by his guests in a procession to the square, Whites Lane, and Eastmans corner, where the Town Clerk, Mr S. J. Parkes, read the ancient proclamation.

'This called upon "all manner of persons to behave themselves quietly and orderly according to the laws, and not make any assault or affray, riot, rout, or unlawful assembly."

'Toasts were drunk in Devon cider, and the age-old custom of handing round gingerbread fairings was observed in the town hall, where guests drank the toast of success to Great Torrington and its fair at the invitation of the Mayor of Exeter, Ald. C. Woodland.

'Throughout the ceremony the emphasis was on the preservation of traditional events. "It would be the greatest tragedy if some of these customs were allowed to lapse," said the Mayor of Exeter.'[3]

With thanks to:
John Down
Dulcie and Bryan Leate
Mike Sampson
Jean Shorters
Gladys and Jack Sing
Pat Wilks

8   What are those Strip Fields across the valley?

From Sydney House (formerly South Street) car park two long thin fields can be seen across the river alongside the village of Taddiport. These two strips, or 'straps', are examples of the medieval field system, a method of cultivation which was once standard practice across the country. These two particular strips are what remain of between seven and a dozen fields (reports vary) which were reserved for cultivation by lepers who lived in the village from the 14th until the 17th century when leprosy was eradicated from Britain. The Tithe Map of 1838 shows that seven strips were still in use, though the lepers were long gone.

'Taddy' is from the Old English 'taddige' which means 'toad' and the name of the village may have had some reference to the scaly skin of lepers who lived at the leper hospital of St Mary Magdalen. 'There are many references to the Chapel or Chantry in the Registers of the Bishops of Exeter, but it is not till 1418 that it is actually named as a Leper Hospital' when a certain Thomas Reymond, in his will dated 8th June 1418, left 4d to 'the Leper house at Torrington'.[1] Only three lepers could be accommodated at the hospital at any one time. They would go from door to door in Taddiport with their begging bowls, using clapper and bells to warn of their arrival, but were forbidden from going up into Torrington. In 1593 the hospital appeared to have its full complement of lepers but no further mention of it can be found until 1645 when the chapel was provided with a bell. There were no longer any lepers at the 'lazar house' by this time.

In 1665 the Magdalen Lands were granted to the corporation for the relief of the poor of the borough. Farmed by the civic authorities over the centuries, the fields gradually began to lose their distinctive appearance as the closely spaced hedges fell away. The fields were made larger during the Second World War to fit in with war-

Above: Leper strips from Castle Hill

Photo courtesy of Linda Downing

Below: Two remaining strip fields

Photo by the author

time food production. The remaining strips were rescued in 1970 by a local benefactor, Mr McKinnon, and public subscription and are now in the safe hands of the Great Torrington Almshouse, Town Lands and Poors Charities.

A programme of works to rebuild the traditional Devon banks and the hedgerows returned the leper strips to their former glory. Using local rural craftsmen to restore the land to its condition when the strips were first created in medieval times, a fascinating piece of history has been preserved.

The appearance of the narrow fields is being safeguarded and also the charities' trustees will ensure the agricultural use of the land mirrors the environmentally-friendly practices of the past. No artificial fertilisers are to be used and the grass is not to be cut until 13th July and summer grazing is to stop by 31st October. 'From an archaeological point of view, what's interesting about them is that the banks themselves contain quite a lot of medieval pottery which was spread on the fields with manure. The hedges act as time capsules'.[2]

To remember the lepers of Taddiport, local artist Shan Miller organises an annual event to raise money for the leprosy relief charity, LEPRA. Local people dress as lepers and take part in a torchlight parade accompanied by the racket of clappers, bells and drums. The chapel of St Mary Magdalen is visited, street performers provide entertainment and mulled wine is served. Participants enjoy a Beggars' Banquet and listen to music by local bands. 2011 was the 10th anniversary of the Taddiport Annual Leper Festival.

With thanks to Shan Miller, author of the pamphlet 'Taddiport: Leper Colony'.

Leper parade   Photo courtesy of Guy Harrop and the North Devon Gazette

9   What is the significance of the Monument on Castle Hill common?

On Castle Hill common, about half-way down between the top of the hill and the river, there stands a monument with an inscription plate said to be made from a cannon brought back from the Battle of Waterloo. This obelisk, with a built-in stone seat on each of its four sides which enables walkers to rest and enjoy the view, was financed by the ladies of Great Torrington and reads:

ERECTED JUNE 1818
TO COMMEMORATE
THE BATTLE OF
WATERLOO
JUNE 1815
PEACE TO THE
SOULS OF THE
HEROES!!!

In this cynical age we wonder about the significance of the three exclamation marks but, probably, they simply denote admiration for men's courage in battle.

Obelisk and Mill Torrington.

Obelisk and Mill   Photo courtesy of Linda Downing

10   Did Torrington ever have a Livestock Market?

The holding of markets and fairs was legalised in Torrington probably before the end of the 12th century. In documents dated 1249 the town was known as Villata de Chepyng Toriton (Town of Market Torrington) so there was certainly an officially recognised market at that time.

When John Leland visited in 1538, he described the town as having a good market every week and the best fair in the area once a year.

A hundred years or so later Tristram Risdon, in his 'Survey of Devon', writes:

> 'This town is indifferently beautiful with buildings, very populous, and flourishing with merchants and men of trade, their market is great furnished from far on every quarter.'[1]

A Royal Charter (1554) allowed the town to have a weekly Saturday market and to hold two fairs a year. 'The grant of the charter with its rights to hold a market and fairs provided a sound legal basis for developing commercial activity. Torrington market became widely regarded as one of the best in Devon.'[2]

The London and Provincial New Commercial Directory of 1830 describes Torrington as

> 'a small but respectable and prosperous market-town and parish in the hundred of Fremington. . .'

White's Devonshire Directory of 1850 states there was a market every Saturday well supplied with provisions, corn, etc. There were cattle fairs on 4th May, 5th July and 10th October and a great cattle market on the third Saturday in March. The dates of the fairs were altered under the Fairs Act of 1873 to the first Thursday in May and the second Thursday in October. 'The October fair has disappeared, leaving the May Fair to carry on under a renewed vitality from 1924.'[3]

To distinguish between fairs and revels: a fair derived its privileges from Royal Grant and involved commerce and business, such as the sale of merchandise, horses, cattle, and so on, as well as the hiring of labour. Some Devon fairs still carry the old names e.g. Bampton Horse Fair, Tavistock Goose Fair. A revel, on the other hand, was a great event in the countryside which appears never to have had any connection with business or trade but consisted of a general holiday to which people of the neighbourhood looked forward for many weeks.[4]

Before 1842 the pannier and cattle markets were held in the streets. An unattributed piece about Torrington in Tudor times describes the bustling market being full of vitality with

> '. . .good-humoured, noisy country folk selling their eggs and cheeses, apples and vegetables. Travelling tinkers and button-sellers, piemen, cider-sellers, showmen, bakers, cobblers, wool merchants, farmers hiring help, tricksters, thieves, fishmongers, scribes, barbers, tooth-pullers, apothecaries, carpenters – all these and more, drawing trade and wealth into the town.'

New Street was converted into a cattle market and some of the iron rings to which animals were tied can still be seen fixed in the wall of the church yard and some of the older houses. There also used to be strong wooden posts with cross-bars in front of many of the houses to keep the animals which were penned on the pavement from breaking the windows.

> 'Pandemonium reigned in the street – sometimes a bullock or cow ran amok through the crowd of dealers and others, scattering them in all directions.'[5]

George M. Doe, writing about Torrington in the late 1920s refers to pig drivers as 'agitatores porcellorum'!

By the end of the 19th century both market traders and livestock dealers had proper permanent premises. In 1842 the pannier market was built at the southern end of the square and in 1890 part of the Glebe land behind the vicarage and alongside School Lane (where the swimming pool is now) was sold to the corporation for £120 and a cattle market was built at a cost of £1,000. This market was opened in 1892 for the regular monthly sale of livestock by Henry Slee, then Mayor of the borough.[6] The swimming pool was built on the site in the early 1970s.

John Down remembers bringing his father's sheep into the market from Chapple Farm between High Bullen and Atherington on the South Molton road when he was a boy. His father would sell their lambs just after Christmas (after 1st January they were called 'hoggarts'). On the day before the market John and one of the men who worked on the farm would set off at around 2pm and drive about 100 sheep to a field at Hatchmoor, which belonged to Mr Sussex, a blacksmith from High Bullen, where they would leave them for the night. It would take them about two and a half hours to walk there, without hurrying. Then the following day they would bring the sheep along Calf Street to the market. John's father would drop them off at Hatchmoor, go and park the car and then walk back to meet them. On one occasion they had reached the top of New Road (where there is a roundabout now – then it was just a wide space) when they met another flock of sheep being driven up from Town Mills. It was impossible to keep the two flocks apart. The man with the other flock was very angry that their two flocks had intermingled but John's father told him it wasn't the fault of his boy and workman. The man was a kind of farmer-dealer who had hoped to slip his sheep in through the grading at the market before anyone knew about it. John had to help his father pick out their sheep once they got to the market. (Theirs were marked with a little black dot in the middle of the back).

After the war there was a gift sale at the market to raise money for the Red Cross to help the troops. Farmers gave corn, potatoes, whatever they could. John's father thought he ought to buy something to help the cause so he bought a little terrier which was getting on in years. He didn't turn out to be quite what they'd expected, 'too much of a townie', because he was hopeless at rabbiting or catching rats, 'but we gave him a good home.'

In the 19th century there was a Torrington Agricultural Association which organised shows known as the 'Torrington Agricultural Exhibition'. In 1895 this was merged with the Devon County Show (which used to be held in different venues around the county) for a three day show which was opened by the Duke of Cambridge, Commander-in-Chief of the British Army. The show was held at Town Park (now a housing estate) on 22nd - 24th May. The Town Council was paid two

Torrington Agricultural Show 1911   Photo courtesy of John Down

guineas for the use of the fields. The early years saw classes for cattle, horses, sheep, pigs and a poultry show organised by a poultry farmer, Tom Buckland. Classes for sheep shearing were well supported with competitors wearing special overalls.

A catalogue for the 1934 agricultural show (costing 6d) at Town Park shows the cost of admission to be 1/6 (i.e. one shilling and sixpence = 7 ½ new pence). The show moved to a site near Burwood Farm in 1937/38 on fields occupied by Frank Bealey and Alfred Burridge. The gates were widened and renewed with new square oak posts. The livestock exhibited were mostly from local farms and were walked to the site and sometimes rested with farmers near the show fields. When the show re-commenced after the Second World War, the show site was at Crowbeare, land farmed by Mr C. Hill and family, and continued on that site until the merger with the Instow Agricultural Society.

With thanks to:
John Down
Margaret Williams

11   When was the Battle of Torrington?

The Battle of Torrington took place in 1646[1] during the English Civil War. It is sometimes called 'the forgotten battle'[2] as it is seldom referred to in accounts of that period but in fact 'the battle is historically remarkable as the decisive one of the final campaign of the West, which ruined the cause of King Charles.'[3]

The Civil War was a time of great upheaval and unrest, 'a stormy period. . . which convulsed the country from end to end between the years 1642 and 1646.'[4] The Royalist army of King Charles I was trying to establish the King's control of the government and the country while the Parliament in London raised its own army in opposition. Families were divided when members supported opposing sides and friends and neighbours found themselves pitted against each other.

At this time Torrington was a busy and prosperous market town with a population of about 2,270. It was in an important location with two river crossings – the 'South Bridge' (Taddiport) and 'West Bridge' (Rothern) – which connected Bideford with Okehampton and Exeter, and Barnstaple and South Molton with Holsworthy.

Torrington was occupied at different times by both Parliamentarians and Royalists. The whole district was in a state of turmoil, taxes were high, trade was disrupted and families had to suffer the billeting of troops in their houses. Many of the local men went off to war and, if they survived, often returned home injured and partially disabled.

By 1646 Torrington was in Royalist hands. Ralph, Lord Hopton, Commander in Chief of what remained of the King's Army in the West arrived in Torrington from Launceston on 10th February and proceeded to entrench and improve the fortifications. Word of what was happening in North Devon reached the Parliamentarian General, Sir Thomas Fairfax, at Exeter who learnt that some of the King's horse from Oxford had penetrated westward and Royalist horse in North Devon was attempting to push eastward to join them in order to relieve Exeter and attempt to recapture the West. With North Devon securely in Royalist hands, they could hope to bring in additional aid from Wales or Ireland. Fairfax, therefore, decided to abandon the siege of Exeter and to advance in person with a force of some 10,000 horse and foot hoping this time to destroy completely the Royalist armies.

On 14th February Fairfax left Crediton with his 'New Model Army' for Chulmleigh. Wet weather hindered their progress. On Sunday 15th Fairfax sent out small parties of horse in the direction of Torrington to observe what was happening. The next day, in order to prevent any chance of a Royalist escape eastward, he stationed a brigade on the Barnstaple road and the rest of the army, after a rendezvous at Ashreigney, marched for Torrington in the early morning.

One of Hopton's best officers, General Webb, was on the lookout for the advancing enemy and kept up a series of skirmishes to try and impede their advance but by five o'clock the Royalists were obliged to evacuate Stevenstone House. Hedge after hedge was fought for until it was too dark to tell friend from foe and at around 8pm Hopton ordered Webb to bring his men nearer Torrington. Foot soldiers were placed along the hedgerows four fields from the town with groups of horse to support them. The main body of horse was stationed at the end of the barricade on the north side of the town and the Prince's Guards were in the Castle Green. The Royalist word for the night was 'We are with you,' and the signal was a handkerchief tied around the right arm.

Fairfax didn't intend doing any more that night than hold the positions already gained so stationed his men in readiness for an assault in the morning. The Parliamentarian watch-word was 'Emmanuel, God with us,' and each man carried a sprig of furze in his hat. When Fairfax and Cromwell were on their rounds at about midnight they heard a noise in the town rather like a tattoo and supposed that the enemy were retreating. As a kind of experiment, a small party of dragoons was ordered slowly to approach the first barricade and fire over it.

'The men were allowed to draw quite close, and then found that there was a hot welcome ready for them. Others now galloped up to their support, accompanied by a forlorn hope of foot to help in bringing them away.'[5]

The reserve, supposing that an attack had been started, came running up without waiting for orders and it soon became obvious that these men would be cut to ribbons unless they were given support. Three regiments of foot were then ordered to the front and fresh horses were brought up in readiness. Pikes and butt-ends of muskets were being used by both sides all along the outer barricade. The Royalists fought bravely but were no match for the energy and discipline of the Parliamentarians and were obliged to retreat, field by field, until the last line of barricades was reached.

There was momentary panic amongst the Royalist defenders of the town which enabled the Parliamentarian foot to obtain possession of the turnpike and, having cleared the way, the horse were able to enter. There was fierce fighting in the narrow streets and townspeople watched, terrified, from upper windows. Hopton and his men made several desperate counter charges and almost drove the attackers out of the barricades but the opportune arrival of fresh horse under Colonel Hammond enabled Fairfax to carry all before him. Hopton's own horse was shot and he himself was wounded and, eventually, he and his men were forced to retreat.

The Parliamentarians drove the prisoners they took into the church not knowing the Royalists were using it as a powder magazine, having stored about 80 barrels in there. Somehow, the barrels of gunpowder were ignited and blew up with a mighty explosion which killed 200 prisoners, guards and citizens and destroyed part of the church and many houses. Fairfax himself had a lucky escape when he narrowly missed being struck by falling pieces of lead. There have been suggestions that the explosion wasn't an accident. One theory is that a villain, Robert Watts, had been paid £30 for setting light to the powder barrels but it is thought unlikely Hopton would have ordered such a deed and the fleeing Royalists had no time to arrange something like that which, in any case, killed a lot of their own men. When the parish church was being restored in 1864 a large quantity of molten lead was found under the floor together with two shilling pieces from the reign of King Charles I.

The streets of Torrington were littered with dying men from both sides and abandoned weapons. When the powder store went up there had been a deafening roar which caused the ground to tremble and echoed around the hills and valleys before subsiding in a long-drawn-out rumble. With the noise of the explosion ringing in their ears, the retreating Royalists fled down Mill Street and over the bridge at

Civil War commemoration   Photo courtesy of Guy Harrop and the North Devon Journal

Taddiport as they made for the Cornish border. The defeat at Torrington had spelled the end of Royalist hopes in the West Country.

In 1996, the 350th anniversary of the Battle of Torrington, there was a series of events in and around the town arranged by an organisation of local people calling themselves 'Fire & Steel 350' to commemorate what happened in the town in 1646.

Over a weekend in February there were various events which were intended as a prelude to the main events at August bank holiday. These included a torchlight procession with members of the Sealed Knot Society and Torrington Silver Band to the town square. Following the reading of the proclamation by Town Crier, Alan Mitchell, there was a short remembrance service by the vicar, Jeremy Hummerstone, followed by a firework display set off at the parish church to represent its blowing up in the original battle. The crowd of townspeople that had gathered then trekked off to South Street, now Sydney House, car park where the ear-splitting cannon was fired. The revelry continued when Devon Dowsers gathered around the mysterious cobbled hump in the churchyard to try and find out whether this was the last resting place of those killed in the explosion. (See 'What is the long cobble-covered hump in the churchyard?'). There was an exhibition of church records of 1646 attended by members of the Sealed Knot who were happy to answer questions. An actor played

Cavaliers' replica of the church   Photo courtesy of Bob Brewer

the part of Hugh Peters, Chaplain to the New Model Army, who had preached to the townspeople in the square from a balcony in the days after the battle, as the church was in ruins. Then the crowds flocked to the Old Bowling Green to witness a spectacular demonstration of drill and tactics of the Civil War.

On three days over the August bank holiday of 1996 there were battle re-enactments by the Sealed Knot in fields on the edge of town and a full-scale replica of the parish church built on the commons was set alight in aid of charity. (See 'Who are the Torrington Cavaliers?'). There were other displays, music, fashion parades, street theatre and living history going on over the weekend. Members of the Sealed Knot walked about the town and drank in the local pubs wearing 17th century costume and speaking in role. Townspeople entered into the spirit of things with some of the shop keepers dressing in clothes of the period. This included Sandford's bakery where my daughter was working at the time. A customer in breeches and leather jerkin strode into the shop declaring to her, 'Mistress, thou art a strumpet!' as she wasn't wearing a 'coif' (bonnet) to cover her hair. I'm not sure what reply she gave him!

The people of Torrington continue to hold a commemorative march each February to mark the Civil War battle which took place in the town. An article in *The Crier*, the community paper, advertised the event for 2012:

'Torrington 1646, in association with the Great Torrington Cavaliers and the Sealed Knot, would like to invite everyone to a day and evening of fun, falconry and fireworks in the 17th Century to commemorate the Battle of Torrington in 1646.

'The event will take place on Saturday 18th February. The day will start with Al Mitchell, the Town Crier, accompanied by the Mayor's Guard, marching around the town proclaiming the event open. Torrington 1646 will be open between 10am-4pm giving a taste of life in the 17th Century, including a living history display and demonstrations of musket and pike drill by the Sealed Knot.

'A musket firing competition will be held in the afternoon (weather permitting). The Falconer will be showing his birds of prey and the Barber Surgeon will also be in attendance demonstrating his very own version of the NHS (No Hope Surgery!). There will be a bar in the grounds of 1646 and the café will be open all day serving breakfasts, light lunches, bacon sandwiches and light snacks.

'In the evening there will be a torchlight parade through the town led by the Great Torrington Cavaliers. The march will start from Great Torrington School car park at 7pm (muster at 6.30pm) and end up in the town square approximately 20 minutes later, where the Mayor will address the assembled troops and public and the Town Crier will read out the proclamation that was read to the townsfolk on the day after the battle. The Mayor will then lay a wreath on the mass grave outside the church of St Michael and All Angels. Everyone is welcome to join in this unique event. Torches will be on sale in the school car park.

'The day will conclude with a fireworks display in South Street car park and free hot drinks at Torrington 1646.

'Please note that this is a free event.'

Today the town is recognised as an important heritage centre for the history of the 17th century and its people can often be seen dressed in costume for historical re-enactments, festivals and celebrations. An interactive Civil War Experience, 'Torrington 1646', marks the town's historically important role. There is also a Civil War Trail around the town.

12   What is 1646?

The 1646 tourist attraction was opened in 1999 to bring to life the fascinating and colourful history of Torrington. The date refers to the final battle of the Civil War in the West Country on 16th February 1646 – a battle uniquely fought at night and in the town itself. The publicity invites us to 'Travel back to the 17th century' and to 'learn a little, laugh a lot.'

1646 at Castle Hill alongside the Sydney House car park provides a living history experience with costumed vernacular-speaking guides. Visitors have the chance to try on 17th century costumes: men can put on armour, women can learn the secrets of the bum-roll and the bodice. 'Ambrose' will demonstrate how to fire a musket and wield a sword and will lead volunteers in pike drill. The treatment of villains is illustrated with a selection of vile instruments and a pillory can be tried for size. 'Master Titus', the Barber Surgeon, will describe with relish the gory details of various surgical procedures of the time. On a gentler note, there is a physic garden where you can learn about 17th century herbal cures. (The whole tour takes about two hours but you can have a separate 30 minute visit to the herb garden).

Characters at 1646   Photos courtesy of David Eadie and The Picture Postcard Company

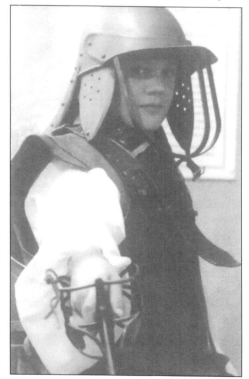 

Costumed wenches serve refreshments in the café between 9am and 4pm Monday to Saturday all year round. These include all day breakfast, light meals, cream teas, pasties, toasted sandwiches, paninis, cakes and lots more. Wherever possible, the food is sourced locally using free range and Fairtrade. There is also a range of gifts including Devon-made biscuits, jams, fudge, cider, books and traditional toys.

The 1646 experience is open from April to September starting at 10am with the last tour of the day starting at 2pm. From October to March tours are only available to schools and pre-booked groups. 1646 is visited by individuals, families, schools, coach parties, groups and overseas visitors and receives a lot of enthusiastic feed-back. ('Excellent. Educational and fun. Learned a lot. Great atmosphere.' 'A fantas-tic hands-on experience that brings history to life.' 'The displays were brilliant, very funny, informative. Stunning setting.' 'Best thing we have done all week.' 'Lovely people. So welcoming.' 'We all had a brilliant time – especially watching our friend being treated for constipation.').

There is an outreach education project where 1646 staff work in schools through-out the South West and give talks to local history societies and other organisations. Subjects include crime and punishment, which is done at GCSE level, witchcraft with the Witchfinder General, Matthew Hopkins, slavery with Sir John Hawkins and, of course, the ever popular Barber Surgeon.

With thanks to:
Kate Henderson
John Wehner (aka 'Sir Basil')

13   How far do the Commons extend and for how long have they existed?

Torrington is surrounded on three sides by 365 acres (146 hectares) of common land.

'The area is freely accessible to all, and visitors can walk the 20 miles of footpaths, rang-ing from the golf course in the north, ancient wood and wild flower meadow in the west, and dropping down to the beautiful River Torridge valley to the south of the town.'[1]

In about 1194, during the reign of Richard I, 'a large waste called the common'[2] was given to the people of Torrington by the Lord of the Manor, William FitzRobert. In 1889 the rights of this land were transferred, by an act of parliament, to an elected Committee of Conservators which now administers the commons. The earliest management was mainly concerned with control over the grazing and quarrying but since 1981 grazing has stopped and various management techniques have taken its place to prevent the area reverting back to scrub and woodland.

'Fifteen conservators, elected on a three yearly basis, administer the Common for the residents of Great Torrington. Their work includes enforcement of the bye-laws, main-taining the public rights of way, conservation measures to preserve the many different environments present on the Common and special work to support some of the rarer species.'[3]

Before the act of 1889, the lords of the manor owned the soil of Torrington common as part of their manor and enjoyed certain rights in relation to the land

Rolle Road   Photo courtesy of Bob Brewer

although they had no right of enclosure. There were often disputes between the lords of the manor and the commoners leading to many misunderstandings and a great deal of bitterness. When Lord Rolle built the canal on parts of the commons in 1827 people wanted assurance that they would not lose their rights of way and wooden bridges were placed over the canal to enable freedom of movement to continue. When the Hon. Mark Rolle wanted to convert part of the old canal into a road, a meeting was held at which the local inhabitants 'denied the cutting of this road from the Town Mills to the Railway Station before compensation had been paid for damages and encroachments made on the commons and terms agreed on for making the road available or otherwise for the use of the inhabitants.'[4] After formal notice had been served upon the contractors making the road, and a defence fund started, several rights of way on either side of this road were again opened.

In 'A Sketchbook of the Commons', Judy Barber mentions many instances of public indignation at accusations of 'stealing' from the commons during the 1800s, such as in 1835 when a man was prosecuted for cutting and taking tree branches. Poachers were caught on Hatchmoor commons, men were charged with removing soil or extracting gravel from the river, and gypsies were fined for camping on the commons. In 1875 the Rolle Estate erected notice boards stating it was unlawful for people 'to cut turf, remove soil, quarry, take stones or commit any other acts of trespass on the Commons'. These boards were torn down and one was paraded through the streets of the town and burnt on the Old Bowling Green by a furious mob of townsfolk. In the 1870s, at the so-called 'Battle of Tanton's Plain', commoners felt the occupying farmer's sawpit was becoming too permanent so they sent the logs rolling down the valley. When the Rolle Estate attempted to re-erect fencing around a small tillage field called 'Barber's Piece', which had been unfenced for five years, angry local people repeatedly pulled it down and eventually made a bonfire of it. A postcard by Dyer of Torrington entitled 'Torrington Commoners Defending their Rights' in 1908 shows a dozen or more men standing holding sticks with children sitting on the ground in front of them.[5]

One of the first Bills to be issued in 1889 prohibited the burning of furze or gorse on the common, known as 'swayling', but this activity appeared to continue judging by the number of fines listed in the Conservators' Minutes for this misdemeanour. Swayling was part of the year's cycle for grazing land. Women would go out and collect 'fuzz-stubs' for faggots and kindling and then the land would be burnt. The alternative was clearing by hand. Before the Second World War one official swayling went disastrously wrong. The wind changed and four thatched cottages in Mill Street backing on to the commons were completely gutted.[6]

There is a variety of terrain on the commons: wild moorland exposed to the prevailing wind to the north and west, steep bracken and gorse covered slopes and sheltered river valleys. Crossing the Common Lake which lies in the valley to the north of the Old Bowling Green is the old Roman Road, part of an old drovers' track from Weare Giffard to Holsworthy which ran straight up the hillside to the Old Bowling Green from where it went down to Taddiport, crossed the river by a natural ford below the bridge and continued between numbers 6 and 8 Taddiport up behind How's Court towards Little Torrington.[7]

Castle Hill with bowling gazebo, monument and Town Mills. Photo courtesy of Linda Downing

The Commons Conservators' Minutes Book shows that many of the paths were cut in the 1890s to give work to the unemployed with the 'Council responsible for all costs'. Barmaid's Walk to the station, said to be where a former mayor strolled with his lady love, was made in 1892 with a £20 grant from the Trustees. Carriage Path was the original route to Bideford before the present road was built in 1928. Centenary Walk was opened by Mayor John Kelly and Clifford Quick in 1989. More recently, paths have been named after local characters who have passed on: George's Path after George Stacey, who used to do voluntary work on the commons, and Alexander Path after Larry Alexander, local builder, artist and founder member of the Torrington Cavaliers. His path passes near to the site of the bonfires that he helped to build. In the year 2000 a path on Castle Hill was named Millennium Path and that same year granite blocks carved with the names of the paths were supplied by Andrew Gist (financed through a Millennium Festival Award) and placed on the commons.

There were far fewer trees on the commons in the 19th and early 20th centuries, as seen from photos and paintings, because of animal grazing. There were donkeys and goats, and sheep were run on the commons until 1981. Dr O'Flaherty's goat ran loose near seats on Castle Hill and the boys of the town enjoyed 'baiting the billy goat'. Opposing football teams called the Torrington team 'The Nannygoats'.[8] There was a duck pond on Mill Street common where the swings were in later years and geese and hens were everywhere. There used to be hunting around Furzebeam and meets at the Old Bowling Green in the 1960s as well as informal shooting and rabbiting. In the Conservators' Minutes of 1899 it was proposed that 80 trees be planted on Castle Hill and the limes and manna ash by Barley Grove car park probably date from this time.

Until 1855 all burials were made in the churchyard of St Michael and All Angels. At a public meeting in August 1852 to consider the question of finding a location for an additional burial ground it was suggested that a piece of the common land at the Bideford end of New Street should be used for the provision of a cemetery and this land was converted for that purpose in 1855. The sum of £60 paid for the ground was invested by Trustees for the benefit of the poor. Since 1894 the Town Council has had management of the cemetery which, in its turn, is now becoming full.

As well as a cemetery, over the years common land also provided 50 acres of allotments (the rents of which benefited poor inhabitants) the Rolle Canal, Staple Vale Woollen Factory and land required by the Southern Railway and North Devon Clay Company. Quarrying went on in the 19th century at Dewslade, just upstream from the railway viaduct over the river, now part of the Tarka Trail, and under Castle Hill near the fishing green. In the Conservators' Minutes of 1893 there was mention of the danger of the hill slipping so it was ordered that no more stone should be taken from there and a fresh quarry was opened up on Marshwood Hill adjoining New Road. During the Second World War the fields called Quiet Possession down by School Lane, which are part of the commons, were planted with potatoes which were dug and bagged by school children.

Various historical objects have been found on the commons and river bank, including prehistoric flints, Victorian handcuffs, clay pipes and swords. Many of these, such as musket balls, pistol and cannon balls, and an Ironside army sword buckle, date from the period of the Civil War. Torrington was a centre for both factions at different times and the commons would have been used for camps, drill and recreation just as they were for tank practice during the Second World War. The Royalist Lord Hopton, who was defending the town at the time of the Battle of Torrington in 1646, erected defensive barriers on the commons.

On the steep slope down from the Old Bowling Green to the Common Lake stream is a spring beside the now overgrown track and surrounded by twisted trees that is the site of an ancient well called Covety's Well. (Coventina is a Roman water goddess). The water from this well was believed to have medicinal qualities especially good for curing eye infections. People would hang bits of rag and threads on the bushes growing by the well and the belief was that as the rags rotted away so the pain would fade. Local doctor Harry Cramp has been quoted as saying that any water containing traces of zinc could, indeed, help with eye problems.[9]

The custom for the young ladies of Torrington to go 'a-Maying' in the early morning of May Day to pick a little bouquet of primroses or beech leaves and wash their faces in the dew went back to the 16th century. It is the tradition for the deputy head of the junior school to collect flowering yellow gorse from the commons to tie on the top of the two maypoles for the dancing at May Fair.

I've been asked if I've heard about the *'eadless 'orseman!* Some local people believe the story about a ghostly horseman who was seen by a number of people riding out of the trunk of a tree on the commons just beyond the archway where Old Maid's Steps lead out of Sydney House car park onto Castle Hill. He was said to be dressed in Cavalier clothing but he had no head and was consequently referred to as 'Headless Harry'!

Football has always been popular in Torrington and in the 1920s each street had its own team and practised on its own bit of commons: Mill Street on Mill Street common, Calf Street on Quiet Possession, Town Boys at Barley Grove and New Street on the Old Bowling Green which was also the location for the annual inter-street finals watched by a large crown. In 1931 the 'Street Shield' was won by Mill Street.[10]

Presumably, the Old Bowling Green was used for bowls at one time before it was played at the present site on Castle Hill. It was certainly used for shinty and women's hockey, as well as football, and as a venue for special events such as the Coronation Sports of 1902.[11]

A nine hole golf course was established on the Old Bowling Green in the 1890s where play continued until the First World War (see 'What Sports are played in Torrington?). After the war, in the 1920s, a new course was made at Darracott and the club moved to its present site at Furzebeam in 1932. As this is part of the commons, there have always been problems with free access to walkers (and their dogs) and, in the past, with grazing animals but the club and Conservators have done their best to compromise and co-operate. 'With its immaculate greens, magnificent views and friendly atmosphere, the club is a major asset to both town and commons.'[12]

The earliest sport played on the commons was 'outhurling', a rough version of football with 25-30 players in each team and goal posts some half a mile apart, which was played down on the muddiest land near Common Lake.

At May Fair the 'Round the Tree' race is run on Castle Hill down to Taddiport and back.

Past generations have happy memories of playing on the commons with their friends, making dens in the bracken and amongst the shrubs, playing 'mothers and fathers', football, hide-and-seek and 'tin can' (hitting each other's legs with a ball). Boys in the 1950s used to trap adders under big square tins acquired from the dairy and kill them with bows and arrows, skinning them and hanging the skins from their belts as trophies! They would swim in the river and go fishing, as commoners used to have the right to fish (the boundary of the commons runs down the centre of the Torridge) and catch eels and have mud ball fights. They went sliding down the small quarry areas on Castle Hill on trays and one particular slope of rock was known as 'Sliding Rock'. There is a seat along Alexander Path, where you can sit and look across the valley to the golf course, which has a little plaque:

'in Loving Memory of
BRIAN TUCKER
(1946-2010)
Whose favourite childhood place was the commons.'

Sadly, it is now extremely rare to see children unaccompanied by adults playing out on the commons.

Commons path

Photo by the author

Cavaliers' Medieval Castle   Photo courtesy of Bob Brewer

The commons have inspired many artists and photographers over the years. These have included Edward Gay known as 'Humpy' Gay because of his crooked back who lived at the end of Halsdon Terrace (in a house since demolished) and was a self-taught naïve painter, Larry Alexander, Philip Dixon, Christine Lovelock and photographers James Ravilious, Dave Sanders, Jayne Poole and Dave Elliott.

The Old Bowling Green is the setting for the Torrington Cavaliers' bonfires. Every few years this band of men build commemorative structures out of wood which they burn in spectacular fashion in front of an audience of thousands in aid of charity. Over the years the themes of these bonfires have ranged from the World's Largest Bonfire and Tallest Guy to scale replicas of the Houses of Parliament, Torrington Church and Nelson's 'Victory' The most recent one, a Medieval Castle burnt in August 2010, raised over £60,000 for charity.

There is a wide variety of flora and fauna to be seen on the commons. B. G. Lampard-Vachell listed 100 different species in his booklet 'Wild Birds of Torrington and District' published in 1944 (while he was Mayor of Torrington). Trevor Beer has written in Town Guides about species to be seen and has advised the Conservators on such projects as the pond made in Common Lake. Judy Barber writes about watching buzzards – which she refers to as 'Nature's Master of the Commons' – from Rice Point, Furzebeam.[13] The Rev. W. Keble Martin (vicar of Torrington 1934-43) compiled 'Flora of Devon' (published in 1939) and his 'Concise British Flora' (published in 1965) became a world best seller. A more up-to-date list of trees, shrubs, flowers, grasses, mammals, birds, bats, butterflies, reptiles and amphibians can be found in a booklet entitled 'Torrington Common: A Guide to the life on the Common

2001-2002' by Michael Collingham (Chairman of the Conservators).   The Conservators have also compiled an attractive and very user-friendly leaflet – 'Torrington Common Tree Trail' – which identifies 53 trees on a circular walk of about 3 km. These include 'most of the trees and shrubs in Britain that are considered to be native' and the length of time each tree has been in this country is indicated. In addition, there is a list of later arrivals which can also be found on the commons.

There are pamphlets available at the TIC detailing walks on the commons and the Torridge Ramblers created a new 20 mile circular walk to celebrate the Millennium.

The commons are a tremendous asset to both townspeople and visitors and, hopefully, will continue to be protected.

With thanks to:
Maurice Cockwill
Michael Collingham
Dulcie Leate
Pat Wilks

14   Who are the Torrington Cavaliers?

The Cavaliers are a band of men who do a lot of voluntary work in the community, organise fund-raising events, drink copious amounts of beer and have fun! The declared aim of one of their founders, Larry Alexander, was 'to put on entertainment the like of which had never before been seen in Torrington.'[1] Their name derives from the period of the Civil War when Torrington was a Royalist, or Cavalier, town. They are best known for the edifices they build on the commons every few years – ships, trains, buildings – which are set alight along with a fantastic firework display. Thousands of people come from far and wide to see these enormous bonfires and huge sums of money are raised for charity. The burning of their half-scale replica of Nelson's Victory in 2005 raised over £70,000.

The Cavaliers were founded in 1970. Plymouth City Council was preparing to celebrate the 350th anniversary of the sailing of the Mayflower to America and many Devon towns were invited to join the celebrations. It was decided by Torrington Town Council Entertainments Committee to send two floats: Carnival Queen and attendants and also a historical tableau involving the parish church.

Larry Alexander, local builder and artist, was one of those detailed to organise the float and he was to be responsible for the people taking part. He had been building marvellous May Fair carnival floats for years and he was the natural choice to design and build the float. He and some of his builder friends created a very impressive float which had a wooden replica of the parish church and a cannon which one of the men, Michael Street, kept letting off, terrifying both horses and spectators in the parade. Stuart Smithson, a Torrington architect, had designed a graveyard on one side of the church, stained glass windows, and other effects. The men dressed in hired costumes as Cavaliers and Roundheads. Sadly, Larry Alexander, having organised the float, wasn't able to take part as he had broken his arm the previous week and was in a lot of pain.

The Victory 2005   Photo courtesy of Bob Brewer

That event was the beginning of the Cavaliers and was marked, as all subsequent events have been, by imagination, hard work, a swashbuckling spirit and enthusiastic drinking. Some of their earlier antics and near accidents would horrify present-day Health and Safety officers! These have included sword fights, flying machines, a human cannon ball, a water carnival on the River Torridge, a wrestling night at the Plough and a snail eating contest!

They are continuing a long tradition of community gatherings around bonfires. Beacons on hilltops warned of the approaching Armada in Elizabethan times. When notices were put on the commons by the Rolle Estate warning against trespass in the 1870s, Torrington people set fire to them as a protest. Jubilees and other events have been celebrated by building enormous bonfires of furze and faggots.[2]

The Cavaliers organised the May Fair Ball for many years at the Drill Hall (now the Plough) in Fore Street. In 1995 a separate group, the Entertainers, was formed and at May Fair sang a selection of wartime classics dressed as characters from 'Dad's Army'. This was done for Larry Alexander, who had been ill, and a tape was made and raised money for cancer care. This has become a tradition on May Fair morning and the Entertainers have performed Country and Western, Songs from the Shows, Sea Shanties and the Dance of the Sugar Plum Fairy (with the Cavaliers in white tutus and tights!).

Cavaliers entertain at May Fair   Photo courtesy of Bob Brewer

The Cavaliers support a lot of local events and do a great deal of unsung work in the town. They hang the bunting and erect the staging for May Fair each year. They organise a firework night at the rugby club for Guy Fawkes night, raising money in the square beforehand with the guy which is made by folk at Woodland Vale. The witch sitting on top of the bonfire last year (2011) looked very realistic, crouching forward as the flames licked all around her. They build Santa's Grotto under the Town Hall at Christmas and hand out some 400 bags of sweets to local children. In the past they have mended toys (donated by townspeople) to give to children and given food parcels and sticks for the fire to elderly people. They get a lorry into the square for concerts on New Year's Eve and organise the march through the town to commemorate the Battle of Torrington each February. They have held scarecrow competitions, built a skateboard park for the youngsters, carried out building work at the primary school and helped pack up artefacts from the museum when it had to be moved out of the Town Hall because of dry rot. They contribute a lot to the enjoyment of life in Torrington.

Here is a list of the Cavalier bonfires there have been over the last 40 years:

1970 'Largest Guy Fawkes bonfire … by the First Company of Torrington Cavaliers in Torrington, Devon, for 5th November 1970' (Guinness Book of Records).
1971 World's Tallest Bonfire.
The first two efforts were conventional bonfires i.e. piles of waste materials to create record heights.
1972 Cacafuego (Fireshitter!) or S. S. Defuego. Spanish galleon encountered by Francis Drake in the Golden Hind in March 1579.

1973 Battleship Bismarck. Dave Kelly, one of the founding Cavaliers, got together survivors of the Bismarck and HMS Hood and two other British ships involved in that battle who came to Torrington to be part of the bonfire celebrations.

1974 Viking Ship with sails made by girls at Sudbury's glove factory.

1975 American Fort Dearborn.

1976 World's Tallest Guy – over 80ft in height, over 100ft when on the bonfire.

1977 Silver Jubilee Celebrations consisted of a conventional bonfire, one of a chain of beacons across the country, the first being lit by the Queen at Windsor.

1990 Houses of Parliament. Dave Kelly managed to get 52 descendants of the Gunpowder Plotters – Fawkes, Catesby and co. – down to Torrington to join in the event.

1991 Great Train Robbery.

1996 Torrington Church before it was destroyed in the Civil War.

2000 Great Fire of London (Pudding Lane). Rumour has it that some visitors to Torrington enquired at an estate agent about the houses with a view to purchasing one!

2005 Nelson's Victory, a truly superb half-scale model of the ship.

2010 Medieval Castle symbolising the one which was once on Castle Hill.

Pudding Lane 2000   Photo courtesy of Bob Brewer

Medieval Castle on fire

Photo courtesy of Bob Brewer

As Judy Barber put it in her book 'A Sketchbook of Torrington Commons', with reference to the Great Train Robbery:

'With pleasure the townsfolk watched the giant engine grow. Yet another imaginative event kept all eyes on the Old Bowling Green. Once more the commons were used "for the enjoyment of the people of Torrington".'[3]

What, and when, will their next construction be?

With thanks to:
Bob Brewer

15   Where was the Old Workhouse?

The system of indoor relief by means of workhouses dates from the early 17th century. Those who found themselves destitute towards the end of the century had their difficulties compounded by the Act of Settlement which prevented people moving from one parish to another in order to find work.

The accommodation of the Torrington poor house was totally inadequate so in 1737 a bridewell or house of correction was built on the north side of Calf Street (spelt

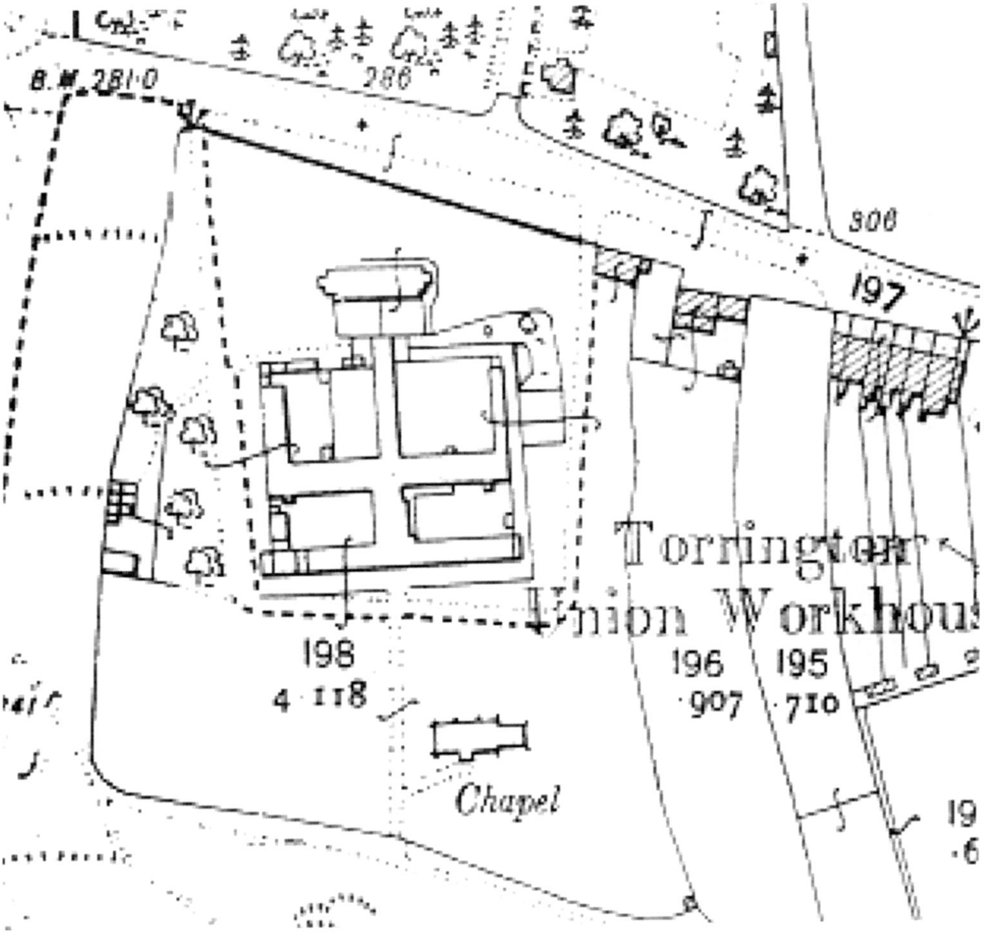
B.M. 281·0
286
308
197
198
4·118
196
·907
195
·710
19
·6
Torrington Union Workhouse
Chapel

PLAN of the old workhouse 1903 Courtesy of Bob Brewer

'Calve Street' at that time) 'for the setting to work and punishing idle and disorderly persons therein, and looms, turns, cards and other necessary tools and implements' were to be provided for the inmates and a governor appointed.[1]

This poor house served its purpose for nearly a century and then it was thought necessary to provide a modern workhouse with more comfortable accommodation for those poor people who were forced to seek shelter there. In 1836/7 a piece of land was bought on the south side of New Street on the western edge of town and a new workhouse, built of stone, was erected at a cost of £3,800. It was designed by Sampson Kempthorne who was also the architect for other Devon workhouses at Axminster, Barnstaple, Crediton, Exeter, Okehampton and South Molton. The workhouse layout was based on Kempthorne's standard cruciform, or square, design which created four courtyards – one each for men, women, boys and girls. It could accommodate 250 inmates. An infirmary was added in 1867, a small edifice of brick and stone to hold 26 inmates which cost £700, and a chapel which could seat 186 was built in the grounds behind the workhouse in 1870. A Master or Governor was appointed as well as a Chaplain, Medical Officer and Matron. The children attended the Board School.

In 1871 there were 113 inmates, twice as many women (32) as men (16) and twice as many children (65) as women. George Sellick was the Governor, John Budd the porter and Elizabeth Williams the nurse. There was also a schoolmaster, Henry Nichols, and a schoolmistress, Emma Acford, for the 36 children listed as 'scholars'. There were 24 children aged under 5, the youngest being just 2 weeks old. One child is listed as 'illegitimate', another as an 'idiot' and a third as an 'imbecile'.

The former occupations of the male inmates included one mason, one accountant, one cabinet maker (also listed as an 'imbecile'), one innkeeper, one farmer, one railway labourer, nine agricultural labourers and three listed as 'idiots'. Amongst the women, there was one former needlewoman, one shoebinder, one cook, one plumber and glazier's wife, 11 gloveresses and 13 servants. Five of the women are listed as 'idiot from birth'. All had fallen on hard times, through lack of work or care from family or general incapacity, and were unable to support themselves or their children. Such was life for the poor and disadvantaged before the welfare state.

In 1894 there were around 95 inmates in the Torrington workhouse and by 1910 there were 48.

An elderly woman, who was a child in the 1930s, remembers attending a concert and tea party each year which she assumes was held to raise funds for comforts for the occupants. She also remembers the bleakness of the workhouse. The grounds were slightly more appealing as the gardens were well kept and vegetables were grown. The bad memories of Victorian workhouses were something of the past and, as local people worked there, it was not without kindness but the place still suffered from inadequate funding. She thinks that married couples were still segregated 'so it must have been rather sad and lonely for the elderly and life was pretty hard.' Dr Bickford (after whom the Bickford Centre for the over 60s was named) was the star turn at the concerts and always sang 'Widecombe Fair'. 'Everyone loved him, he was a great and kindly man.' People who attended the concert had to supply sandwiches, sponges and other food items, as well as paying for their ticket, and 'we, as children, were warned by our parents not to eat too much as it wasn't OUR PARTY!'

When the building ceased to be a workhouse it became the Torrington Public Assistance Institution. Then it was Torridge View nursing home and 'housing with care' – eight bungalows, one and two bedrooms, including mobility standard and wheelchair properties. The chapel behind the workhouse, which hadn't been used for some time, was demolished to make way for these bungalows. The old, rather forbidding workhouse building was demolished in the mid-1990s and the single storey Woodland Vale was built on the same site and opened in January 1997. This residential care home and day care centre is run by Devon County Council.

With thanks to:
Brian Nash
Angela Newcombe
Pat Wilks

16   Which are the Oldest Streets in the town?

All the main streets of Torrington date back to well before the Civil War and are mentioned in early deeds e.g.

> Calf (formerly Calve Strete) 1283
> Calvesford 1283
> Castle Street 13th century
> Cornmarket (Cornstrete) 1345
> Mill Street (Mylstret) 1405
> South Street 1561
> Well Street 1585

Even New Street (Nywystret) is mentioned in a document dated 1382.[1]

At the time of the Civil War in the 1640s the physical extent of the town was much smaller than it is today. Apart from a few outlying habitations, most of the population lived close to the town centre in houses lining the main streets – Mill Street, Well Street and South Street. There was scattered residential development along New Street but little on Calf Street which was mainly barns, linhays and gardens.[2]

The Hearth Tax of 1674 lists only 316 houses. Given the same sized population as in 1646, this would make an average of seven people per house so the built-up area of the town was much more densely populated than at present.[3]

New Street   Photo courtesy of Margaret Trounson, Roy Beer and Dave Kelly

Town square   Photo courtesy of Dave Kelly

Torrington commanded an important crossing of the River Torridge and served as a market centre for the surrounding area. Originally, there were only two bridges – the South Bridge (Taddiport) and the West or North Bridge (Rothern). There were four distinct old main roads running almost due north, south, east and west where they leave the town:

- School Lane to the north was the old road to Bideford via Weare Giffard, Gammaton and East-the-Water. It was named after the school set up by John Lovering in 1671 in Weare Giffard. This was also the route to Barnstaple either by way of Gammaton Moor and Bideford or across the commons in the direction of the old parsonage at Priestacott. (The really ancient road to Barnstaple – 'Barum' – was by another old pack-way from Calf Street down what is now Gas Lane to Brent Bridge and on by Coombe Cross).

- Taddiport Bridge to the south took the old road to Plymouth which climbed a steep hill to Little Torrington.

- To the east the old road to Exeter went from Well Street by way of Caddywell and Shallowford and back up to North Healand.

- The old road down over the commons at the western end of town crossed the Torridge at Rothern Bridge and went up to Frithelstock and on to Hartland and Stratton (which facilitated communications between monastic establishments).[4]

Street (and place) names in Torrington reflect the activities that took place there in the past. Limers Road was an old pack road along which lime, coal and other supplies were transported after being unloaded from vessels and barges that had sailed up the tidal part of the Torridge to Weare Giffard. This road, whose function was replaced by the Rolle Canal in 1827, came across the commons from the Weare Giffard road, over the stream near Common Lake and up to the Old Bowling Green and then down to Taddiport. Preceding the bridge, there was a ford further downstream where the weir is called Fordham (or Stoneyford) to which Limers Hill led straight down. Such fords could only have been used in dry periods when the water was low.[5]

Mill Street led down to the ancient Manor Corn Mill which was later rebuilt further upstream by Lord Rolle. The name of Rack Park up on the hillside above Mill Street is connected with cloth manufacture for which Devon was once famous. This was where the woollen cloth was hung out on racks to dry. The scoured serge was brought up from the fulling mill by the river and stretched out on wooden racks on the south-facing hillside to dry in the sun and catch the prevailing wind which swept along the valley from the west.

Castle Street marks the approach from the town to the site of the medieval castle which was reduced to ruins by the 17th century although there were still 'good lands held in Castle-Gard'.[6] In the 1940s the land around the castle site was still known as 'Castle-garden Fields' which are now the Castle Hill Gardens housing estate. Barley Grove refers to the bailey of the castle, the outer wall and the court enclosed by it surrounding the keep. In 1883 this land was known as the Yeo as it had been laid out and planted as ornamental ground by three times mayor, John Yeo. This area of land was conveyed by the Rolle Estate to the Town Council along with the bowling green which was part of the castle site.

Castle Street 1905   Photo courtesy of Linda Downing

Potacre (often called 'Pottyacre' by Torringtonians) either refers to 'a potter's field' or, a more modern meaning, 'Apothecary's Street'. The Shambles, an open courtyard in Cornmarket Street, at the rear of the Town Hall, was the site of the old meat market. The Old English word 'scamel' meant a bench which referred to the stalls and benches on which the butchers laid out their meat for sale. Goose Green refers to a grassy spot, perhaps a village green or a piece of common land, where people could keep their animals. Caddywell comes from the Old English word 'weille' meaning spring and so refers to Cada's spring.

Rothern Bridge has been variously known in the past as Rotherna, Rodenford and Rothernford. A bequest was made to the Bridge of Rothernford by Sir William Hankford in his will of 1423 and, before the bridge was built, there was a ford there. (Old English 'hryther' meaning ox or cattle, so 'a cattle ford').[7] It is believed that the bridge was built by the masons who built Frithelstock Priory in the 13th century.[8] The bridge has been widened on both sides but the original medieval bridge remains.

Before 1825 the only road from Torrington to Bideford was via Weare Giffard, Gammaton and East-the-Water. In 1824 it was suggested that a new road should be constructed on the west bank of the Torridge via Landcross and this came into being as a turnpike road in 1825. When it reached Bideford, instead of going along the quay it was routed up Torridge Hill and along Buttgarten Street, the reason given being that most traffic along the road came to Bideford market and this was the quickest route. Eventually, New Road was opened along by the river which charged tolls until 1876 when turnpike tolls were removed.[9]

The old road from Rothern Bridge to Torrington was up Carriage Path on the commons parallel to the present road which comes out at the Old Bowling Green. When Torrington railway station was built in 1872 the route to Bideford had to be diverted by a winding course to Rothern Bridge and this necessitated the felling of four fine Scotch pines which were a landmark on the commons.

In 1928 this road was altered again by Devon County Council and the new Rolle Bridge was built upstream from the old Rothern Bridge. One could now cross the river with a full view of the traffic on either side and dangerous corners had been removed on the Station Hill and the road widened in different places. It was thought that not only the borough but the county would benefit from the improved means of communication. The new structure provided a solution to the problems of flooding suffered by the low level approach to the old Rothern Bridge and was designed to take 'the great loads that were imposed upon the roads today'. The design was approved by the Ministry of Transport who had made a contribution of £9,000 towards the cost. At the opening ceremony a civic party walked in procession to the bridge, headed by Torrington Town Band. Sir Ian Amory of Knightshayes Court, Tiverton cut the ribbon entwined around the chain stretched across the road with a pair of silver scissors and afterwards unlocked the padlock connecting the chain and threw away the key signifying that the bridge would remain open.[10] Station Hill was reconstructed to yet another new line in 1969.[11]

Taddiport Bridge is a medieval bridge probably dating from the 13th century and certainly mentioned in documents in the 14th century. Indulgences were granted by bishops to parishioners for donations raised for the building and upkeep of bridges. Fairfax mentions both Taddiport and Rothern bridge in his dispatch to the Speaker

Station Hill   Photo courtesy of Margaret Trounson and Roy Beer

of the House of Commons, February 1646, as routes of escape taken by Royalist soldiers after their defeat at Torrington. Taddiport Bridge has three arches with cut-waters and was widened by means of 'heavy additions'[12] on the west side in 1879 at a cost of £900.[13] Town Wardens' accounts show numerous entries for repairs of the two town bridges such as in 1693-94 'paid for repairing; Rotherna and Town Bridge as ordered and particulars £6 0 0', and between 1705-6 repairs needed after both bridges 'damaged by great waters'. There have been a number of floods over the years: in November 1894 when the flood water swept over the parapet walls of the bridges and more recently in December 1994, January 1999 and October 2000 (see 'Is Taddiport part of Torrington?'). Extensive work was done on Taddiport Bridge in 1959 when water had scoured out shingle under a pier of the bridge to a depth of 6-8 ft. It took five weeks for Len Jackson, Divisional Road Engineer and Surveyor for the Torrington District and his foreman, Bert Sussex, and their men, working in difficult conditions below the surface of the water using a coffer-dam, to carry out the necessary repairs and save the bridge.[14] Both Taddiport and Rothern bridges are now scheduled as ancient monuments and their upkeep is the responsibility of Devon County Council.

New Bridge by the New Manor Mill (Town Mills/Orford Mill) was built in 1843 at the instigation of John Lord Rolle. It is a three-arched bridge built of dressed local stone from quarries at Halwill Moor and Dolton with granite copings to the parapet walls whose style was in keeping with the nearby New Manor Mill built in a castellated form with battlemented gables and parapet walls surrounding an inner yard. Together, they form 'a picturesque feature that fits in well with the beautiful surrounding scenery.'[15] A new road was cut from there up Mile Hill to Little Torrington,

Above: Town Mills   Photo courtesy of Linda Downing

Below: Well Street pre New Road   Photo courtesy of Linda Downing

Merton and Hatherleigh which was opened in 1844 and, since then, Taddiport Bridge is no longer on a major thoroughfare and used only by local travellers. The gates of the toll house by the bridge were in existence as late as 1879.[16]

Torrington roads are now expected to carry far more and far larger vehicles than they were designed for and traffic hold-ups and parking problems are an ever-present feature of the town. New Street which 'has, with some justification, been likened to the main street of a mining village. . .'[17] carries a constant stream of heavy through traffic but the town square is tucked away from the main road which gives the centre of town a nice, rather intimate feel. There are lots of terraces and groups of houses, old and new, hidden away in corners of the town, such as Providence Row (1866), Glove Court, Lynn Terrace, Tavern Mews, Alice Court, Louise Terrace, Elizabeth Court, Kitchener's Row, Cavalier Court, Old Inn Mews and Tannery Row, which can be spotted on a walking tour of the town.

With thanks to Graham Truepenny

17   How old is the Drinking Fountain in the square?

The drinking fountain in the High Street was a gift from the Honourable Mark Rolle in August 1870. It bears the inscription:

'Presented to the Town of Torrington by the
Honourable Mark Rolle, 1870'

and

'This fountain was restored by public subscriptions
during the Mayoralty of Thomas J. Dyer, 1928-9'.

It was restored and cleaned in the 1970s and again in recent years and Gabriel Hummerstone has repaired some of the ornate stonework.

I've been told by someone who was a teenager in Torrington in the 1980s that 'everyone climbed the fountain on New Year's Eve!'

The fountain is built of stone and granite and consists of a Gothic style square on plan with a crocketed spire of carved stone and a round basin for drinking water on each face. It no longer functions as a drinking fountain and these four basins are now filled with flowers which have been maintained for years by local florists, Ken and Irene Daniel. They have now handed over this duty to Val and Mick Knight. The structure is 18ft (4.5m) high and approached by two rows of steps. In the higher portion is a clock with a face on the north and south sides. The clock needs to be wound twice a week and this was done for many years by Derrick Reed (along with the church clock). Colin Beer is now the clock winder.

There used to be two-way traffic in the square which went either side of the fountain.

Torrington Square from the Market.

Rolle Fountain from the Pannier Market   Photo courtesy of Linda Downing

Next to the fountain in the pavement is a small manhole cover which is 16ins (40cms) square. This covers a well which used to feed the fountain. In the mid-1990s this well was explored by Pete Sawyer, son of the then publicans at the Black Horse. It is hard to imagine an adult being able to squeeze through the opening but Pete somehow managed it. His diving equipment was handed down to him once he was through and he climbed down a ladder the fire brigade had let down into the well. I had heard tales that he'd discovered arches and tunnels which were part of the sewers rather than the secret tunnel that many people believe runs under the square from the church to Castle Hill. I'd also been told that, before Pete went down, the well had been 'seeded' as he'd found the scull of an animal and a pair of red glittery scanty knickers! However, I learnt from Pete himself that in fact the well went straight down into the earth. He'd hit water at a depth of 2 metres and silt at about 6 metres. His main memory of the experience is how very very black and mucky it was down there.

With thanks to:
Colin Beer
Roger Hickman
Alistair Kimber
Pete Sawyer

18   What Industries were there in Torrington in the past?

Torrington as a borough dates from the late 12th century and in its early days the town flourished on its markets and fairs: it was reckoned to be the best market town in Devon, except perhaps for Honiton.

Agriculture was Torrington's primary industry when the main essential was the cultivation of land and the production of food. As the population increased other important trades would follow.

By the 13th century England's main source of commerce was the supply of unmanufactured wool sold to the Flemish and other foreign merchants. Until the middle of the 14th century all our clothes were imported but a statute of 1327 during the reign of Edward III prohibited the export of wool and the wearing of imported cloth and this was the beginning of the great woollen industry in England.[1]

In Devon the manufacture of cloth gradually became very important and by the 15th century 'Devonshire kerseys' had become famous. John Leland, in around 1538, described Torrington as a trading centre and said it had

'a good market every week and ons a yere upon S. Michal's day the best fayre in al those quarters. . . the most parte lyvith there by making of cloth.'[2]

In around 1570 the 'new draperies' appeared in England. They were light fabrics of the worsted type which were first made in Flemish towns. The new fabrics reached Devon by the end of the 16th century, in and around Barnstaple to start with where baize was made. Soon after 1600 the manufacture of serges and 'perpetuanos' (so called for their hard-wearing qualities) started in Devon. Tiverton still concentrated on the kersey trade in which Peter Blundell (1520-1601), founder of the school, made his fortune. Tristram Risdon in his 'Survey of Devon' (1630s) described Torrington as

'indifferently beautiful with buildings, very populous, and flourishing with merchants and men of trade, their market is great furnished from far on every quarter.'[3]

By the beginning of the 18th century the woollen industry was well-established in Torrington, the cloth produced described as 'bayes' (baize, single and double) and 'frizadoes' (a plush-finished fabric). The town was 'now a rich and populous Place full of Merchants who carry on a good trade to Ireland and other Places'.[4]

Place names in Torrington reflect the manufacture of woollen cloth:
- Tucking Mill meadow;
- Staple Vale down by the old station where there was an extensive manufactory;
- Reed's Field, down by the Puffing Billy cottages, between the commons and the Tarka Trail, is named after a Mr J. B. Reed who was manager of the Staple Vale manufactory;
- Two places called 'Rack Park' – fields where cloth and serges were stretched out on racks to dry – one at the western end of town near Warren Lane and the other by the river which was part of the Staple Vale property.

A woollen mill building of considerable size at Weare Giffard belonged to a Mr Turton who produced what were then known as 'Turton blankets' until about 1850. Water was conveyed by a mill leat from the River Torridge which worked a water wheel for the woollen manufacture and later, up to the 1930s, a large flour mill.

Above: 'Peace Party' for glove workers at the end of WW2

Photo courtesy of Ben Jones and the North Devon Journal

Vaughan-Tapscott glove factory

Photo by the author

By 1777 the woollen industry in Torrington had greatly decayed and many of the town's inhabitants were suffering through unemployment. Attempts were made to revive the industry and the manufacture of cloth appears to have lasted at Staple Vale well into the 19th century. (The manufactory was sold to Lord John Rolle in 1802). By 1833 the manufacture of woollen goods was confined to the production of a few serges, blanket and some coarse cloths.[5]

When the wool trade was past its peak it was replaced to a certain extent in importance by animal skin curing for the making of kid and chamois which was carried out during the first three decades or so of the 19th century in what was known as 'The Yard, Torrington'.

Allied to this was glove making, which had developed during a thriving wool industry in the 17th century and which replaced it as the town's major employer in the 19th century.

'There used to be a number of establishments and premises in various parts of the town where gloving was carried on, much of which was done by outworkers, who periodically brought in the work which they had done or collected from others in the neighbourhood, the work extending over a radius of 30 miles'.[6]

By the 1830s some 3,000 women were employed in the making of kid, chamois, beaver (called Woodstock gloves) and other sorts of gloves for the London and foreign markets. In *White's Gazetteer* of 1850 are listed the names of 13 glove makers in the town. As the smaller establishments disappeared machines began to be introduced into the larger ones, at first worked by hand on the premises until hot air, steam and gas engines were introduced. One factory alone had more than 600 employees – both factory workers and outworkers – in the 1880s. By the 1940s there were three factories in the town, though a lot of gloves were still made by women and girls in their homes. Tapscott's in New Street amalgamated with Vaughan's in Whites Lane in 1989 and this factory, which was sold to Bennett Safetywear from Lancashire, continued to operate until 2002. The last working glove factory in the town was Sudbury's which had moved from its premises in Villa Road up to Greenbank and taken over Vaughan-Tapscott. It closed some five years ago and the building was sold in 2011 and has been demolished to make space for housing.

The lime burning industry started to be of great assistance to agriculture from the 17th century onwards. Lime was the only fertiliser used on farmland, apart from farmyard manure, and its use was so widespread that there were at least 20 kilns working between Weare Giffard and the mouth of the River Torridge. Some of the limestone came from quarries in North Devon but most of what was burnt in these kilns came from South Wales, shipped in small coastal vessels that landed their cargoes at quays up the River Torridge. Risdon, writing in the 1630s says:

'Of late, a new invention has sprung up, and been practised, by burning lyme, and incorporating it for a season with earth, and then spread upon the arable land, hath provided a plentiful increase of all sorts of grain amongst us, where formerly such never grew in any man's memory.'[7]

The fertility of the soil was greatly improved and large amounts of wheat, barley and oats were exported from Bideford between 1817 and 1820.

In Torrington parish there were three kilns employing a number of men. One near Town Mills and another near Taddiport bridge were both built by John Lord Rolle at

Old lime kilns, Rosemoor

Photo by the author

the time when the Torrington Canal was constructed from the navigable part of the river at Annery to the New Manor Mills at Torrington and limestone was brought inland on barges drawn by horses. The Staple Vale kiln would have been a later construction brought about by the extension of the railway to Torrington in 1872 and it kept working until 1910. The use of artificial manures, less corn being grown and the larger portion of farmland laid down to grass led to the quarrying of limestone and burning in local kilns to be abandoned. Limers Hill reminds us of this important local industry and remains of kilns can still be seen at Annery, near Weare Giffard, and at Rosemoor, where the canal continued from New Manor Mills out beyond 'Rowe's Moor' through Darkham Wood to rejoin the River Torridge.

Tanning was a flourishing industry which provided steady employment to many men and contributed to the prosperity of Torrington in the 17th century. There were a number of tanneries working in the 19th century up to 1850. One which was situated on the eastern side of Stoneman's Lane and another on the north side of Mill Street were both owned by a Mr John Bound Kingdon and had ceased working by 1875. The Bullring Tannery in Church Lane consisted of an extensive range of buildings with a large house facing the High Street (where Ferry's hardware shop is now). The large bark shed was converted into a cinema which, in turn, became a bingo hall and was eventually demolished to make way for the properties called Tannery Row. Originally, this was the site of the bullring where bull baiting took place. Chapple's tannery was at the top of what is now New Road and incorporated the large building which still stands behind McColl's store and Sing and Gist where chamois leather was produced. Remains of an old tannery for horse tack can still be found behind number 4 Castle Street. There was also a small tannery out at Caddywell, owned by John Rude, and one which belonged to the Adams brothers in South Street remained working until 1925 and was then taken over by a market gardener.[8]

These tanners were also 'curriers' – currying being the process of putting a fine face on the leather by rubbing it with oil and Russian tallow after which the leather was dyed to the required colour. Using English hides they turned out, by a somewhat slow process, a leather of fine quality and endurance. This was eventually replaced by leather made more rapidly from foreign salted hides treated with chemicals as well as with water saturated with oak bark. Gradually, work in the old tanneries ceased and the buildings were converted to other uses or fell into decay. Workers migrated to larger establishments in towns and cities. Other industries affected by the decline of local tanneries were: coppice workers cutting trees for stripped bark for the tanner's crushing mill; the village cordwainer or shoemaker whose hand-made footwear was replaced by machine-made boots and shoes; the harness maker whose product as late as the beginning of the 20th century, 'with its fine tooling, silver mounts, and excellent craftsmanship was a joy to behold'.[9]

There were one or two clockmakers in many of the old Devon towns and villages who made and repaired clocks and watches and, sometimes, also worked as gunsmiths. Their industry included the making and installing of clocks for parish churches and other public buildings but their craftsmanship will be mostly remembered for their output of long-case or 'grandfather' clocks of which many were produced. In around 1797 a clockmaker called John Oatway was working in Torrington and a man named Dennis is also mentioned. *Pigot's Directory* of 1830 lists two watch and clockmakers: John Dennis (and silversmith) of High Street (possibly a descendant of the Dennis previously mentioned) and James Langbridge, also of High Street. In 1844 a Richard Passmore of High Street is listed. In *White's Gazetteer* of 1850 three clock and watchmakers are listed in Torrington – John Dennis, High Street, William Saunders, South Street and John Williams, Potacre Street – but by this date these tradesmen were probably only selling clocks with their names on them and not actually making them. *Kelly's Directory* of 1866 lists Hubert Bartlett (watchmaker and photographer) of High Street, John Passmore Rowe (watch and clockmaker) of South Street and Allan Taylor (watch and clockmaker) of High Street.

In the 17th century there were several potters in Torrington who were able to sell their wares at home and abroad. Like the potters of Bideford and Barnstaple, they used Fremington clay which would have been shipped up the River Torridge and then brought the rest of the way by packhorse.

In her book, 'North Devon Pottery', Alison Grant mentions 17th century potters Luke Deane, Harry Rice (who sent pottery to Ireland as well as more local places) and Jeremiah Robbins (quite likely the maker of tiles marked with the initials IR found in the locality). There was also a local potter at this time called John Elsworthy (who died in 1704) and another John Elsworthy (married in 1705) so church floor tiles with the initials IE, found in parishes near Torrington as well as in a domestic hearth in South Street, could have been made by either of these men. Another potter, Peter Elsworthy, died in 1797 so this family worked at the trade for over 100 years. Peter and Samuel Redecleave were both Torrington potters in the 18th century. There is thought to be a 17th or 18th century kiln site in New Street, somewhere near the Torrington Arms, but there has been no excavation.

Quantities of tobacco pipe clay were sent to Bideford by ship in the 17th century. It seems there was no pottery in Weare Giffard at that time but one was built in the 19th century right by the river at Annery. Salt-glazed stoneware was made there, which was not in the North Devon tradition, but it did exhibit 'pipe clay and common potter's clay' at the Great Exhibition of 1851. White clay from Peters Marland tempered with flint etc. could now be used for stonewear. Annery Pottery's most lucrative sales were drainage pipes which were sent to London and other cities.

Some pottery sherds were found on Torrington commons so, at the beginning of the 21st century, a short rescue dig was held in Torrington led by archeologists from Devon County Council. Grant reckons there was probably a pottery at Caynton House, Mill Street, just above where kiln remains had been noticed by a builder, though too late to save them, where three houses were built in the garden. The pottery was from a waster heap. Tile fragments were found and matched tiles in local churches that make it likely that this was a Deane pottery. Tiles were marked LD, ID and DD. The Deanes leased a tenement and garden and some land beside the river at Taddiport in the 17th and 18th centuries and, maybe, they then moved up to a town site. The dig produced some small 'trailed slip' pieces, perhaps from the early 18th century.

Alison Grant includes in her book a list of 'Potters from Great Torrington and the villages' from the 17th century to the 21st.[10] She has excluded some notable potters of the present day, such as Nick Chapman and Helen Lamprey, and ceramic restorer Philip Dixon.

There are many old Torrington crafts and trades which are no longer in existence or practised in a very different, probably mechanised, way including the following: glover, pewterer, heelmaker, cardmaker, ropemaker, thongcutter (for sewing leather, not scanty knickers!), brickmaker, packsaddler, cooper, worsted-comber, fuller, felt-maker, maltster, spoonmaker, nailmaker, tallow-chandler, soap boiler (though hand-made soap continues to be produced by the Soap Kitchen up at Hatchmoor and sold in their shop in South Street as well as on the Internet), charcoal burner, ostler, sawyer, straw hat maker, tanner, currier, blacksmith, whitesmith (a worker in tin, also polisher or galvanizer of iron), watch and clockmaker, wheelwright.

With thanks to:
John, Tilly and Alistair Kimber

19   What Industries are there in Torrington?

Torrington has long been a factory town, with its woollen, glove making and tanning industries in the past, but large factories have deserted the town in recent years. In the second half of the 20th century the main factories in Torrington employing a large proportion of the town's population were the Dairy Crest creamery down in Taddiport, Dartington Glass and the North Devon Meat factory, both standing to the north of the town.

Torridge Vale Dairy 1960   Photo courtesy of Bill Brook

The presence of three fairly large, labour-intensive employers was a strength from the 1960s to the 1980s but by the early 1990s had become a weakness – too many eggs in too few baskets[1] – and all three were badly affected by the recession.

There had been a dairy at Taddiport since 1874 but in 1993 the milk factory moved its production elsewhere which meant the loss of 134 jobs (see 'What is that Derelict Factory down in the river valley below Torrington?'). In 1992 Dartington Glass had to put its 250 staff on short-time (see 'Why is the glass factory called Dartington Crystal?'). In its heyday, North Devon Meat, which opened in 1967, was the largest meat factory in Europe and employed 400-500 people. In the early 1990s 100 workers were made redundant and then the building burnt down in 2001 when 250 people lost their jobs. The company was taken over by St Merryn Foods based at Bodmin in Cornwall.

Peninsula Proteins, on the site of the meat factory rendered offal into other products such as fertiliser and bonemeal. It was a source of misery to the people of Torrington for many years because of the smell produced by its processing methods – especially when blood boiling was going on to make dried blood, fish and bone. In 1979 an action group was formed to fight the 'disgusting' smell. Finally, filters were installed which solved this problem but, not long after this was achieved, Peninsula

Proteins closed down and sold off its filtering machinery. Another company, Prosper De Mulder Ltd, set up a meat rendering factory and, once again, people living nearby were complaining of an acrid smell believed to be coming from there.[2] It seemed the obnoxious odours which had previously plagued the town for 30 years had returned.

Many old factories and businesses have closed down. Years ago there used to be an ironcraft business, Gush and Dent, where Castle Hill Gardens is now. Cobbledick's seed merchants up at Hatchmoor were taken over by BOCM Paul animal feed supplier which, in turn, has closed. All the glove factories have closed: Vaughan's in Whites Lane, which closed in 2002, still stands empty and deteriorating as it waits for its future to be decided and Sudbury's up at Greenbank has been demolished to make way for housing (2011).

AMP opened up an electrical connector manufacturing site in Torrington in the early 1980s when they needed more floor space than their Bideford factory provided. This was up at Greenbank where Advanced Pallet Systems is now and 100-150 people were employed doing assembly work and plastic injection moulding. It was AMP who invented and made telephone jacks to plug into the wall. The Torrington branch closed in 1997/98 and some of the employees moved to the Bideford factory which became Tyco in the early 21st century and is now known as TE Connectivity.

Dave Kelly, who started work at 15 in the early 1960s says, at that time, there were jobs for everyone in Torrington whatever their level of educational qualifications. He remembers the thunder of hobnail boots in the early morning as men made their way to the station to catch the train out to the clay works at Marland and both men and women worked in the glove factories. He worked in the office at Sudbury Gloves when it was in Villa Road where there were seven glove cutters, originally men in suits and bowler hats, and the gloves were made up by women. They made what they called 'mitts' for debutantes, long silk gloves with pearls on for Fownes in London. An order for two thousand dozen gloves could be completed in a week. Materials were kept upstairs where the windows were covered so no sunlight was let in to spoil them. As well as smart, elbow-length gloves, they made industrial gloves and gloves made out of leather or astrakhan. There was also an 'arrant boy' attached to the factory who would make tea, wash cups and generally run about doing odd jobs.

Dartington Crystal is the major employer in Torrington though the lease on the factory site will run out in the near future and a new location will be sought. Other big employers are Simon's Plastics, established in 1958, and K & J Plant Contractors out of town at Yarnscombe.

At the eastern end of town, on the Hatchmoor trading estate, there are a number of businesses: R. W. Simon Ltd ('Simon's Plastics'), the Soap Kitchen, which has an outlet in South Street and a thriving online business in environmentally friendly cleaning products, S. Mitchell – Tipper and Plant Hire Ltd, Torridge Tyres and Batteries, Torrilitho Printers, Clearwater Brewery, ASI, Merchant Dice Ltd, Tempex ISP, Karen Lambert Workwear, Hatchmoor Veterinary Practice, S. W. Dispatch, Decorating Dimensions, Alfie's Country Supplies, Lyndale Plastics, Tamar Trading Co. Ltd, Waghorn's Wheels, Watson Fuels Co. U.K., CMG, Beran, Helitune, Denis Wright Ltd and, at Greenbank, Advanced Pallet Systems Ltd. M & D Transport are based at the old dairy down in Taddiport. There are two long-established building companies: J. E. Stacey & Co. Ltd, formerly at Goose Green and now based up at Hatchmoor at Tamar Trading, and W. H. Tolley & Son Ltd at Caddywell.

There are lots of small businesses and independent traders in Torrington, the majority of which have fewer than ten employees. These include builders, plumbers, carpenters, gas engineers, electricians, double glazing fitters, painters and decorators, hairdressers, beauticians, aromatherapists, accountants, funeral directors, TV installers, cycles for hire, chiropodists, solicitors, travel agents, chiropractors, window cleaners, childminders, architects, gardeners, estate agents, printers – and many family owned shops.

With thanks to:
Dave Kelly
Danny Ryan
Clive Ward

20   Where does the River Torridge rise?

The name Torridge comes from the old word 'toric' meaning 'noisy' and 'violent, rough stream' as opposed to its companion river, the Taw which means 'smooth, placid'. The sources of the two rivers are about 26 miles apart and they follow very different routes before meeting in a broad estuary.

The Torridge doesn't have one definite source, no single bubbling spring that can be said to be where the river starts, but rather three headwaters that combine to form the river: a stream starting in a small pool in the middle of a rushy field below Newlands Farm just over the border in Cornwall, two other streams which combine below Brimford Bridge, and a rather more impressive tributary that rises on Deptford Moor and joins the Torridge above Horton Bridge. So, in general terms, the River Torridge rises on the border of North Devon and North Cornwall, just east of the A39, only some 15 miles from where it meets the sea.

Brimford Bridge is the first of the Torridge's many bridges and, in its upper reaches, the river is very secretive losing itself in a tangle of willow and reeds. Kismeldon Bridge is the first bridge of any importance. It was constructed of iron girders in about 1912 and replaced an old narrow, humped-back bridge. In the 16th century it was called 'Kissington' by the locals and in the 13th century was known as 'Kistmelebrigge'.

Cory Manor which dates back to the 13th century has views over the Torridge valley at West Putford and the river flows under Putford Bridge which is said to have been built in 1900. It has a single main arch with a smaller one offset to one side which may be either a relief arch for flooding or to carry a mill leat. There are secluded pools and a series of loops and curves as the river widens between tree-lined banks on its way to the attractive little Haytown Bridge. This is a well built, single-arched bridge of roughly-dressed local stone. The older bridge was called 'Hey Bridge' ('hey' meaning 'hedge').

Above: Haytown Bridge

Photo courtesy of Graham Truepenny

Below: Sheepwash Bridge

Photo courtesy of Graham Truepenny

Woodford Bridge could be said to be the first public appearance of the Torridge as, before it gets here, it has been hidden in the countryside with its banks overgrown by trees and bushes, brambles and rushes. Between Haytown and Woodford Bridge 'the young Torridge is sheer beauty, its gently wandering course marked by alders, sallows and sycamore'[1] and immediately above Woodford Bridge is a stretch between water meadows and woodland which is popular with fishermen.

At Newton Mill, in a wooded valley below Newton St Petrock, a rusting iron footbridge crosses over the river, the only one along the entire length of the Torridge. The next crossing of the river is at Gidcottmill Bridge, west of Shebbear, which is believed to have been preceded by a clapper bridge. The Torridge is joined by the River Waldon just above Bradford ('broad ford'). Then comes the single span bridge at Dippermill, a pretty spot where the river broadens into pools and shallows with a shingly beach and overhanging trees but which is notorious for flooding.

A farm bridge with two arches which may well date back to the mid 18th century, or earlier, crosses the river near Black Torrington and, further downstream, the narrow, ancient Sheepwash Bridge joins the villages of Sheepwash and Highhampton. Built in the 17th century with four arches and a dry arch, this bridge would have provided an important route for Sheepwash out to the south and west when it was a thriving market town.

Below the village of Meeth the Torridge is joined by the River Okement bringing waters from Dartmoor. The railway bridge carrying the branch line from Torrington crossed both the road and the river on its way to Hatherleigh station near Hele Bridge, a graceful structure but narrow. It has been widened since it was originally built, but that was over 40 years ago, and larger lorries have to give and take. This bridge was given English Heritage Listing (Grade II) in 1988. It is a fine three-arched bridge built in dressed sandstone of a faint red colour. It lies at the foot of steep Friar's Hele Hill about 1½ miles to the north of Hatherleigh where the river swings upstream to the west.

It is possible to stop and park the car by the Torridge at Newbridge east of Huish near the estate of Heanton Satchville, home of Lord Clinton. In the churchyard of Huish church within the parkland, there are memorials to many members of the Rolle and Trefusis families. Newbridge lies on an important minor road between Dolton and Higher Lodge which is a junction with the A386 Torrington to Okehampton road. There is evidence of a bridge existing in the 17th century but the present bridge was built in 1879 and repaired in around 1960. One of the problems suffered by many bridges on the Torridge is when trees float down the river and get wedged under the arches. This happened on one occasion at Newbridge with a whole oak tree. It was a difficult job to get it to the river bank, cut off the eight large limbs in the water and then manoeuvre the huge trunk out of the river. The timber had damaged the cutwaters in front of the piers.

Downstream from Newbridge, the Torridge makes a big loop on its way to Beaford Bridge near the former Beaford Mill where it is possible to walk along by the river on a public footpath. Beaford Bridge is on the site of an old fording-place and Len Jackson, former Devon County Council Divisional Road Engineer for the Torrington Division who supervised a lot of work on the roads and bridges of North Devon, calls it 'an almost secret bridge in a delightful setting.'[2] A well-constructed bridge, believed to have been built in the mid 19th century, it nestles under a wooded hill and is largely hidden by riverside trees.

From Beaford Bridge the river performs a series of large bends through wooded countryside, with little habitation and no public access, until it reaches New Bridge at what used to be called Town Mills and is now known as Orford Mill at the junction on the A386 where the B3124 turns off to Exeter. Before arriving there it has run over a weir alongside Darkham Wood, which marks the place where the Rolle canal ended its journey from the estuary at Bideford, and passed the old lime kilns at Rosemoor. New Bridge is

'a truly majestic structure and is very high above the water.'[3]

This is because of the provision of a dry arch to take the canal which was on a higher level than the river. There are two dry arches and three main arches, the latter being of a rather unusual circular design.

'The arches are semi-circular with paved inverts to complete the circles; the faces of the piers and abutments are curving to rounded ... There is a curved high-level causeway connecting the bridge to the foot of Mile Hill, the one-time turnpike road to Little Torrington but now the A386 main road to Okehampton.'[4]

The river then flows along the base of Castle Hill on which stands, high above, the town that has taken its name – Torrington – with flat water meadows on the opposite bank. There was a bathing spot in the river here and a concrete platform and changing shed were built in the late 1920s paid for by the ladies of the town. It is said that the river was clearer and deeper in those days without so many rocks on the bottom by the edge.

The next bridge to cross the river is the one at Taddiport which is first mentioned in documents from the early 14th century and was probably built during the previous century. Before there was a bridge here, the place was known as 'Fordham' as it was an important fording-place and focal point of several routes: Barnstaple to Plymouth, Torrington to the west side of Bideford, the northerly route to Cornwall, and the route to Hartland. It was originally known as Town Bridge and has been strengthened and altered many times over the years. Massive repairs were made in the 18th century and it was widened on the downstream side in 1879. Tie rods, dated 1911, can be seen clamping the widened portion of the bridge to the main structure and in 1938 the County Council carried out some protective work to the foundations. In the years following the Lynmouth Disaster of 1952, successive bad floods caused deep pits to be cut into the river bed below the arches and beyond which gave great cause for concern. In 1959 Len Jackson was in charge of tackling this problem on the Taddiport side abutments with his chief foreman, Bert Sussex, a mason of considerable experience, to direct the work. The foundations were found to be in an appalling state so permission was given to undertake underwater repairs to the whole bridge. Further strengthening work was carried out in the following years. The 'violent, rough' river has flooded here on numerous occasions with the water reaching over the top of the bridge and flowing into the houses of Taddiport. The occupant of the large whitish house on the left of the bridge which still bears faintly the name of the Buckingham Arms had to live upstairs and proposed that the bridge should be torn down and new flood defences built to better withstand the rising

Floods at Taddiport, November 2000

Photo courtesy of Mark Deneven and the North Devon Journal

waters in the event of flooding. Getting from Taddiport to Torrington to do the shopping would have required a long round trip! However, after its repairs (in the late 1950s), despite parts of the parapets and roadway being swept away, the bridge has stood firm. 'By its rugged resistance it has survived the ravages of the River Torridge for over seven centuries.'[5]

A 700 foot long wooden viaduct once spanned the Torridge valley. It was built in 1880 by the Marland Clay Company to carry their narrow gauge trains and was replaced by a more conventional iron structure when the line was converted to standard gauge in 1925 and extended to connect with the Southern Railway system at Halwill Junction. The passenger service closed in 1965 and clay traffic ceased in 1982 and this bridge is now part of the Tarka Trail walking and cycling trail. From here, looking downstream, in the foreground is Kruger's or Kruser's Island which used to be a favourite spot for picnics amongst tall trees and a popular site for swans but is now just a bank of shingle.[6] The river passes under Rolle Bridge, opened in 1928, which was built in reinforced concrete with three arches, one of which is partially dry to allow cattle to pass from field to field. Then it flows under the old Rothern Bridge which, with Taddiport Bridge, was one of the town's original bridges and dates from at least the 14th century. At one time it became so dilapidated that it was threatened with demolition but there was such an outcry that Rothern Bridge is now a scheduled ancient monument.

The river continues on to Weare Giffard, looping through woodland and meadows and crossed three times by the Tarka Trail. At the second river crossing a heron can

Halfpenny Bridge   Photo courtesy of Graham Truepenny

often be seen standing motionless by the weir or further along the bank and it is also a popular spot for fly fishermen to cast their lines. From the third river crossing you can look upstream at Beam Bridge, with its five semi-circular arches set on tall, elegant piers, which was built as an aquaduct for the canal to cross the river but is now a roadway leading from the Torrington to Bideford road to Beam House.

Weare Giffard marks the tidal limit of the River Torridge but being low-lying along by the river the village has suffered flooding on many occasions. Chopes Bridge is at one end of the village and the river flows along past the Tudor Weare Giffard Hall to 'Ha'penny' Bridge at the other end. This bridge was built in the mid 1830s and until at least the end of the 19th century a halfpenny toll was charged to cross. A tiny toll house of stone with a slate roof was built by local builder Walter B. Cock at a cost of £33. It stood adjoining the north-east approach walling but was demolished in the 1950s. The bridge has three flat arches and is set high above the river to give fair clearance during floods. Adrian and Hilary Wills who live in one of the Annery Cottages near the large lime kilns are working to restore the water channel coming off the river which once marked the beginning of the canal.

The River Yeo joins the Torridge at Landcross (purported to be the smallest parish in Devon) and the river, much wider now, is crossed by the former railway bridge now carrying the Tarka Trail which follows the river bank into Bideford ('by the ford').

Bideford Long Bridge dates from the latter part of the 15th century and has been widened at various times and in a variety of ways to cope with the demands of modern traffic. Before the building of the present stone bridge, there were at least three different wooden structures which were in use from the late 13th century and often in need of repair. Prior to these bridges, crossing the estuary would have been by boat or via the ford at Ford Rock which would have been dangerous at the best of times and impossible at high tide or in wet weather. Much east-west traffic had to be routed through Torrington during the Middle Ages to use the town's two stone bridges.

In his book Len Jackson writes: 'The original Bideford stone bridge was very narrow and intended only for use by travellers on horseback, with pack animals, or on foot. When built, it was constructed around the original trestles of the wooden bridge, which was done to obtain continuity for the traffic crossing the river. Following the collapse of the western arches in 1968, I was promised as a memento a small slice of the old oak trestles which had come to light inside the collapsed pier. Alas, on drying out the timber completely disintegrated. The bridge was strengthened and widened in 1790, in the 1860s, in 1924-5 and in 1968-70[7] when cracks appeared and the two arches at the western end collapsed. More work has been done on the bridge in recent years: in 1998 the coping stones were rebedded, in 2002 the cutwaters were repaired and in 2009 the arches were strengthened.

The arches of the bridge are of different sizes and there are numerous theories about the reasons for this: that it depended upon the size of the donation given towards the building of the bridge, the length of building timbers used or where the firmest areas of the river bed were to support the foundations. Whatever the reason, it is an amazing structure and a much-loved local landmark which has withstood centuries of traffic.

Further downstream is the new Bideford bridge, a soaring curve high up above the river which was opened in 1987 to relieve the pressure of traffic on the Long Bridge and in the narrow streets of the town. The Taw and the Torridge meet just beyond Appledore and Instow and flow together out through Barnstaple or Bideford Bay to the Atlantic. (The first suicide from this bridge was in 1988).

Bideford Bridges   Photo courtesy of Mark Deneven and the North Devon Journal

An otter on the River Torridge   Photo courtesy of the Guardian

The 'land of two rivers' inspired Henry Williamson to write his classic 'Tarka the Otter' which mentions places along the Torridge including Canal Bridge (aqueduct at Beam), Beam Weir, Halfpenny Bridge, Annery Kiln, Never-Be-Good Woods and Landcross ('Landcarse') Pill. A film was made of 'Tarka the Otter' in the 1970s directed by David Cobham and narrated by Peter Ustinov in which local people took part and in 2008 wildlife photographer Charlie Hamilton James spent a year filming on the river to make 'On the Trail of Tarka' for the BBC Natural History unit. This film goes in search of Tarka's descendants to see if they still fish in the same pools as their forebears. In Williamson's day otters were treated as vermin and were trapped and hunted for sport. Today the otter is an endangered species and our attitudes towards it have changed and the film explores whether the lives of modern otters reflect this shift. It is a charming combination of well-loved fiction and modern-day fact and is a wonderful evocation of the changing seasons and the wildlife on the River Torridge.

With thanks to:
Graham and Janet Truepenny
Rosemary Anne Lauder, author of 'A Tale of Two Rivers' from which I have borrowed extensively for this section.

21   What are the Great Torrington Almshouse, Town Lands and Poors Charities?

These charities originated in the 17th century from benefactions by the great and good of Torrington. Over the centuries public-spirited people have given some of their private fortunes to be used for the benefit of those in need of help. The most recent benefaction was 23 years ago from a Mr Pointon. By 1970 the number of charities involved had increased to 22 but in 1971 these were reduced to three by amalgamation. The Trustees' 'Bible' is a manual entitled 'A Scheme' (1971) which gives instructions on how the Trusts and Trustees are to operate.

Above: Almshouses, New Street   Photo by the author

Below: Old almshouses demolished 1958 (where Rolle Court, New Street is now)
                    Photo courtesy of Margaret Trounson and Roy Beer

There are 15 people on the present Board of Trustees: the vicar of the parish church (ex officio), four representatives of the Town Council who are appointed for four years, and ten other co-opted Trustees who are appointed for five years. The criteria for being a Trustee is to have a specific knowledge of, or interest in, Torrington and candidates are suggested by the existing Board of Trustees. Their suitability is then debated and they are selected by the Board.

The Trustees meet monthly to determine all matters. They have a peripheral involvement with the Town Council (as already stated, four Trustees are members of the Town Council) but operate entirely independently. They are responsible for a considerable amount of investment in the stock market and in property. The Trust owns around 40 properties in the town, both commercial and domestic, as well as several acres of land. When the Trustees sell income-producing endowments, they have to replace it with similar. For example, when they sold land for building at Torrington Gate, they purchased seven properties to let. The accounts of the Trust are very complicated and are audited by chartered accountants for ultimate approval by the Charity Commission.

Chris Styles was 'Steward and Receiver' for the Trust for over 40 years and was responsible for the day-to-day management of all affairs with direct responsibility to the Trustees. He was aided by his administrative assistant, Val Hunt. Sadly, Chris finally lost his long battle with cancer and died in January 2012 aged 72. The Trustees employ in total five part-time people to deal with administration, caretaking and cleaning of the Town Hall, the almshouses and the office which is adjacent to the Town Hall.

Torrington people are favoured when it comes to choosing tenants for the many properties owned by the Trust. There are eight almshouse flats in New Street which have recently undergone a £300,000 refurbishment. The four elderly occupants of the flats when alterations began lived in one half of the building while work was carried out on the other half and they then moved into the completed part. Now all eight almshouse flats are occupied.

On the second Friday in December each year there is an annual distribution of the fund for the sick and aged at the Plough Arts Centre. In excess of 500 people attend and, in 2010, those who were eligible received £14 per household.

The Trustees receive many requests for funding. These are considered on a one-to-one basis with the circumstances of the individual being taken into account. Grants totalling up to £60,000 are given annually according to estimated income to various organisations in the town for upkeep and maintenance, such as the parish church, the Town Hall, the Plough, the Town Band, Scouts, Guides, playgroups, chapels, etc. As well as giving aid to the elderly who are struggling financially, help is also sometimes given to young people for educational or training purposes.

I suggested to Chris Styles, when I spoke to him, that it must be very rewarding for the Trustees to be able to distribute largesse to deserving local people and causes. He agreed that they derive great satisfaction from doing good for the town and that the Trust is like local government used to be, 'compassionate and people-orientated.'

With thanks to:
Chris Styles

22   What is the Tarka Trail and where is it?

The Tarka Trail is a recreational route opened in May 1992 which describes a figure of eight, centred on Barnstaple, through the beautiful countryside of North Devon. It extends for 180 miles (290 km) and different parts of the trail can be covered by rail (the Barnstaple to Eggesford section of the Tarka Line), on foot or by bicycle.

The part of the Tarka Trail that is nearest to Torrington follows the route of the old railway line which was opened in 1872 but fell to Beeching's axe in 1965, although freight continued to be transported until 1982. About a mile out of town on the A386 towards Bideford, at the bottom of the hill, is the old Torrington railway station, now a pub called the Puffing Billy. Nearby is Torrington Cycle Hire and families can often be seen cycling along the trail at weekends and holidays on bikes and tandems or with children pedalling along behind on small attached bicycles or riding in special covered trailers.

Going in a southerly direction, you can walk or cycle, via Watergate Bridge, East Yarde, Petrockstowe to Meeth Halt. (Torrington to Meeth is 11.4 miles/18.3 km). In the other, northerly, direction the trail crosses over the River Torridge on numerous occasions as it winds through the meadows and woods. You pass the village of Weare Giffard, which follows the far side of the river, go through an echoing tunnel and then cross the river via an iron bridge and on alongside the Torridge estuary to Bideford. (Torrington to Bideford is 5.3 miles/8.5 km).

Crossing the Torridge on the Tarka Trail   Photo courtesy of Bob Brewer

Torrington to Watergate   Photo courtesy of Bob Brewer

Beyond Bideford you come to Instow, which overlooks the Taw and Torridge estuary, and then Fremington, once an important port, and alongside the River Taw, at a distance, to Barnstaple. The cycle track crosses the river and, on the other side, leads on to Braunton which marks the end of the stretch where it is possible to cycle. Beyond Braunton to Croyde, Woolacombe, Ilfracombe, Combe Martin, Lynton and Lynmouth the trail is for walking only and is partly along the South West Coast Path. You can then follow an inland route back to Barnstaple.

From Torrington, in the southerly direction, it is possible to cycle as far as Meeth but, before Meeth, the trail continues, for walkers only, to Dolton, Iddesleigh, Hatherleigh, Jacobstowe to Okehampton and on to Belstone, Sticklepath and South Tawton on Dartmoor and then, via North Tawton and Bondleigh to Eggesford where you can catch the train back to Barnstaple.

The Tarka Project was set up in 1989 by Devon County Council, four district councils and the Countryside Commission with the aim of protecting and preserving the environment which led to the creation of the Tarka Trail. Its name was inspired by Henry Williamson's classic novel, 'Tarka the Otter' (1927) and takes the traveller through the contrasting landscapes of 'Tarka Country' described in the book: peaceful countryside, wooded river valleys, rugged moorland and dramatic coast. Tarka was born and died near Torrington so, in one sense, this is the beginning and end of the trail.

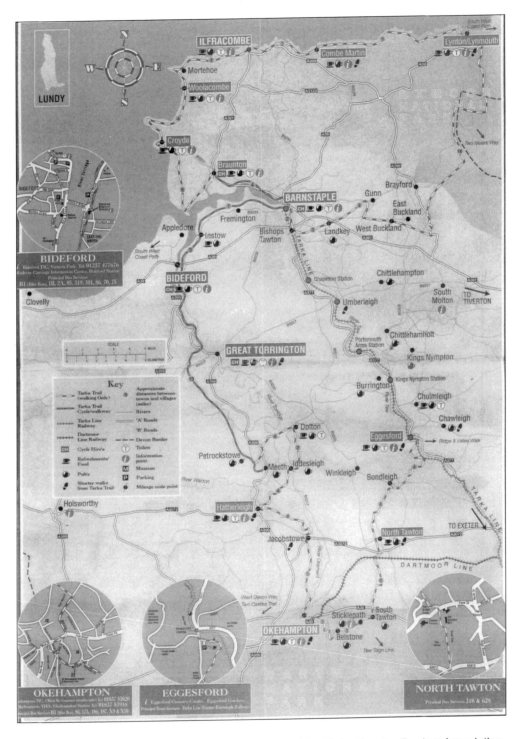

The Tarka Trail

Map courtesy of the Tarka Country Tourism Association

Distances on the Tarka Trail from Torrington

Bideford station to the tunnel (going south)	2 miles	3.2 km
Tunnel to Torrington station (Puffing Billy pub)	3.3 miles	5.3 km
Bideford to Torrington station (about one mile from Torrington town centre)	5.3 miles	8.5 km
Torrington (Puffing Billy) to Watergate Bridge	1.8 miles	2.9 km
Watergate Bridge to East Yarde	2.7 miles	4.3 km
East Yarde to Petrockstowe Station	3.5 miles	5.6 km
Petrockstowe Station to Meeth Halt	3.4 miles	5.5 km
Torrington to Meeth	11.4 miles	18.3 km
Bideford to Meeth	16.7 miles	26.9 km

TARKA TRAIL
Train: Eggesford (from Exeter) to Barnstaple (with 4 halts)
Cycle/walkway: Barnstaple to Braunton
Walkway: Braunton to Croyde to Woolacombe to Ilfracombe to Combe Martin to Lynton/Lynmouth to Barnstaple
Cycle/walkway: Barnstaple to Bideford to Torrington to Meeth
Walkway: just before Meeth to Dolton to Iddesleigh to Hatherleigh to Okehampton to North Tawton to Eggesford.

23　　How long has there been a Community Hospital in Torrington?

The idea of a hospital in Torrington was first suggested by William Vaughan, owner of the glove factory in Whites Lane, and a fund was set up in 1887 for this purpose. By 1897 this fund had increased, with donations from the Hon. Mark Rolle and other subscribers in the town, to £500 15s 7d and a hospital was established in January 1898 at 181 New Street (opposite Lidl supermarket). Vaughan lent the house, rent free, for three years. Subscribers would be able to nominate a patient for a month for one guinea. Until recently there was a pair of white double doors to the right of the front door which led into a Marland brick walled space that had been the mortuary. The present owners (2011) have divided the house into two and replaced the white doors with wooden panelling, windows and an entry door leading to the living area of what is now a one up, one down property, number 181A. A bus shelter stands right outside.

In 1903 a declaration of trust was made and four trustees appointed, the trust property then consisting of furniture in the house in New Street, a credit balance at the bank of £73 13s 6d, and the residuary estate of another benefactor of Torrington, William Frederick Glubb, who died in 1897. It took about six years for this bequest to be sorted out and money to be released because of disputes between the trustees of the hospital and the executors of the will.

Old cottage hospital   Photo courtesy of John and Tilly Kimber

In February 1907 a piece of land at Goose Green was given by Mark Rolle with the consent of his trustees and conveyed to the trustees of the hospital,

> 'upon trust to permit the same to be used for the benefit of poor persons suffering from accidents or non-infectious disease who cannot be properly attended to in their own home, and primarily for those resident in the town and district of Torrington.'[1]

On this land the trustees were authorised by the Board of Charity Commissioners to build a hospital which cost £1,300 and was officially opened on 5th August 1908 by Lady Gertrude Rolle. Despite the fact that neither William Vaughan, William Glubb nor Mark Rolle lived to see their vision of a hospital, a plaque commemorates the opening and the three men who brought it to reality.

There were three wards – men, women, accidents – each containing three beds and a cot, operating room, surgery, consulting room and matron's apartment. Records of the time show the hospital dealing with such ailments as 'mitral incompetence', crushed fingers, injuries from a gunpowder explosion and someone needing the amputation of a big toe.

In 1939 four wards were added for the use of paying patients, the cost of building being provided by a gift of £1,000 from retired GP, Dr Mark Jackson, whose family had lived in Torrington for many years. He gave the money in memory of his father, mother and wife who had given him 'unforgettable and happy years of my life', as recorded on a tablet on the building. These wards later became a maternity ward.

During the two world wars many wounded and convalescent soldiers were treated at the cottage hospital.

In the 1970s the hospital was threatened with closure but these problems were overcome and in the 1980s it underwent major building reconstruction, remaining open throughout the building work. A League of Friends was set up which still supports the hospital today.

There continue to be periodical threats of closure and in the last few years the number of beds has had to be reduced from 14 to 10. For a small hospital there is a wide range of services for both in-patients and out-patients and it is a great help to the people of Torrington, especially the elderly, to have a local hospital where they can be treated and visited by relatives and friends without having to traipse over to the North Devon District Hospital in Barnstaple. Chiropody and physiotherapy are provided for out-patients and consultants hold clinics at the hospital dealing with ear, nose and throat problems, breast treatment, family planning, optometry, paediatrics, continence and rheumatology. Day cases are also treated for blood transfusions or intra-venous infusions. A member of the volunteer service comes into the hospital two or three times a week to organise activities with the patients.

Torrington is possibly the only small community hospital to have a separate dining room and day room where patients are encouraged to go for their meals and to sit together and talk or watch TV (provided by the League of Friends). At May Fair the Torrington Silver Band stops outside in the street to play for patients in the day room and they can also watch the carnival parade go by.

On 3rd August 2008 the hospital celebrated a centenary of serving the community. To mark the special anniversary Lord and Lady Clinton unveiled a commemorative stone and a fête was held in the grounds of the hospital, organised by staff and members of the League of Friends. It is to be hoped that this valuable asset to the community will be able to continue its work for many years to come.

With thanks to:
Jacintha ('Cin') Richards
Ann Ayre
Chantell Oversby

24   Is Taddiport part of Torrington?

Taddiport, which lies in the valley of the River Torridge, is, strictly speaking, in the parish of Little Torrington which is out of sight over the hill to the south. Great Torrington looks down upon the village from the hill to the north.

Between the 14th and the 18th century it was known variously as Taddy-Ford, Addiport, Taddyporte or Taddypitte. 'Taddy' from the Old English 'Taddige' means 'toad' and 'port' refers to a 'door' or 'entrance' rather than a 'port'. Toad was thought to have some reference to the scaly skin of the lepers who lived in the village, or there may have been toads coming up from the river, thus 'Toadpit'. It tends to be a damp place at the foot of two steep hills, often filled with early morning mist, and has been flooded badly on occasions.

'Litelorilanda' in the Domesday survey has been identified with the site of the Magdalen Hospital. The first mention of it is in 1311 when a priest was appointed as chaplain 'to the chantry of St Mary Magdalen, juxta pontem de Chepyng Toritone' i.e. close to Great Torrington bridge, which was most probably built during the previous century.

In 1423 Sir William Hankford of Annery left money in his will for the upkeep and repair of several local bridges including 'Toriton' (Taddiport) and 'Rothernford' (Rothern) down by the Puffing Billy.

John Leland, who visited Torrington twice at the end of the 1530s, entered the town over Taddiport Bridge (which he refers to as the 'South bridge') and left by way of Rothern Bridge (which he calls 'West bridge') when he went on to Hartland and Cornwall on his first visit. On his second visit, he refers to Rothern Bridge as 'North bridge' when he travelled on to Bideford.[1]

After the Battle of Torrington in 1646, the remnants of the defeated Royalist army fled to Cornwall by way of the bridge at Taddiport.

Taddiport (or 'Town Bridge') and Rothern Bridge were the only two bridges over the Torridge connecting Torrington to the outside world until New Bridge at Town Mills was built by Mark Rolle in 1843 and Rolle Bridge was constructed down by the station in 1928 when Rothern Bridge could no longer cope with the heavy traffic that used it. Before these new bridges were built, the main road out of Torrington to the south passed through the village of Taddiport. At different periods it has been used by pack-horses carrying clay, carts collecting lime or coal from the canal boats or, later, bringing milk to Sandford's dairy, wagons carrying timber and many other conveyances. It is still a popular short cut despite the steep, narrow lane up Dick Baker's Hill.[2]

45916. TORRINGTON, FROM SOUTH.

Torrington from Taddiport 1930s   Photo courtesy of Linda Downing

Chapel of St Mary Magdalen

Photo by the author

In 1665 Tristram Arscott, who had purchased Annery and other estates belonging to the Hankfords, became 'Hereditary, sole, and perpetual guardian of the Hospital of St Mary Magdalen, Taddiport.'

'He conveyed the hospital with its revenues, "in the vacancy of Lazars and Leprous people" to the Mayor and Burgesses of Great Torrington and the Church Wardens and Overseers of Little Torrington, to be equally divided for the relief of the poor of those parishes.'[3]

During the 18th century the income of the charity was spent on clothes for the poor and the rent of the chapel field was paid to the rector of Little Torrington on condition that he had divine service in the chapel twelve times a year. In the 1940s the Borough Council were the Trustees of the Great Torrington portion and grants from the revenue were made from time to time to various charities. Little Torrington kept the cottages belonging to the Trust in repair and provided clothing for the poor, which was distributed at Christmas, and blankets for the winter which were stored in the rectory.[4]

The little chapel of St Mary Magdalen still retains traces of its early origin as the chapel for the leper hospital which stood nearby. At the west end is a small embattled tower, measuring 5ft (1m 50) square, and a north-east transept is thought to be the earliest part of the building. The nave is only 30ft (just over 9m) long and there is seating in the church for about 40 people. The east window with its traceried head is

86

relatively modern, the south-east round-headed window is 18th century and there is a 17th century window with wooden mullions inserted over it. There are also two square-headed windows but the building tends to be rather dark inside. The south doorway is not the original, which was further to the west by the font and only 5ft (1m 50) high. The thickness of the walls denotes the great age of the building and the only ornamentation consists of some carved oak wall plating below the rafters in the transept. Two image brackets remain on the east wall and a recess shows the position of a piscine (a stone basin near the altar in Roman Catholic and pre-Reformation churches for draining water used in the Mass). The font is comparatively modern. On the east and south walls there are texts painted in 18th century style and restored in 1971: the Twelve Commandments and a passage from Micah. The stained glass south window commemorating the leper hospital was created by Chris Sing in 1972. The window is richly coloured in green, brown, yellow and red and depicts lepers working in the fields, lying ill in bed, walking in pairs with heads bowed and kneeling before a priest being blessed. Around the edge it reads:

'REMEMBER THE LEPERS WHO LIVED AND WORSHIPPED
HERE AND ALL WHO BEFRIENDED THEM IN THE
15, 16 AND 17 CENTURY OF OUR LORD'.

The 'Chantry Chapel of St Mary Magdalen' was called either a 'chapel' or a 'chantry' to indicate that it was not a parish church. 'A weekly mass was said for the poor folk, and its bell tolled daily to call people from the fields for meals.'[5]

The chapel was set in order by the Rev. T. McClelland, Rector of Little Torrington (1894-1908), and it was served by its own reader and regular services were maintained (certainly up to the 1940s). It is now part of the responsibility of the parish church of St Michael and All Angels in Torrington which serves the chapel by invitation.

There is an interesting 'saint' up near the altar where the communion elements were left so that the lepers could take part in the sacraments without (as it was wrongly believed) passing on the leprosy to others in the village. Lepers were segregated from their village communities as their condition was considered to be 'catching'. Judy Barber tells us in her book how, when workmen were bringing electricity to the village some 50 years ago, they dug up some bones. They promptly downed tools for fear of contracting leprosy. The cable was re-routed.[6] Some myths endure for centuries.

'In living memory, much of the village was thatched. There was a pound, a saw-pit, smithy, inn, carpenter's shop, infants' school and chapel.'[7] The cottages had 'hatches' (half-doors) over which residents would lean and chat to their neighbours. An old shop front survives advertising that it was licensed to sell tea, tobacco, coffee, pepper and snuff. The last place to close was the Post Office and shop in around 1995. Further up the street next to 'Daisy Cottage, is a cottage called 'Leper Cottage' which has a donation box fixed to the wall.

To the left of Taddiport bridge before you cross over into the village is the former toll-house, a Grade II listed building. When it came on the market in May 2009 the

Leper window

Photo by the author

Taddiport bridge

Photo courtesy of Dave Kelly

advertising blurb stated that it had been named one of the five best toll-houses in the *Daily Telegraph* which also described it as a 'pint-sized property with lots of character'. It was built when the canal was filled in and Mark Rolle hoped to open the section from the station to New Town Mills as a toll road. However, potential loss of trade for the town made it politically inadvisable and plans were abandoned. The pretty two up, two down cottage has been badly flooded on several occasions when the river has broken its banks – 1893, 1955, 1980, 1994, 1999, 2000, 2009 – and one year water forced its way in through the back door and was seen pouring out through the letter box in the front door. The building to the left of the toll-house, on the opposite side of Rolle Road, was one of the canal warehouses which was converted into a cottage. As well as floods, there have been tragedies down by the bridge including the drowning of a young boy in the late 1990s and a man in 2011.

On the far side of the bridge, facing the toll house across the river, is a large square white building, formerly a coaching house called the Buckingham Arms which, until the late 20th century, sported the black horse of the brewery Starkey, Knight and Ford, one of the last surviving in the area.[8] You can still make out the name on the front of the property and on the side by Watery Lane you can see the words 'Buckingham Stables.' The former owner was forced to live upstairs for several years because of the danger of the property flooding.

On the right hand side of the bridge is 'Sanctuary House', the home of Torrington Town Crier, Alan Mitchell ('Big Al') and his partner, Ian. Big Al was born in the village and contributes a lot to the local community. He has had a colourful history and enjoys a varied life which includes singing in a rock band, 'The Bandits', helping to maintain the commons, sometimes supervising young offenders on community service, and restoring gypsy caravans. He also works at 1646, the Civil War centre, playing the character 'Ambrose' wearing 17th century costume and demonstrating how to fire a musket, amongst other things, as well as giving talks further afield about the Civil War. Al and his friend Katie Robinson have found various artefacts dating from the Civil War in the locality including lead musket balls, iron cannon balls, a broken rapier blade, a cavalry spur and a horse-bit. Their largest finds were two lumps of stone, one carved with a bishop's crozier, the other shaped like a head.[9]

When the Rolle Canal was in operation the Canal Company had its main headquarters at Taddiport basin. It was a busy place with canal boats arriving to unload lime and coal to be taken inland and returning with bricks, clay, grain and oak bark. Clay was dug from pits at Peters Marland and brought down to the canal basin at Taddiport by pack-horses. Then it was loaded into the tub boats for transport to the local potteries or shipped from Bideford to potteries in other parts of Britain and the continent. The canal basin was overlooked by the company offices from where the Clerk of Works managed operations and employees – 'office staff, shipwrights, general maintenance men, lime burners, stable hands, store men and workers in the company's corn, saw and bone mills and their iron foundry'[10] as well as boatmen, lock and incline keepers. The basin was ideally situated next to the main road over the bridge to Okehampton and Plymouth in one direction and up the steep Mill Street into the centre of Torrington in the other.

'The original canal map shows that the basin had a central island which may have been designed as a safe place to store the large quantities of coal needed in the area. Three lime kilns were built along the bank between the canal basin and the river ... The basin was surrounded by warehouses for the storage of goods ranging from corn and hides to timber and other building materials. There were also covered sheds for clay and oak bark awaiting transport down the canal, as well as a barge repair yard, a foundry and a sawmill.'[11]

'There were lime kilns, malt kilns, a carpentry shop, a boat building yard for making and repairing the tub boats, a blacksmith and. . .stabling for the canal horses and for the donkeys employed about the yard.'[12]

Robert Sandford, a member of a well-known Torrington family, established the Torridge Vale Dairy Factory in 1874 on the site of the Rolle Company's stores near Taddiport Bridge. The factory was surrounded by gardens which produced flowers, fruit and vegetables grown for the local markets. The Sandfords had been engaged in that business for many generations in Torrington and Sandfords Gardens off Mill Street is named after the family. It was a pioneering butter factory and eventually became the Dairy Crest Creamery – main producer of Clover – which closed in 1993 with the loss of 134 jobs. In 1998 a co-operative of 50 farmers started up in part of the buildings producing milk, clotted cream, yogurt but that, in turn, has closed and moved elsewhere. The factory buildings remain, stripped of their machinery, full of rubbish, vandalised, and are an eyesore in the midst of this lovely Devon valley.

The population of the hamlet of Taddiport was under 120 in the 1890s and the question of closing the school comes up frequently in the Minutes of the school managers at that time. The combined population of Taddiport and Little Torrington was 412 and yet there were two schools. The number of children on the school register was 30, of which 11 came from Torrington, and some of the children were under five years old. The average attendance was only 21. Taddiport School finally closed on 14th March 1901.[13] Its premises became the village hall which is much used for local events.

In 1643 a certain Luke Deane paid £25 for the lease of a tenement and garden at Taddiport. The site appears to correspond to what is known locally as 'Crockers Court'. Before renovation number 19 Taddiport had four ovens and its garden backs on to Crockers Court. Luke was the first of at least three generations of Deanes who were potters in Torrington. Dr Alison Grant, in her book 'North Devon Pottery', says Taddiport was an ideal site for a pottery with its supply of fresh water, wood and gravel. 'Tobacco-pipe clay' for slip probably came from Peters Marland to Weare Giffard to be shipped down to Bideford and returning carts could deliver heavy raw materials via Bideford. The road from Barnstaple to Holsworthy and Plymouth crossed the bridge so a good deal of pottery could have been marketed along this route.

With thanks to:
Lynn Barratt
Alan Mitchell
Louise Punchard
Chris Sing
Pat Wilks

25   How old is the Pannier Market?

The pannier market was built in the 1840s and refurbished in the late 1990s.

Originally, Torrington market traders set up their stalls in the streets and the butchers sold their meat in an open courtyard at the rear of the town hall known as 'the shambles'.

'Farming folk came into town from the countryside around to sell their produce. Those who arrived the earliest secured the best pitches and each vied with the other to call out the loudest.
'Rosy red apples! The sweetest you'll find!'
'Fresh cut flowers, buy a bunch for yer missus!'
'Luv'ly parsley!'
'Farmers' wives set out their eggs and cheeses and home-baked pies and pasties on trestle tables and gossiped to each other in between selling their wares. Fishermen from Bideford and Appledore and as far away as Hartland came to sell their slippery, shining, pungent catch. There were chickens crammed into crates, pecking and clucking, rabbits huddled in boxes, wide-eyed and quivering, and a rough-looking man with a litter of puppies of indeterminate breed tumbling around his heels.'[1]

Victorian market

In 1842 £2,990 was raised and a proper market place was built by local mason W. B. Cock to provide accommodation for the sale of farm produce, meat and fish which offered protection from the cold and wet days of the winter months. Facing the High Street was added a handsome hall with a gallery above the market arch. This large hall was let for lectures and exhibitions, the occasional ball and concerts, and in 1936 became the public library. Since the library moved to Castle Hill it has been used to display pictures from the Beaford Archive, as an antique showroom run by a local family in aid of a Romanian care home for children, by a toy library and by local photographers and artists as a workshop and gallery. The narrow market which was reached by passing under the arch was well used and had a good reputation for meat, poultry, butter and eggs from the two rows of stalls lining the central alley. The iron gates at the entrance were made by Richard Baker, a blacksmith in the town. In 1892 the market was glassed over, mainly paid for by the Hon. Mark Rolle.

Goods for sale in the pannier market in the early days used to be brought in pannier bags slung on the side of horses. Above the haberdashery, 'Crafty Needles', on the left of the entrance can be seen the table of tolls and rent (printed in traditional old money).

An elderly lady who was a child in the 1930s remembers Saturday being market day at the pannier market where the farmers' wives brought their eggs, chickens, rabbits, vegetables, honey, jams and other produce. She says the women were all dressed in their best clothes with spotless white aprons.

The original Victorian structure gradually deteriorated during the first half of the 20th century. Local legend has it that the glass roof was dismantled during the Second World War so that moonlight reflecting on it wouldn't attract the attention of German bombers but the actual story is rather more prosaic. According to Owen Warne, who has lived in Torrington all his life, the pannier market was a smelly place because it wasn't cleaned properly and the three butchers shops at the entrance added to the general stink. Taking the roof off freshened the market up a bit. It was said that the glass was in a poor state and some of the wood was rotten but it didn't lie around for long and Owen reckons it was used to build a number of conservatories in the locality! After that the market was merely an unprepossessing lane of shabby cabins which were sealed up for much of the week when not open for trade.

In 1996 Torrington won a one million pound award under the government's Rural Challenge scheme (one of just six places to be chosen) to improve country areas. The town square was packed when the announcement was made that Torrington's imaginative Genesis Project (a scheme devised by the Community Development Trust aimed at restoring Torrington's great past and encouraging tourism – see 'What is the CDT?') had won the challenge in competition with hopeful schemes from all over Britain. The prize money that came to the town, and its 24 surrounding parishes, was to be doubled by contributions from partner organisations in the public and private sectors. The project included refurbishing the Castle Hill Hotel and putting in a Civil War Centre, Tourist Information Centre, modernised library and telematics centre (the Thomas Fowler IT Centre). The Victorian pannier market would be reconstructed and given a new glass roof. Genesis project manager, Peter Hood, said, 'Once work is completed, the scene will not be dissimilar to that of the 1890s.'

The refurbished pannier market was officially opened in 1999. Renewed at a cost of £670,000 the new building both reflected its ancient past and provided an airy, glass-roofed shopping mall in the centre of town. There are 12 permanent shops and,

Present-day market   Photo by the author

at the top end, a large hall used for the weekly market (on Thursdays, Fridays and Saturdays), monthly auctions and other events such as the 'Big Sing' at Christmas. New public lavatories were installed. Firemen's ladders, which used to be stored along the walls of the hall, have been moved elsewhere.

The Mayor at the time, Harry Cramp, and Mayoress, Anne Tattersall, and other local dignitaries paraded through the new market mall led by the town's Silver Band and accompanied by members of the Torrington Garrison of the Sealed Knot Society and staff of the 1646 Heritage Centre dressed in 17th century costume. Dr Cramp said that when the original market was built in 1842 it was part of a programme of building which had helped to regenerate the town. 'Now, 160 years later, we are passing through another exciting regeneration programme in Torrington.' Torridge District Council chairman, John Rawlinson, unveiled a plaque and the building was blessed by the Vicar of Torrington, Rev. Jeremy Hummerstone.

With thanks to :   Owen Warne
                     Pat Wilks

26   When was there a Railway Service to Torrington?

A passenger rail service to Torrington was in operation for nearly a hundred years. Built as an extension from Bideford, the line was opened in July 1872 and passenger trains ran until 1965 when the service was axed by Beeching.

Torrington station wasn't in a terribly convenient situation being about a mile out of town at the bottom of a steep hill on the road to Bideford. However, the railway service was used by a lot of workers and school children travelling to the girls' grammar school in Barnstaple and the boys' grammar school and Edgehill in Bideford. Pat Wilks, who travelled to school by train in the 1930s, remembers how beautiful the rail journey was with its numerous crossings over the River Torridge, running beneath wooded slopes, by green meadows at Weare Giffard and alongside the estuary into Bideford. She says there was a 'station bus' that went from New Street and remembers the driver being very trusting. If it was wet on the way home and you didn't have the fare, he would let you ride up into town and pay the next day.

There were proposals for a railway line to Torrington as early as 1831 but, although surveys and plans were commissioned and drawn up, no initiative was taken to put the plans into action.

There was a lot of enthusiasm for a railway connection with Torrington during the 1860s and in 1865 the London and South Western Railway (LSWR) was authorised to build a standard gauge extension up the Torridge valley from Bideford to Torrington (5½ miles). The work would be difficult and expensive involving compensation for land through East-the-Water, engineering works including a tunnel, a viaduct and numerous bridges, and more compensation required for using the bed of the Rolle Canal which was to be bought. There would be a new passenger station at Bideford at the end of Bideford bridge to supersede the old broad gauge station at Cross Parks (retained for goods traffic). Work started in 1867 but in 1868 and 1869 the LSWR sought to abandon the Torrington extension because of expense.

Above and below: Torrington station being built   Photos courtesy of John and Tilly Kimber

It was at this stage that the Lord of the Manor, the Honourable Mark Rolle of Stevenstone House, stepped in and fought hard lobbying Parliament to authorise the Torrington Extension Railway. 'The idea of a canal owner and major landowner fighting vehemently for a railway to be built on his canal is an amusing one to say the least.' It was reported that he 'would be glad to see the canal superseded by a more useful and convenient mode of transit and communication' and he performed a valuable service to the people of Torrington.[1]

The railway from Bideford to Torrington opened on Thursday 18th July 1872 to the delight of local people who celebrated with a holiday and festivities. There were hundreds of spectators at the station and a loud cheer was given to the many people who had come from Barnstaple and Bideford and even further away for a day out to Torrington. There were speeches, processions of the North Devon Hussars, the Bideford Rifle Volunteer Corps, the town officers and tradesmen and parties on the commons. Houses and inns in the town were decorated with flowers and greenery and a dinner was provided at one o'clock for the 'working class and poor' men of the area in the pannier market where some 600 were fed and watered. There were sports on Castle Hill where visitors enjoyed the scenery as well as the activities after which between 1,600 and 1,700 were entertained to tea in three sittings in the Market House. In the evening there was a banquet in the Town Hall to which the Mayor and Town Council had invited a great number of distinguished guests. The Mayor, Mr N. Chapple, proposed the main toast of the evening to the Hon. Mark Rolle for all he had done for the poor of the area. After that there was dancing till the early hours.

In his book 'Lines to Torrington' John Nicholas describes the route of the Bideford to Torrington extension:

> The new line 'commenced at a junction outside the old Cross Parks broad gauge station, controlled by the Bideford Junction signal box with junction signals mounted on a tall wooden post. The line climbed up behind the old Bideford Station which retained the extensive goods traffic, and squeezed its way through Bideford East-the-Water, between Barnstaple Street and Torrington Street on the one side by the Torridge, and the steep hill on the other. Two overbridges and three underbridges in rapid succession kept the line clear of the busy streets ... Leaving Bideford (New) Station, the line passed market gardens, lime-kilns and the gasworks, keeping to the east bank of the Torridge Estuary until it reached Landcross. Here was the first of four bridges over the Torridge, Landcross Viaduct being a long iron structure. The line then passed through a short tunnel, and from here on it used part of the bed of the Rolle Canal, then crossed and recrossed the River Torridge on masonry viaducts of four arches, until arriving at Torrington Station near the old Rothern Bridge at Staplevale. The Rolle Canal had originally passed through the site now occupied by the station, which had been built as the new terminus of the LSWR North Devon line with an engine shed and turntable, but with limited siding accommodation.'[2]

The initial passenger service on the North Devon line in August 1872 comprised six trains each way as far as Torrington, three from London, Waterloo, one from Yeovil and two from Exeter, with another between Barnstaple and Bideford. The 2.10pm express from Waterloo (1st and 2nd class only) took 6 hours 51 minutes for the journey of 225 miles to Torrington. There were extra services to and from Barnstaple on Fridays which was market day.

When the Torrington Extension Railway had opened in 1872 and the Holsworthy line in 1879, it was felt locally that the line should be extended southwards as soon as possible to complete a through route from North Devon to Plymouth and to serve the Marland Brick and Clay Works, some six miles away from a railhead. At that stage, clay and bricks were brought to Torrington station by road, using early traction engines, but better transport facilities were required if the works were to prosper. The new Torrington station had been designed to convert easily to a through station but the LSWR were in no hurry to extend the line so, once again, local initiative was required to bring the rails south. The manager of Marland Clay Company, Mr F. Holwill, contacted an engineer, Mr John Fell, who specialised in the construction of light railways to survey a line between Torrington Station and the Marland Clay Works – 3 ft gauge, 6 ½ miles, £15,000 (in contrast with the 5½ mile Bideford to Torrington line which cost £100,000). The line was built without an Act of Parliament which kept the cost down. Mr Holwill had negotiated with the four landowners concerned and obtained their consent – Lord Clinton, Hon. Mark Rolle, Mr J. C. Moore-Stevens and Mr Johnson.[3]

The ceremony of cutting the first sod of the Torrington and Marland Railway was held on Torrington common opposite the LSWR station at 12 noon, Wednesday 26th May 1880. There were two major engineering works on the new line: 1) a short tunnel out of LSWR goods yard under the main road and 2) a long wooden viaduct on stone piers over the River Torridge, both at Staplevale. Elsewhere on the line, earthworks were kept to a minimum by following the lie of the land (which required sharp curves and steep gradients) and by the use of timber trestle structures instead of embankments.[4] The line was completed by the end of December 1880 (in only seven months). It was a private mineral line and, at this stage, there was no intention of running a public passenger service. On 1st January 1881 the first train of bricks and clay ran down the Torrington and Marland Railway from the Marland works to Torrington goods yard.

Official passenger services were restricted to the workmen's trains, the first of which left Torrington at around 6.30am. About 50 men boarded at Torrington while six joined at Watergate and another 20 at Yarde. At around 9am the Torrington engine would return with the first load of clay and another two or three trainloads would be dealt with during the day. The last movement of the day would be at about 6pm when the workmen's train returned.[5]

The Torrington and Marland Railway of the North Devon Clay Company was in use for 44 years until the opening of the North Devon and Cornwall Junction Light Railway in 1925. Much of the trackbed of the 3 ft gauge line was used but the narrow gauge system was retained within the clay works for another 45 years until it finally closed in 1970.

During the First World War Torrington station saw a lot of hay and timber traffic for war supplies as there was an artillery training area on the commons.

In 1925 standard gauge rails finally pushed south from Torrington and connected up at Halwill Junction to the rest of the network. A new steel viaduct over the River Torridge near Torrington station was built alongside the old wooden viaduct of the Torrington and Marland Railway which was subsequently demolished and the new line followed the course of the narrow gauge line as far as Dunsbear, where it veered

Marland and Rothern Bridge 1893   Photo courtesy of the Francis Frith Collection

away slightly to the west to avoid the Clay Company property, then headed through Petrockstowe, Meeth, Hatherleigh, Hole and on to Halwill Junction where it met up with the Bude, Okehampton and Padstow lines. There were three trains each way between Torrington and Halwill on weekdays but none on Sundays.

This railway system wasn't the success that had been hoped for. The mistake was to make the link westwards between North Devon and Cornwall rather than south to Mid and South Devon via Okehampton, as had been the original idea. That would have connected Torrington and North Devon with Plymouth and Exeter and thus given a direct link to the main railway network. This would have provided more through freight and passenger traffic and opened up trade in North Devon to a wider market. In reality, the North Devon and Cornwall Junction Light Railway was built more as a through tourist route than as a local service. During the Second World War there was a reduction in passenger services on the line but goods services increased and Fremington Quay had its busiest year in 1942.

A substantial flow of traffic from Torrington station was milk for the London market. For many years it was transported in milk churns in luggage compartments or special vans. During the 1930s and 1940s the Southern Railway built a number of glass-lined milk tank wagons in conjunction with dairy companies, together with loading and unloading facilities at the terminals. In the late 1940s such a depot was established at Torrington at the end of the goods shed road, and from then on milk tank wagons became a common sight on the Torrington to Barnstaple line. Milk was brought to the station by road tankers from the extensive creamery at Torrington, operated at the time by Cow and Gate.[6]

The existence of the Southern Railway came to an end after 25 years when the new nationalized British Railways came into being on 1st January 1948. The large concrete name board announcing 'Southern Railway – Torrington Station' lasted for many years. There were no significant changes made on lines to Torrington after nationalization until the early 1960s when traffic on those lines was declining. Passengers were travelling in their own cars or by bus, particularly between Barnstaple and Bideford where there was a frequent service which was more convenient for both town centres. Freight traffic was also declining, including much of the extensive cattle business which had been lost to road transport after the 1955 ASLEF strike. Inevitably, there were cuts to services.[7]

1963 saw the final transfer of all the former Southern Railway lines west of Salisbury to the Western Region and by the end of summer 1963 timetable there were no through services at all and the Barnstaple to Torrington and Torrington to Halwill lines were both worked as self-contained branches. The Western Region of British Railways struck the first blow to all the Southern lines west of Exeter when the 'Atlantic Coast Express' and other through trains from Waterloo ran for the last time on Sunday 5th September 1964, thus ending a century of through train services between Bideford, Barnstaple and Waterloo.[8]

From 7th September 1965 freight facilities were withdrawn from nearly all stations west of Exeter (Watergate and Dunsbear Halts had already closed from 2nd May 1960 and Torrington had lost its locomotive shed back on 2nd November 1959).

The age of the diesel locomotive began on 7th May 1963 when a North British Locomotive Type 2 diesel ran up from Plymouth to Halwill, Torrington (where it suffered a failure), Barnstaple and Taunton.

On 6th September 1964 the Western Region introduced a new pattern of diesel services on former LSWR lines west of Salisbury. The train from Waterloo to Exeter, St David's had no onward connections. Diesel trains ran between Exeter, St David's and Ilfracombe in connection with an express service from Paddington and a connecting diesel service ran between Barnstaple Junction and Torrington. However, passenger services on both lines to Torrington were destined to end in a matter of months.

The government brought in Dr Richard Beeching from ICI to make major improvements to the rail industry and he produced 'The Beeching Report' in March 1963. 'This recommended the development of freight and fast passenger services on main lines, concentrating on the profitable bulk flows of traffic and the elimination of large numbers of stations and branch lines. In North Devon the effect was devastating with the withdrawal of passenger services on three of the four routes to Barnstaple, with only the Barnstaple to Exeter line being retained.' The lines to Torrington had two bulk flows of traffic that were retained – clay from Meeth and Marland and milk from Torrington – so the Barnstaple to Meeth section was retained for clay and milk traffic. Passenger services were completely withdrawn. By 1963 passenger traffic at both Torrington and Bideford had dropped to only about half its pre-war level and, as Nicholas says, 'on trains between Torrington and Halwill, a passenger was something of a rarity. The travelling public had taken to road transport'.[9]

Trains at Torrington station

Photo courtesy of the North Devon Journal

The year 1965 was a bleak one for lines to Torrington as both passenger services and general goods services were completely withdrawn. The last passenger train on the Torrington to Halwill line was the 6.20pm on 27th February 1965 from Halwill which consisted of a three coach diesel multiple unit carrying some 200 passengers to commemorate the event. An enthusiasts' excursion train, the 'Exmoor Ranger', five coaches hauled by Ivatt 2-6-2 tanks ran up the line from Halwill to Torrington and Barnstaple on 27th March 1965 a month after it was officially closed below Meeth but by May 1966 the track had been lifted between Meeth and Halwill. Remaining passenger services to Halwill Junction on the North Cornwall and Bude lines were withdrawn when lines closed on 3rd October 1966 and all the tracks were removed by December 1967.[10]

In February 1965 the withdrawal of passenger services on the Barnstaple to Torrington line was announced for the following autumn. Three buses were to run daily between Torrington and Barnstaple via Bideford to help workers and school pupils.

General goods services from Torrington, Fremington and Bideford ceased on 6th September 1965. The milk depot at Torrington and quay siding at Fremington stayed open but Bideford (Goods) closed completely.

The passenger service between Torrington and Barnstaple was withdrawn after the 1965 summer season. On Saturday 2nd October 1965 the last regular passenger train ran from Torrington to Barnstaple witnessed by 30 - 40 passengers and the signals at Bideford were pulled off by Mayor, Mrs Ethelwynne Brown. On the following day the last steam train ran between Barnstaple and Torrington – a portion of the 'Exeter Flyer' from Waterloo hauled by a British Rail locomotive.[11]

Freight continued to be transported on the line after 1965 (milk until 1978 and fertilizer until 1980). Clay traffic on the railway ceased completely in 1982. Fremington Quay had closed in 1970 and clay was no longer transported by rail but by lorries or dumpers.

Special trains were put on for particular events, such as an excursion to Portsmouth for Bideford football club and to London for Bideford school. The first locally organised trip from Torrington was on 29th April 1979 when a Torrington May Fair special train ran first to Barnstaple and then to Meeth with a picnic stop at Petrockstowe.

The last railwayman's post on the line went on 19th September 1980 when Mr Harry Beer retired at Torrington. From then on all necessary duties – opening and closing gates, operating points, coupling and un-coupling wagons – were carried out by train crews.

There was a considerable amount of local interest in the possibility of reopening Bideford station for regular passenger services by extending the existing train service between Exeter and Barnstaple in the late 1970s and early 1980s. Concern about all the extra lorry traffic on the roads around Meeth and Hatherleigh prompted a meeting at Torrington Town Hall on 8th October 1982 by the North Devon Railway Line Development Group to discuss the closure of the railway line but the numerous proposals came to nothing because of lack of funding.

The 'Last Train to Torrington' run by British Rail itself was on Saturday 6th November 1982. It went from Bristol (Temple Meads), Bridgwater to Exeter (St David's) and Barnstaple. Leaving Barnstaple the train consisted of a Class 31 diesel (leading), 15 coaches carrying 843 passengers and another diesel (trailing). This was the longest and best-patronised passenger train ever to run into Torrington station. At the station the train was met by the Mayor, Councillor Clifford Quick, and a party of townspeople including Mr Harry Beer, the last railwayman to work at Torrington, and Mr Tom Mill who had been the fireman on the first passenger train to Halwill in 1925.

The passengers slowly disembarked to view the station and its surroundings and some took the free coach up the long hill to the Torrington Arms, formerly the Railway Inn, for refreshment. A BBC radio team recorded interviews which were broadcast in the West Country on the following Monday. The train was due to depart at 1515 but it was not until 1607 that Councillor Clifford Quick was able to wave the green flag to signal the departure of the last train from Torrington.[12]

Last Train fare prices (return):

£7.50 from Bristol, Temple Meads, £6.00 from Bridgwater, £5.00 from Exeter, St David's, £3.00 from Barnstaple.

The North West Devon Railway Preservation Society was established after this event with the aim of acquiring the Barnstaple to Bideford section of the line and on

27th January 1983 a single coach diesel car ran from Barnstaple to Torrington and back. A request to the EEC for financial assistance for the line was turned down in March 1983.

The Torrington station building, which had been unoccupied for some time, was sold at a public auction in October 1983 and in May 1984 its new owners opened it to the public as 'The Puffing Billy' pub and restaurant.

In June 1984 track-lifting began at the Meeth end of the line. Most of the old track bed has been incorporated into the Tarka Trail, a footpath and cycleway covering approximately 180 miles of old railway and established footpaths in North and Central Devon, named after Henry Williamson's well-known book about the otter of that name. A length of track remains in Torrington station on which are parked a small locomotive originally from the clay works as well as a railway carriage, brake van and clay truck.

There are still hopes to revive parts of the old railway line. The Tarka Valley Railway Group was formed in 2008 and their declared objective is 'to build and operate a steam railway based at Torrington station and to extend the railway up the line in the Bideford direction'.

With thanks to the following two authors on whose books I have based this section:
Rod Garner – 'The Torrington and Marland Light Railway'
John Nicholas – 'Lines to Torrington'
and also Pat Wilks

27 Why is the glass factory called Dartington Crystal? (as Dartington is in South Devon)

The company was founded by the Dartington Hall Trust, a charity which aims to assist the economic regeneration of rural areas through business, education, the arts and country crafts. The trust was originally set up in the 1920s by a wealthy American heiress and her husband, a Yorkshireman, Dorothy and Leonard Elmhirst at Dartington Hall near Totnes, South Devon.

In the early 1960s the trust had become concerned that North Devon was becoming depopulated as a lack of job opportunities forced people to move elsewhere to find work. The glass-making factory was intended to be a solution to this problem, conceived as a centre of employment giving local people a reason to stay in the area.

To achieve this vision the trust recruited Eskil Vilhelmsson, a Swedish glass manufacturer, to be the company's Managing Director. A team of Scandinavian glass blowers came with him to Torrington, some of whom are still here to this day, and the factory opened in June 1967 under the name of Dartington Glass. To start with, there were just 35 employees. Homes were built for the Swedish glass blowers near the factory (Eskil Place) as well as at the eastern end of town (Dartington Fields). The Swedes were gradually accepted into the community and the first marriage between one of them and a local girl took place in 1972. Fourteen more were to follow over

Glass blowing

Photo courtesy of
Dartington Crystal

the next ten years. Dartington would not have survived without the talent and commitment of the original Swedish glass blowers.

In an article in *Devon Life* magazine in 1971 entitled 'Made in Devon', Robert Marshall described what went on at Dartington Glass:

> 'Inside, the scene is typically Swedish: teams of sweaty, clogshod men, some in shirt-sleeves, others bare-chested, move rhythmically around gaping, yellow hot furnaces in the ritual of glassmaking. At the core are some thirty glass blowers imported from Sweden to produce glass commercially, thus providing employment for British grinders, cutters, inspectors and packers, and to train Devon lads in the ancient craft.'[1]

One of the first five apprentices, appointed when the factory opened, was Peter Smithson (1952-1989). He went on to qualify as the first English master blower in 1978. Linda and Stuart Smithson have dedicated their book about the first twenty years of Dartington Glass to his memory.[2]

The factory developed under the guidance of Eskil Vilhelmsson and the Design Director, Frank Thrower. The first piece of glassware to be produced was a tankard engraved with the reference number FT1 (Frank Thrower 1). Funds were nearly exhausted after a difficult first year but Frank Thrower devised a clever advertising plan that helped establish Dartington Glass on the industry scene and caught the attention of their first customers: the renowned John Lewis Partnership and an interesting new shop called Habitat. The company thrived from here growing into a worldwide brand recognised for its quality and design-led manufacturing. Frank Thrower created some of the most important glassware designs of the 20th century, such as Sharon, Exmoor and Dimple.

'Stemming the Tears'

'A Very Heavy Drinker'

Glassware designed by Frank Thrower   Photos courtesy of Linda and Stuart Smithson

'Beau Bells'

'Pitter Platter'

Frank Thrower started his design career while working for Portmeirion Pottery. He learned that the Trustees of Dartington Hall were looking for projects that might provide craft jobs in North Devon and by 1962 Frank had joined the small development team. The Dartington and Frank Thrower partnership was successful from the beginning. Only two years after production began in 1967 he received his first prestigious design award. He actively encouraged the development of young talent and established the Dartington Design Bursary with the Royal Society of Arts in 1982. He was appointed MBE in 1987 and made a Fellow of the Royal College of Art for his services to design in British industry. He died in June 1987 at the age of 55 after a long battle with cancer.

Since 1967 thousands of individual products have been designed and manufactured at the glass factory. Eskil Vilhelmsson said, 'We like to give quality glass that people can afford. Hand made glass is always a piece of art to be enjoyed in the home.' Apart from modern electric furnaces and mechanical aids, hand glass blowing is one industry where traditional methods are still used. The glass blowers are grouped into different teams of between three and eleven men, depending on the complexity of the item being made. Each man has his special function and rank. There is one master blower, the chief of the team, one deputy master blower, one blower, three gatherers and several assistants in a team. The finished object becomes a minor work of art and the charm of handmade glass is that no two articles are exactly alike, each bearing evidence of the maker's skill. It takes ten years to become a master blower.

By 1970 the Dartington workforce numbered 84 with manufacturing and distribution centred on two large sites in Torrington and the company had made its first steps into the lucrative tourist market. 5,000 visitors passed through the factory in the first week it opened to the public. During the 1970s 2-3,000 pieces of glass were made every day and, with 75% of Dartington's production sold domestically, the design was what might be called 'English-tempered Swedish'. The glass was exported to some 30 nations – primarily Australia, Canada and the United States – including Sweden. Demand outstripped production and the factory had to be expanded and the workforce grew to 330 for a time. By the 1980s the modern image of Dartington had attracted the attention of Wedgwood who took up a large stake in the business, allowing for further expansion.

Business continued to boom in the late 1980s and early 1990s until it was affected by the recession and in 1992 the factory had to put its 250 staff on short-time, working two weeks out of three. The business underwent a management buy-out in 1994 from Rockware and by the end of the 1990s manufacturing had declined from twenty glass kilns to three, with much of its stock imported under the Dartington name. The company was taken over by US giftware giant, Enesco, in 2004. By now the company was called 'Dartington Crystal' and it underwent another management buy-out in April 2006, safeguarding many skilled jobs in the area. Dartington Crystal bought Scottish-based Caithness Glass in October 2006 and also owns Royal Brierley Crystal which is based in the West Midlands.

Dartington Crystal celebrated its 40th birthday in June 2007. It has played an important role in regenerating the regional economy of North Devon. It has had a chequered history going from success through the doldrums to today's position as a leading tourism draw as the only remaining crystal factory in the UK welcoming 300,000 visitors every year to its popular Visitor Centre, factory tour and large shopping area. It is Torrington's major employer, employing 142 people at present (Feb 2011) and the whole site has an annual turnover of £1.5 million.

Dartington products have been exhibited around the world and over the years the company has received numerous design and industry awards. It now creates a variety of unique commissions and counts British Airways, Boots, Cartier, Disney, Marks & Spencer, Porche, Rolls Royce, Sunseeker, Tiffany, P & O Cruises and Harrods amongst its clients. Individual pieces have been created for royal birthdays, weddings and anniversaries and there have been some unusual commissions

Above: Glassware designed by Hilary Green

Photo courtesy of Dartington Crystal

Below: Dartington glass shop

Photo by the author

ranging from an engraved crystal iceberg presented to Pope John Paul II to mark the 50th anniversary of his ordination to commemorative tankards honouring the Queen's Silver Jubilee, the Battle of Britain and the 100th anniversary of the FA Cup.

In September 2010 Dartington Crystal won the licence to manufacture and supply crystal and glass tableware and giftware for the London 2012 Olympics. Royal Salute, the world's leading luxury Scotch whisky brand has commissioned Dartington to make hand crafted decanters for their 62 Gun Salute blend, each decanter being mouth-blown and hand finished using the finest midnight blue crystal, then decorated with 24 carat gold and crowned with a cut crystal stopper. In 2010 Dartington invested in a new website to meet the demand to buy goods on the internet and in the first twelve months sales have already risen by 33% through its website.

In a few years' time the lease on the factory will be up and the search for a new site has already begun. Dartington Crystal has had a great impact on the town of Torrington.

With thanks to:
Hilary Green

28   Where was Sydney House?

Sydney House was situated in South Street between the gateway to the former Castle Hill Hotel (now the library, tourist information centre, council offices, 1646, etc.) and the Conservative Club. This site is now the entrance to Sydney House car park (formerly known as South Street car park but renamed by the Town Council in June 2006).

The house was built by William Vaughan, a wealthy glove manufacturer who owned the factory in Whites Lane. The house was enormous, built of local cream-coloured Marland brick and Ham stone in the Modern English Renaissance style with turrets, pinnacles and gabling. A Torrington woman remembers the house as being 'a beautiful building, like a fairytale castle.' The Vaughan family moved into the house, which they called 'Enderley', in 1889.

The 1891 census shows Enderley being occupied by William Vaughan and his wife, Catherine, their eight children (seven daughters and one son), William's brother, Thomas, and four servants. A gardener, his wife and niece lived in a staff cottage behind the main house.

In May 1903 William Vaughan collapsed and died on his way to the factory and his family didn't live at Enderley for much longer after that. His son subsequently lived at West House, Rolle Terrace at the western end of New Street.

In 1914 Enderley was put on the market by Lord Clinton who had inherited most of the estates of Mark Rolle. The house was described as a mansion suitable for a man of means or for conversion into a hotel, school or institution but it failed to find a bidder.

Sydney House

During the First World War Enderley was used rent-free by the Red Cross as a hospital for sick and wounded soldiers and the first group of men arrived in April 1917. Eventually, 100 patients were accommodated. The hospital was supervised by William Martin of Chulmleigh who had made his fortune in the wool trade in Australia. He paid off the outstanding mortgage on Enderley for the Red Cross in the spring of 1918 and undertook the upkeep of the hospital. The house was renamed 'Sydney House' in his honour for that was where he had gained his wealth. At the end of the war patients were gradually sent home.

In June 1919 the Red Cross offered the lease of the house to Devon County Council who used it as a residential school of recovery for delicate children suffering from pre-tuberculosis and asthma, known as an 'Open-Air School'. One of the outbuildings was converted into a laundry and fruit and vegetables were grown in the garden. The regime in the school was strict and the conditions spartan and children often felt homesick. When the Second World War started the Devon children were joined by evacuees who needed special care.

On 19th February 1942 a fire broke out in Sydney House during the evening. The girls slept on the first floor while the boys were on the top floor in four dormitories, one in each corner of the building. Between them was the linen and ironing room and it was here that the matron believed afterwards that the fire had started, caused by a short circuit in the electrical wiring or problems with a faulty iron.

The fire spread rapidly, the open stairway acting as a funnel which created a draught and the highly-polished pitch pine panels and stairs feeding the flames which could be seen for miles around. It was feared that in the war-time blackout the

Hospital for wounded soldiers 1914-1918

Photo courtesy of Elaine Weeks

flames might attract enemy bombers which were going to and from South Wales and the Midlands. Ten fire engines were on the scene and they had difficulty with water supplies on an icy night and even laid pipes down Mill Street to the River Torridge.

The staff tried to get all the children downstairs and they were taken next door to the Conservative Club. When a roll-call was made, it was discovered that five boys were missing, all from the south-east dormitory on the top floor. Heroic efforts were made by the matron, firemen, police and local people to find the boys, returning with great difficulty three times to the top floor where they found the bodies of three of the boys but no sign of the other two. They were found dead in the rubble of the building the following morning.

There were 59 children in Sydney House at the time of the fire. 54 survived physically unscathed but many bore the emotional scars of the experience for the rest of their lives.

Sydney House remained a ruin for the next eight years and, although it was a dangerous site, children liked to play there. Demolition started in October 1950 and as building materials were in short supply after the war a lot was sold off and used in the locality. One pair of wrought iron gates was first used at the entrance to the children's playground in Calf Street but they are now at the Warren Lane entrance to Rack Park Gardens. A local man told me that the other pair was put at the entrance to the football club but went missing in the early 1980s. 750 of the Marland bricks were bought for ten shillings and used to build an outside toilet for a family home in Calf Street. Marland brick was much sought after and was sold for £2 10s 0d per lorry-load. The extensive buildings at the rear of the house – caretaker's cottage, laundry, stables, various stores and workshops – were unaffected by the fire. They were used as living accommodation and, for a short while, as billets for American soldiers. They remained until 1967 when they were demolished to make way for South Street car park.

Some people in Torrington had long felt there should be a memorial to the five boys who died in the fire. When there were plans to develop the entrance to South Street car park, the Town Council set up a working group to create a memorial and also to mark the grave of Tom Shute, unmarked until then in Torrington cemetery. Relatives of four of the boys were found and attended the commemoration ceremony 60 years after their deaths, together with survivors and staff from Sydney house and North Devon dignitaries. On 18th May 2002 a stone was placed at Tom Shute's grave in the cemetery and a memorial plaque was unveiled by David Stark, survivor of the fire and former deputy Lord Mayor of Plymouth, and dedicated by the Bishop of Exeter at the entrance to South Street car park. The large slab of stone to which it was attached had been sold off at the time of demolition and was being used as the doorstep to a stable, to prevent horses from slipping, at a farm in Little Torrington owned by Fred and Doris Hooper. Mrs Hooper donated the stone for the memorial.

The inscription on the memorial stone reads:

IN MEMORY OF THE CHILDREN

RONALD DOOLAN
AGED 8 YEARS (COLLIERS WOOD, LONDON)

GEOFFREY DRAKE
AGED 8 YEARS (UFFCULME)

DAVID LAWREY
AGED 8 YEARS (TEIGNMOUTH)

TOM SHUTE
AGED 7 YEARS (BROCKLEY, LONDON)

PETER WILKINSON
AGED 7 YEARS (PAIGNTON)

WHO LOST THEIR LIVES IN THE FIRE
AT SYDNEY HOUSE ON THIS SITE
THURSDAY 19th FEBRUARY 1942

It also says: 'This stone was part of Sydney House'.

Rear view of Sydney House   Photo courtesy of Dave Kelly

The final paragraph of the book on Sydney House by Susan Scrutton and Harry Cramp reads:

> 'The working group has throughout been very conscious of the possibility of reawakening unpleasant and painful memories. The vast majority of those making contact with the working group have expressed gratitude that a suitable tribute is being paid to the boys who lost their young lives and feel that it finally closes a tragic part of Great Torrington's history.'

A Secret Memorial Garden has been created on the site of Sydney House which is 'open to anyone looking for a tranquil space in which to collect their thoughts, sit and read, or simply to wander around taking in the sights and smells of a wonderful variety of plants and herbs.' A bronze statue of a boy sitting on a boulder reading a book is a tribute to the memory of the five young boys who lost their lives in the fire. A mosaic created by local children and a mural created by a local artist are mounted on the wall. 'It is truly a community garden, created with a community spirit.'[1]

With thanks to the following two authors on whose book I have based this section:
Susan Scrutton and Harry Cramp – 'Sydney House'
and also:
Pauline Baker
Linda Downing
Dave Kelly
Dulcie Leate

29   How many Churches are there in Torrington?

The Parish Church of St Michael and All Angels is in the centre of town and its tall spire can be seen for miles around. Torrington Methodist Church is at the top of Mill Street. Great Torrington Baptist Church is in New Street, set back a little between the houses. The Holy Family Catholic Church is in Gas Lane. The Howe Church in Castle Street is where the Congregationalists used to meet for worship but that building is now the Torrington Silver Band concert hall and a private house. There is a Jubilee Church held at Winslade, 2a Burwood Road, a Torrington Community Church which meets in the Blue Coat school hall and a Gospel Hall in Whites Lane next to the old glove factory.

There has been a parish church in Torrington since at least the 13th century. The building has suffered partial destruction on a number of occasions in the past and been rebuilt at different times but parts of the present building date from the 14th century. The latest work to have been done is a development of the tower area to provide toilets, a kitchen, and a new ringing room which was completed in November 2008. (See 'How old is the Parish Church?'). There was also a Chapel of St James in the 13th century castle at Torrington which was still standing when Henry VIII's antiquary, John Leland, visited the town in about 1538. By the time Tristram Risdon wrote his Survey of Devon a century later the chapel had been converted into a schoolhouse.

Methodism had a struggle to become established in Torrington and Methodist preachers faced considerable intolerance and persecution in the district in the 1790s. An appointed Methodist preacher, Richard Drew, was given permission to preach in a courtyard in Taddiport but he was interrupted at once by Henry Stevens of Cross House, a local magistrate, who pulled the preacher down off the chair on which he was standing. This encouraged the crowd to give the preacher some rough treatment and he was thrown into an old quarry pit, urged on, it is said, by Stevens. Both men ended up in the pit and when, having scrambled out, they were walking down a road leading to the river, the crowd said they would throw the preacher into the water. Learning that his persecutor was a magistrate, Richard Drew appealed to Henry Stevens to protect him from the violence of the people and informed him that it was, in fact, his duty to do so. Feeling he had no alternative, Henry Stevens ordered the people to leave the preacher alone and he walked on, unmolested, to the common on the north side of Mill Street where he addressed a large congregation. After this, shaken and exhausted, he went up to the town and rested for the night at the Globe Hotel. Henry Stevens was reported to the Court of the King's Bench (by the Wesleys) and he was so mortified by proceedings against him that he left the neighbourhood and Cross House remained unoccupied for some 30 years. This action stemmed the tide of intolerance in the Torrington area for a time.[1]

In about 1808 a preacher, William Beale, who had been appointed a missioner in the Bideford circuit came to Torrington to preach in a room in a cottage in Mill Street but he and his congregation were interrupted by a hostile mob gathered out in the street and the preacher had to take refuge in another place. Again the result was determined by legal action and some of the rioters were bound over to appear at the next Quarter Sessions for the county. The next time William Beale came to Torrington, some 40 years later, he had the pleasure of preaching in the roomy and comfortable Wesleyan Chapel at the top of the same street in which he had been persecuted on the previous occasion.[2]

The interests of Methodism remained at a low ebb for many years and it wasn't until 1833 that Richard Drew again visited Torrington and was able to inspect a new chapel built the previous year on a piece of land at Windy Cross with plentiful seating and schoolrooms attached which served as a place of worship for the combined Methodist and Wesleyan congregations. The Register of Baptisms began in 1841. In 1874 a minister's residence and garden was provided alongside the chapel. This is now a private house, Ramla, with its entrance in Villa Road. Sunnyside, number 204 New Street was then used as the Methodist manse but that house has now also been sold and the manse is up at Kingsmead.

The most recent ministers have been David Sheriff, John Bradley, Ian Hill, David Gregory, Graham Slingo.

The Methodist church underwent extensive refurbishment in 2000/2001 which included the removal of old pews and the building of a new playschool. It took a year, cost £393,000 and was re-opened by the oldest member of the congregation on 16th June 2001. All the money was paid off within two years. At one time there were railings along the front wall but it was felt they didn't make the church look very welcoming and so they were dismantled. For the same reason, the solid front doors were replaced with glass ones so people could see inside the church and feel more inclined to enter.

Methodist Church, Mill Street

Photo by the author

In around 1865 the Bible-Christian Methodists erected a chapel on a site purchased from the Torrington Town Trustees in South Street on which formerly stood an inn called the Boot and later added a building at the rear for Sunday School, which had a library of some 200 books, and a residence for the pastor. This chapel was opened for public worship in October 1866. In 1927 the Bible-Christians united with the United Methodist New Connection which, in turn, united with the Wesleyan Methodists in 1932. Public worship was discontinued here and the chapel building was sold to the Torridge Vale Dairies Company to be used as a packing station and store. In 1949 the building became the Unigate and Torridge Vale Dairy social club.

The first Baptist Church in Torrington was formed in 1820 but, before a resident minister had been appointed, a prominent preacher, Charles Veysey of Barnstaple, frequently preached to a small congregation in Torrington and about 16 people were said to have been baptised.

In 1818 the Rev. George Charles Smith, the naval and sailor missionary of Penzance, a noted Baptist, came to preach in Torrington. A contemporary account of his visit to the town states he, 'narrowly escaped being burnt to death, while preaching in the market-place, such was the opposition of the people that they fiercely attacked him, and were eager for his life, but he was mercifully preserved'.[3]

In 1819 the first minister was appointed, the Rev. Thomas Pulsford, who found a few disciples in Torrington but no church. On 25th June 1820 six people were baptised in the river and, together with the 16 previously immersed, formed the first Baptist Society.

Thomas Pulsford, with Charles Veysey as co-pastor, converted an old building on a site now occupied by numbers 7 and 9 Mill Street into a meeting house. As the numbers grew, it was found to be too small and the Baptists moved up to New Street where a dwelling-house, garden and land was conveyed upon trust for a public meeting-house for them. The two ministers worked together until 1839, preaching to their congregation in Torrington as well as in ten villages in the surrounding country. It is said that Charles Veysey travelled more than 50,000 miles – a remarkable feat of endurance – and, not surprisingly, he died on 15th March 1857 utterly worn out as a result of his labours for the church.

Alexander and Hooper writing in the 1940s say:

'The present church is a plain building with a seating capacity of about 400, built on the north side of New Street, bearing the date 1829. It was erected on land conveyed by James Williams and his wife Sarah, to Thomas Snell, 30 April 1819, and 1 May 1819, and by Thomas Snell to Charles Veysey and others on 4 October 1828.'[4]

There used to be a cottage in front of the church to the left of the present entrance where 'Hutchy' lived. She subsequently moved to Stonemans Lane.

A new organ was installed in 1885 and during the incumbency of the Rev. G. F. Owen new extensions were added to the church in 1896 providing a lecture hall, schoolrooms, vestry, etc. At the rear of these buildings was a small cemetery where interments were made from 1830-1855. The first minute book records that Elizabeth Veysey, who died on 4th January 1830 aged 37, was the first person buried there and the last was James Snell who died on 17th August 1855. A new burial ground was opened on the edge of town and so all interments both in the parish churchyard and the Baptist cemetery ceased. A manse for the resident minister was built in New Street. This is now a private house called 'Underhayes' and on its front wall is a plaque which reads:

'Baptist Manse
Pulsford Memorial
1913'

Recent refurbishment of the chapel took place in the mid 1990s when a vestibule was created which included new toilets (previously out at the back and inaccessible), new doors, and pews were removed and replaced with chairs.

The latest minister was an interim paster, Graham Pestridge, a retired man on a short rolling contract. Baptists have local management. Deacons, now called 'leaders' are voted into position of responsibility and they organise preachers who are booked in advance. The last full-time minister was David Eadie and before him was David Flower. There was a gap between him and the previous minister, the charismatic Keith Judson whom many people were very sorry to see move away from Torrington.

The first meeting house of the Independents in Torrington was somewhere in Well Street in the second half of the 17th century. It wasn't until 1672, under the Declaration of Indulgence, that Nonconformists could worship openly. Joseph Baller was appointed minister of the Independents in 1763 but such preachers had to struggle and earned very little money. When he left in around 1775 the Independent cause declined. Nonconformists had established other forms of worship such as the

Baptist Church, New Street   Photo by the author

Baptists and Wesleyans who were preaching to congregations in the Torrington area. John and Charles Wesley had been visiting the West Country though at that time the only Nonconformist place of worship was the Independents' meeting house in Torrington and it was not until 1785 that the Methodist preachers, Drew and Sandoe, visited the town.

In 1806 the Independents acquired a vigorous pastor in the Rev. Ephraim Jackson During his ministry a dwelling house in Castle Street was registered for religious worship in 1810 and later, possibly on the same site, new premises were erected. The building was

> 'very nearly square and quite unpretentious, the interior furnished with two galleries, a partition behind the pulpit shutting off that portion of the building used as a Sunday School and vestry, the windows were of plain glass, and the music was supplied by stringed instruments.'[5]

Rev. Jackson died in Torrington in August 1833. The Independent following increased rapidly during the three succeeding ministries of Evan Davies, John Chapman Davie and John Poole and in 1836 the church enlarged the gallery to accommodate the increasing congregation. The building was enlarged again and opened for worship on 1st August 1837. The first recorded marriage in the church took place on 10th August 1838.

Howe Church, Castle Street

Photo courtesy of John and Tilly Kimber

The Rev. James Buckpitt, began his ministry in Torrington in June 1842. As well as being an outstanding minister and caring for his flock, he took an interest in the life of the town and did a lot of work to improve the lives of its inhabitants. His ministry was so successful that the Independent church once more needed larger accommodation and, further land adjoining the existing chapel having been obtained, the old building was demolished and funds were raised to provide a more spacious chapel. On 1st October 1857 the foundation stone was laid for the Howe Chapel which still exists in Castle Street. It was named after John Howe, the Puritan divine, chaplain to Oliver Cromwell and the perpetual curate of the Torrington parish church from 1654 to 1662 when he was ejected under the Act of Uniformity. It consisted of a chapel, school and lecture room together with a minister's house at a cost of £1,500. After 24 years of untiring effort on behalf of the people of Torrington, Rev. Buckpitt died in March 1866. In 1875 the Torrington church was affiliated with the Congregational Union.

The Howe Chapel ceased to be used as a church in the late 1990s and became the Torrington Silver Band rehearsal and concert hall. The Howe Manse at the rear of the building was bought as a private house in 1998. The Congregationalists met at the Gospel Hall in Whites Lane for a while and then shared the Catholic Church in Gas Lane until Christmas 2009. Their minister, Rev. Cecil Jones, had died and they had a variety of visiting ministers, congregation numbers had dwindled to about 11 and the deacons and congregation finally decided to disband. They now worship with the Methodists.

There was once a mission church in Calf Street (where Goose Green garage was subsequently) which was known as 'the iron church.'

Mass has been celebrated in Torrington since 1930. At first Catholics met in the public library and later in a room over a corn merchant's shop in New Street (above where Tracey's restaurant used to be, now a private property called Church End). During the war when a lot of Americans were stationed in the district, mass was celebrated for them in the local cinema. After the war a large back room of number 88 New Street was used for services and Sunday school. A new Catholic church was built in Gas Lane in 1964 and opened by the Bishop of Plymouth on 25th March 1965. A very generous parishioner paid for the church and the church bell was presented by the Archdeacon of Appledore as an ecumenical gesture. The applewood candlesticks were made at Buckfast Abbey. The statues of Our Lady and St Joseph on either side of the chancel are of Italian carved wood and were given by the late Sir Maurice and Lady Lacey. The mosaic representation of the Stations of the Cross was designed, made and given by early visitors to the church.[6]

At the end of 2011 there was no full-time Baptist or Congregational minister or Catholic priest and the Methodist minister was living out at Shebbear. Before Lawrence MacLean came to Torrington, there was a period when there was no minister of the church resident in the town.

With thanks to:
Doug and Lorraine Eade
Dave Kelly
John and Tilly Kimber
Mary Short
Linda Smithson
Pat and Nigel Stark
Ron and Betty Sussex
Elaine Weeks

30   How old is the Parish Church?

No-one really knows how long there has been a church in Torrington. We do know from the Register of Bishop Bronescombe ((Bishop of Exeter 1258-80) that Humphrey, a priest, was instituted as vicar on 22nd February 1259/60 so there has certainly been a parish church here for 750 years, and probably longer than that. The oldest parts of the present building date from the 13th and 14th centuries.[1]

John Leland, in his 'Itinerary', refers to the church in around 1538: 'In the toune is but one paroch chirch, Dr Chaumbre is personne thereof.' (John Chambre, 1470-1549, was the last of the Torrington rectors. He was also a member of the Privy Council, Doctor of Medicine and Physician to Kings Henry VII and Henry VIII). In 1510 Henry VIII granted the rectory and advowson of Great Torrington to Cardinal Wolsey who appropriated them to his foundation of Christ Church, Oxford and since 1549 the perpetual curates (more recently called vicars) have been appointed by the Dean and Chapter of that College.

The older rectory had been at Priestacott (off the road to Huntshaw Mill) but when Margaret of Richmond became Lady of the Manor 'she pitied the long path that the rector had from the church' and in 1491 presented to the rector, Thomas Burswell, and his successors, her 'manor house here with lands thereunto belonging'.[2] The

Vicarage, New Street

Photo by the author

house was surrounded by a moat 'traces of which are rapidly disappearing', according to the Rev. Frederic Colby in 1875. The present vicarage which stands on this site dates from 1841.[3] Lady Margaret also gave the church a library which is mentioned by Risdon in his description of the building:

> 'The church is spaciously fair, and decently kept, whereupon a library belongeth; in which church are divers exquisite epitaphs, made to the memory of the deceased.'[4]

During the Civil War at the Battle of Torrington in February 1646 there was an explosion in the church which killed some 200 people and destroyed part of the building as well as many of its records of other events. In his despatches, Sir Thomas Fairfax refers to the church as being 'quite blown up' but his report was written immediately after the event when the building was a wreck and still smouldering. The blast came from the south transept (the old tower) in a north-westerly direction but a good deal of the church survived. The pillars at the east end of the nave are thought to date from the 14th century and the small Tudor room at the east end of the south aisle (c1485), once called the 'south room' and now used as a vestry, survived intact. This was possibly the Tudor library, although the books have long since disappeared.

Some writers speak of the church being wholly rebuilt in 1651 but this was not the case. Once restoration was begun it was found possible to repair the ruins and at both the east and west ends older work was retained. The lower part of the old south tower survived the explosion while the upper part and the spire disappeared. The

Tudor room

church had previously had a leaded broach spire similar to the 14th century spires of Barnstaple and Braunton. In 1651 the tower had been sufficiently repaired to enable the erection of a second spire which remained at least until 1786 as it is mentioned by the Rev. John Sweete in his tour of North Devon at that time, '. . .this brought me to the centre of the Town by the Church side, the tower of which is rendered a conspicuous object at a distance, possessing a handsome spire cased with lead.'[5] At some time between 1786 and 1830 this spire was blown down by a gale and fell through the roof causing much damage and the remaining part of the spire was converted into the curious cupola shown in the old engraving of 1830 with a bell hung on the outside.

It was decided that a new tower should be built at the western end of the church and the work was done by a local builder, Walter Brown Cock,

'good work, but of the conventional Devon type, rising in three stages, with buttresses set square, having an embattled parapet ornamented with crocketed pinnacles, the whole surmounted by a lofty spire, which the elevated position of the town renders a landmark for many miles. The west doorway has a pointed arch, the dripstones embellished with the heads of a lady and a bishop. They may have been intended to represent Cardinal Wolsey, Archbishop of York, and Margaret of Richmond, but they are purely conventional in style.'[6]

From an engraving of 1830   Picture taken from Alexander and Hooper

The work cost £1,600 and was paid for by public subscription and grants made by the Feoffees of the Town Lands jointly with the Town Council. Four years after completion, there was a storm which blew down the top of the newly erected spire which had to be repaired by the builder between 1836 and 1838.

At the time of rebuilding, the old tower was converted into a transept and after the restoration of the church in 1864 it accommodated the schoolchildren and seating was put in for that purpose. In 1938 the seating was removed and the transept was furnished as a side chapel and memorial to the late vicar, the Rev. Frank Emlyn-Jones, who served as parish priest from 1894-1934. It is named the Chapel of St James after the demolished chapel of Torrington Castle.

There are three grotesque terminals to the hood-moulds over the south-east window near the vestry which are the oldest carvings on the building (thought to be late 13th century) and probably set in as ornament at some time of restoration. West of the Tudor vestry is a small priest's doorway which leads into the eastern end of the church. Beyond this is the south transept, originally the tower, used for military purposes and barrels of gunpowder stored there caused the explosion. On the west side i.e. right of the present main entrance, is a stone, with the town arms on it, inscribed:

'This chvrch was blowen vp with Powder Febry ye 16th ano 1645 and rebvilt Ad 1651.'

There are old lead rain water pipes and hoppers decorated with the borough arms and dated 1655.

West doorway

Photo by the author

The church is set a little apart from the bustle of the town square and the church-yard contains some handsome trees and shrubs. There are no tombstones which go further back than the 18th century. Inside the church there are no tombs or monuments earlier than the 17th century – those of an earlier date than the Civil War have all disappeared.[7]

Inside the church 'the effect is of largeness (107 ft long)[8] and bareness.'[9] The fine roof is of the 'waggon-shaped' pattern typical of this part of England. The pulpit with its carved cherubs and gilded lions' heads is typical 17th century work. During the restoration of 1860-64 (when the old galleries and box pews were removed) the pulpit was moved and the sounding-board discarded. Someone later rescued the sounding-board from a builder's yard and gave it to the Victoria and Albert Museum in London. It remained there until 1960 when the Mayor of Torrington, Colonel J. E. Palmer, arranged for its return to the church. It is still, technically, the property of the museum and is in Torrington on loan.[10]

The Willis organ is one of the finest organs in the West Country. It was built by Henry 'Father' Willis (1821-1901) for Sherwell Congregational Chapel in Plymouth in 1864. He was one of the most celebrated organ makers who built 2,000 organs, 20 of them for cathedrals, and in 1871 an organ for the Royal Albert Hall. In 1989 alterations planned at Sherwell meant that the organ had to come out and perhaps be destroyed. Lucian Nethsingha, organist at Exeter Cathedral, told people at

Parish church   Photo courtesy of Ron Andrews

Torrington church that the organ was available as he knew they were looking for a replacement for their own organ. Dismantling the organ and rebuilding it at Torrington was undertaken by Lance Foy of Truro and, to keep costs down, much of the work was done by parishioners under Foy's supervision. It is a fine-sounding instrument and much treasured in its new home at Torrington.

The six silver altar candlesticks are the gift of the late Fr Malcolm Pearce. They had been intended for a church dedicated to King Charles the Martyr which was never built but have found a home in a parish which suffered the ravages of a battle between King and Parliament.

The rood which hangs under the chancel was installed in 2002 and was formerly in St Oswald's, Small Heath, Birmingham. It was given to St Oswald's in 1920 as a war memorial and more recently has been coloured and gilded. Before being installed in St Michael's, the figures were restored by Philip Dixon.

The bronze figure of St Michael at the entrance to the chancel is by Mother Concordia of St Mildred's Abbey, Thanet and given in memory of James Bastin, Churchwarden. The wooden figure of Our Lady facing the main door was carved by French nuns and given in memory of Phyllis Hearn.

In the Chapel of St James in the south transept the altar is the 17th century Lord's Table. In the reredos (from left to right) are the figures of St Michael (for Torrington), St Giles (for Little Torrington), St Mary and Virgin, St James, St Mary Magdalen (for

Taddiport) and St Gabriel (for St Gabriel's Mission Church in the town, 'the iron church', which was dismantled and re-erected as a teashop in Westward Ho!). The large oil painting above the altar is a copy of Caravaggio's 'Ecce Homo' made by Catherine Doe who was born in Torrington in 1818 and studied in London.

The icon to the left of the altar is a copy of the famous Byzantine icon known as Our Lady of Czestochowa, the original being in Poland. There was controversy about this icon (referred to as the 'Black Madonna') when the Rev. Hummerstone introduced it into the church in 1983. The Chancellor of the Diocese had refused permission for its installation but in 1984 this decision was reversed.

The window is a memorial to Thomas Fowler the apothecary and inventor who died in 1843. The decorative border shows two of his inventions: the thermosiphon (foundation of central heating systems) and a calculating machine. (See 'Who was Thomas Fowler?').

The eight bells in the tower, six cast by Abraham Rudhall of Gloucester in 1716, and later added to and rehung in 1884 and 1934, are one of the best peals in Devon. The original bell from the old tower now hangs in the spire and strikes the hours.

The white ensign by the organ was used in the Normandy landings in 1944 and presented by Captain Sutcliff R.N. whose daughter, Rosemary, has made Torrington famous in her novels.

The 14 Stations of the Cross originally belonged to a religious community and were an anonymous gift to the church.

The crucifix on the pillar behind the pulpit was carved at Oberammergau in 1934 by Willy Bierling who was St John the Evangelist in the Passion Play that year.

There are two monuments on the north wall, one to Mrs Penelope Johnson and another to Mrs Palmer (in a family tablet) both relations of Sir Joshua Reynolds who used to visit them in Torrington. Another, in the sanctuary, commemorates Sara Gooding who was born by caesarian section in 1671.

The war memorial contains fragments of glass from Westminster Chapter House salvaged after bomb damage.

The glass is mostly 19th century. In windows at the west end appear the arms of the Patrons (Christ Church, Oxford) and the Borough. The fine east window shows a series of Old Testament and New Testament events in parallel.[11]

October 2008 saw the completion of interior work which provided toilets, a kitchen and a new ringing room in the tower area. These new rooms greatly improve the building for use by the local community for events, meetings, concerts, church services, and the new stairs and balcony blend very sympathetically with the existing church interior.[12]

Perpetual curates, or vicars, of Torrington parish church have included Theophilus Powell who was the incumbent at the time of the explosion during the Civil War. He was ejected from the benefice the same year. After the Restoration he became Rector of Langtree in 1662 where he died in 1666. Hugh Peters, Chaplain to the Parliamentary army, 'preached at Torrington to the people from a balcony, the church being blown up' in February 1646. Active in Commonwealth affairs, his voice was often raised in favour of peace and toleration. However, under suspicion as an agitator soon after the Restoration, he was committed to the Tower of London and soon afterwards condemned and executed in October 1660. John Howe, a notable Puritan

Divine and Chaplain to General Fairfax was appointed perpetual curate at Torrington in 1654. In 1656 he became perpetual curate at St Saviour's, Dartmouth. On a visit to London he preached before Cromwell who appointed him his domestic Chaplain with the stipulation that he should spend three months in each year in his North Devon charge. He remained Chaplain to Richard Cromwell on whose deposition he returned to Torrington in May 1659. In 1660 he was informed against as having preached sedition and treason, and was bound over by the Mayor of Torrington to appear at the next Sessions, was tried and acquitted. Howe was among the ministers ejected under the Act of Uniformity in 1662. Samuel Johnson was licensed Vicar of Torrington with St Giles-in-the-Wood in September 1713 and instituted Rector of Little Torrington in 1720. He has been described as 'a thoughtful, able and pious man, who commanded the respect of his contemporaries.'[13] He was vicar for 30 years and died in March 1746. His son, who was three times Mayor of Torrington, married Elizabeth, sister of Sir Joshua Reynolds. Frank Emlyn-Jones was elected to Torrington in October 1894. He was subsequently appointed Rural Dean in March 1906 and Prebendary of Exeter Cathedral in February 1918. He was vicar of Torrington for 40 years. William Keble-Martin was instituted to Torrington on 21 March 1934. He wrote and illustrated the famous 'Concise British Flora in Colour.'

The most recent vicar, the Rev. Jeremy Hummerstone, retired in April 2010 having been at St Michael's and All Angels Church for 30 years. He and his wife, Clarissa, were well-known figures in the community. He would often be seen riding around the town on a huge motor bike, clerical robes flying, and his wife was very involved in local events and helping people. Everyone has their memories of Clarissa and mine are of her wheeling a very squeaky wheelbarrow through town, preparing refreshments at concerts in the church and also, around the time of Palm Sunday, leading a donkey through the streets accompanied by local children.

Rev. Jeremy Hummerstone   Photo courtesy of Mike Southon and the North Devon Journal

Clarissa Hummerstone

Photo courtesy of the
Hummerstone family/
John and Tilly Kimber

Local resident, Dr Jean Tyler, said the couple would be missed in very many ways:

'The regularity of Father Jeremy's home and hospital communions are treasured and valued beyond price.

His right hand woman, Clarissa, has been a tremendous support to him and given unstintingly to the local community. The vicarage has been an open house for anyone in need as well as an ideal setting for more formal entertainment. They take our love, thanks and our heartfelt wishes for a good Yorkshire retirement.'[14]

Sadly, news was received in the town that Clarissa Hummerstone died of a stroke on 27th October 2011. A memorial mass was held for her in the parish church on 8th November.

The Induction and Institution of the new vicar, Father Lawrence MacLean by the Bishop of Exeter, the Right Rev. Dr Michael Langrish, took place on Monday 5th September 2011. He and his wife, Jacqueline, have moved to Torrington from Florence in Italy where he has been serving for the past nine years.[15]

Fr Lawrence MacLean
Photo courtesy of the N. Devon Journal

31   What Shops are there in Torrington?

Early in 2011 Torrington was highlighted as one of the UK's top five towns for independent shops. It still retains many individual, family-owned businesses and was listed the fourth most independent town by the New Economics Foundation. Devon had mixed results in think-tank NEF's survey: Exeter was named the UK's third most 'cloned town' while Crediton ranked just behind Torrington for having many independent shops and Totnes was praised for the support it gives to local businesses.

The Torrington Town Traders brought out a comprehensive guide to the local shops early in 2011 but by the end of the year there had already been several changes. While I've been writing this book shops have opened, moved, closed, and premises have been used for different purposes. Small businesses have been affected by the recession as well as by competition from supermarkets selling more than just groceries but local traders say all it takes is a little custom to keep them going and that having unique, independently run shops makes Torrington a far more friendly town. In 2011 the Torrington Town Traders won this year's good citizen award which is given by the Mayor to mark work within the community. Former Mayor, Sue Mills, said she had worked closely with the traders group, who were not yet a year old. She said, 'Their enthusiasm and drive for this town is wonderful.'[1]

Torrington is a Fairtrade town. The Fairtrade Mark, established in 1994, guarantees that farmers and producers in developing countries are paid fairly and treated properly. It guarantees fair wages and prices for products, good working conditions, no forced or child labour, contracts are agreed and adhered to, a commitment to the environment, an extra 'Fairtrade premium' payment to the producer community or co-operative and producer support. Fairtrade products and refreshments can be found in many shops and other venues in the town and a Traidcraft stall is held in the Plough on the first Saturday in the month.[2]

There are 13 small shops and a café in the pannier market which was roofed in and refurbished in the late 1990s.

There are lots of family run businesses in Torrington which give the town its individual and friendly character. Londis is run by two generations of the Nijjar family, Ferry's hardware store is also into its second generation, and Sing and Gist carpets is into the third generation of the Sing family. Ware brothers, Reg and Steve, worked with their uncle, Stanley Brown, in the butcher's shop on the left of the entrance to the pannier market and then started up on their own in South Street opposite the Co-op. Reg has now retired, although he often helps out, sister Ruth is on the staff and Steve's son, Robert, has joined them after serving in the army.

The very popular Sandford's bakery opened in June 1981. Before that the shop was a greengrocer and florist run by Owen and Joyce Warne who had moved there from 7 South Street which they said had been like living in a lighthouse as 'every room was upstairs!' That shop had originally been a nail store for Heywood and Hodges (ironmongers where the Mole and the Haggis is now). The Warnes moved to Potacre Street in 1960 because the former saddler's shop offered larger premises. It became known as Sandford's greengrocers named after Owen's aunt and family who grew fruit and supplied much of Torrington with apples and plums. In 1981 they were

Sandford's bakery family members

Photo courtesy of Mike Southon and the North Devon Journal

joined by their daughter and son-in-law, Mary and Nick Lovering, and turned the shop into a thriving bakery with some of the savoury snacks provided by Mary's sister, Sue Parish. In 2008, Amy, the eldest daughter of Mary and Nick, joined the bakery team making Sandford's a business spanning three generations.

The Mole and the Haggis has been a bookshop since 1984 named by the couple who owned it with reference to themselves – she a Scot (haggis) and he a photographer who spent time in a darkroom (mole). Lisa D'Alberti ran the shop after they left, keeping its distinctive name, and the present owner, Roger Hickman, took it on in 1993. Before being a bookshop it was Heywood and Hodge, ammunition dealers and ironmongers, an 'Aladdin's cave' that supplied local quarries with explosives which were kept stocked in the basement! The building is known as Heywood House.

The bookshop was mentioned in the *Guardian's* directory of independent bookshops in October 2011 which states that Roger has built up 'an eclectic array of publications'. It goes on to say,

> 'Classics mingle with textbooks and rare finds, while self-publishing authors from north Devon jostle for shelf space with local interest tomes. The unchallenged bestsellers are the Ordnance Survey maps for Devon and Cornwall. The space may be tiny, but it holds a day's worth of browsing material in its nooks and crannies.'

Roger is retiring in June 2012 after exactly 19 years. With his bow tie and easy charm, he will be greatly missed in the town not least by local authors who have been grateful for his support. The premises will be taken over by Adrian and Amanda Shearing who run Jack and Molly's Trading Company. I understand they intend to continue the book ordering service and to stock Ordnance Survey maps and books by local authors.

Above: Heywood & Hodge

    Photo courtesy of Roger Hickman

Left: Roger Hickman of the Mole & Haggis

Photo courtesy of Mike Southon and the North Devon Journal

Alan and Heather Stacey of Xanadu fruit and vegetable shop believe that their happy and successful lives are due to 'hard work, give and take, and loyal customers.' They took over Xanadu where Heather's mother worked in 1986, Alan continuing with his milk round for a year to subsidise the business. Their two boys would come in after school to pre-pack potatoes and do other odd jobs. They invested in a van and Alan would go to Bristol market for produce twice a week, setting off at 2am and arriving back at 8am when an employee would off-load the stock and Alan would have a few hours' rest. They started supplying the Black Horse pub with produce and this side of the business started to grow and today they supply shops in outlying villages, restaurants, schools and residential homes throughout the area. Alan and Heather are grateful to loyal customers who helped them build their family business and some of the customers who shopped with them years ago now enjoy home deliveries. As well as fruit and vegetables, Xanadu stocks a large variety of health foods and this side of the business has grown following customer requests. Alan says, 'We are always happy to stock something our customers want to buy on a regular basis as this keeps people shopping in the town.' Alan and Heather are now stepping back a little and letting their son, Giles, run the business but Alan continues to work part-time as he still enjoys his work and is not ready yet to pack up completely.[3]

Alan and Heather Stacey of Xanadu
Photo courtesy of Rob Tibbles and the North Devon Journal

Green Lantern

Photo by the author

The Green Lantern cake shop in the town square is up for sale after 27 years in the same family (2011). Pam Kent is selling up because of health problems, physically exhausted after being on her feet for up to 13 hours a day, six days a week and lifting heavy baking trays. She began working in the café with two other women before becoming the sole owner in 1984. The café is famous for its homely atmosphere, its cups of tea for 45p and for her father, Roy Handford, who is still working at the age of 87. Upstairs is a great location for watching the May Fair procession and crowning of the May Queen and, for those who book, there is a cold meal laid on. Pam's daughter, Samantha, also works at the café and recalls when a car drove through the window in 2007 and cakes and buns flew out of the shop. She says, 'It was like a Carry On film, it was so funny.' Laura Churchill in the *North Devon Journal* under the title 'Car makes cracking entry' refers to 'Torrington's first pasty ram raid'. The elderly man driving an automatic car had possibly mistaken the accelerator for the brake. Pam assures her customers that the café won't close until a buyer is found. 'I don't want people thinking I'm just walking out and leaving the place,' she says.[4]

Around Christmas 2011 a notice appeared in the window of Cosmi-Cuts, the popular discount store at 25 South Street, which read:

Cosmi Cuts with descendant of Thomas Andrews in the doorway

Photo courtesy of Ron Andrews

'DUE TO RETIREMEMT, AFTER 34 YEARS TRADING AS COSMI-CUTS,
THE SHOP WILL CLOSE ITS DOOR FOR THE LAST TIME ON NEW YEAR'S EVE.
'WE WOULD LIKE TO THANK YOU FOR YOUR LOYAL SUPPORT OVER THE YEARS.
'WE WISH YOU HEALTH AND HAPPINESS FOR THE FUTURE.

'FROM THE WATKINS FAMILY, MANAGERESS KAREN AND ASSISTANT JILL.'

A lot of people are very sad to see the closure of this useful shop with its friendly staff. These premises had previously been a greengrocer's, an antique shop and Andrews photographers. (Thomas Andrews took many photos in and around Torrington which were used as postcards).

Old directories from the mid 19th century list many different shops and trades. In the 1830s there were three bakers: Catherine Browne in Well Street, Elizabeth Evans also in Well Street and Mary Howe in New Street. There were nine boot and shoe makers, six butchers and three china, glass and earthenware dealers. There were two druggists, one in South Street who also dealt in spirits and one in High Street who also distributed stamps. There were six grocers and tea dealers, all in South Street and High Street, and five ironmongers. One of these was Thomas Fowler who is listed as being a 'patentee for an improved mode of heating conservatories, picnics, hot houses and large buildings with boiling water.' There were six linen and woollen

India and China Tea Company   Photo courtesy of Linda Downing

drapers and six milliners and dress dealers. There were two perfumers and hair-dressers, both men, two saddlers and two watch and clock makers and ten people listed as being 'shopkeepers and dealers in sundries'. In terraced houses facing on to the street, a lot of people had a little shop in their front room.

People who have lived in Torrington for many years say there used to be far more shops than there are today stocking a wider variety of goods. That was in the days before people had cars and were able to drive to Bideford or Barnstaple and buy everything they needed in one go at a supermarket.

Pat Wilks lived in Torrington during the 1930s when her father, Stanley Webb, was manager of the Midland Bank (subsequently HSBC which closed in December 2011 and put on the market for £15,000 per annum leasehold).[5] She lived with her family in the flat above the bank and retains amazingly vivid memories of her years in Torrington. In her day there were four banks: Midland (previously a stationery shop and, before that, Mr Beck's chemist) Lloyds (now Lloyds TSB), National Provincial (now NatWest) and Barclays (previously a butcher's).

She recalls Tickle's garage in the square where you could buy petrol, Sparks' seed and flower shop near the Rolle fountain just past the Town Hall, and the wonderful smell in Blatchfords which sold tobacco and cigarettes. Mr and Mrs Louis Reddaway had a butchers near the (old) Post Office (which then became Farm Fresh and is now Steve Gladwin's). She also remembers a butcher's shop in New Street run by Mr and Mrs Burridge whose two sons, Lester and Peter, were both soldiers in the Second World War, Peter taking part in the abortive Norwegian landings. Mr Burridge made wonderfully tasty sausages and his wife read a lot of books. She and Pat's mother were always discussing their latest literary find. Mr Lyle kept a high class grocers in the square (where the present Post Office is). His shop had the sort of small container fixed to a wire pulley system by which cash was returned to the till which was fashionable in those days. He sold bacon, cheese, flour, dried fruit, biscuits etc. and wrapped his sugar in triangular-shaped dark blue paper packets. Mr and Mrs Langlois kept a newsagents on the corner of New Street and Halsdon Terrace and let Pat and her sister read the magazines without always having to buy them. Miss Mountjoy was 'a lovely little lady who kept a tuck shop near the school' and sold sherbert fountains and liquorice laces and non pareil drops (chocolate drops coated with hundreds and thousands) 'and many more delicious sweets'. Pat says Miss Mountjoy 'always insisted on good manners!' Grocer, Mr White, sold wonderful home-made ice-cream with an added dab of clotted cream. The Misses Doe kept a china and glass shop 'at the bottom of South Street.' Pat had a Saturday job dusting and tidying up in their shop and, when she and her family left Torrington, they presented her with a lovely china robin which she kept for years.

Residents up at the eastern end of town have long wished for a local shop. There used to be a general store at Dartington Fields, but that closed, and a launderette which local people have been fighting to keep open. There has never been a shop at Burwood – I suppose no-one wants it next to their house. The nearest convenience store is 'Happydays' in Calf Street. The building was originally an old shippen which a man called Ernie Gilbert turned into a shop and his son, Alec, ran the shop which was named after their family. Alec is remembered as being very funny and having a nice smile and a gap between his front teeth. Derek Jewell bought the shop from the Gilberts in 1969/70 and ran it for ten years as Centra Food Market. He remembers a local lad trying to leave the shop with a suspicious bulge under his jumper. When asked what he had up there, the lad replied, 'Nothing', and when he was asked to demonstrate this fact by lifting up his jumper, several packets of biscuits fell out onto the floor. When asked how he thought they had got there, he replied, 'They must've fell up there, mister!' Two different lots of people took on the store after the Jewells, still as Centra, for the next two or three years. It then became Spar and then Masons and at one time was called Eight till Late before the present shop. It is much used by pupils at the nearby school, by passing motorists and by local residents who pop in for provisions. A notice has appeared in the window – 'No admittance to people in pyjamas'!

Shops have changed many times over the years. Where Fresh and Fruity is now used to be the Central Garage and at the back was the coffee tavern (which is why the development of houses in behind the High Street is called Tavern Mews). It was upstairs and reached by quite a steep staircase which would probably be considered a Health and Safety hazard nowadays. Lots of people would meet there, especially when the market was flourishing and farmers and their wives came into Torrington with their livestock and produce to sell.

There were four toy shops at one time, sweet shops, shoe shops, drapers, dress shops and gents' outfitters. There was a Co-op in South Street for 83 years where Londis and the shop next door (previously Computers At Torrington) are now. It used to sell furniture and clothes as well as general foodstuffs and closed in 1983. There was also a Co-op in Well Street for a time, on the left hand side after crossing New Road. Now we have a Co-op once more after it took over Somerfield.[6]

White's Stores (now Co-op)   Photo courtesy of John and Tilly Kimber

There was Boots the chemist from the late 1930s until the late 1960s next to the old Newmarket pub where HQ hairdressers and Designers florist and giftware at 12 and 12A South Street are now. Spar used to be Sussex's gas showroom and, before that, Neal's dress shop and, prior to that, Webber's drapers. There was Downing's drapers on the corner of Well Street and Potacre Street which is now Paul Donner optician and the neighbouring Nationwide building society (previously the Portman).

A & J optician on the opposite corner used to be Great Torrington cards and balloons and, before that, Eastman's ironmongers. Just along Fore Street a little way is Studio C which was officially opened in July 2011 by Mayor and Mayoress of Torrington, Richard and Helen Rumbold selling an 'eclectic and interesting mix of goods' collected by the owners mainly in France but also from Italy, Mexico, China and other places.[7] This shop, which had stood empty for several years, had previously been a series of newsagents, the most recent being Martin's.

Further along Fore Street next to the former HSBC bank is Toyzone which was once the electricity showroom, SWEB, and before that a baker's run by Mr Luxton. Ferry's home hardware is on the site of an old tannery which extended back to where Tannery Row is now in Church Lane. It was a grocer's at some time around the beginning of the 20th century, a gas showroom with maintenance being carried out at the back, Pow furniture store and, since about 1980, a hardware shop, the present owners buying the business in 1984.

Brown's delicatessen at the top of South Street is run by the son of the former owners of Brown's restaurant and his wife. The shop had been Brook's shoe shop, a dress shop and, before that, a lawnmower repair shop run by Ron Juniper who first came to Torrington as an evacuee.

Many former shops have closed and are now private houses such as, in New Street, Darch's butchers/The Soup Kitchen at number 50, Mrs Fisher's Stores/Allen's Stores at 85A, Dave Ward's electrical shop at number 58, Sussex hardware (plumbing equipment) which is now four properties to the right of Stonemans Lane, and Tracey's restaurant (formerly Cobbledick's animal feed) at number 12, Church End. In South Street, number 48 between the former CAT and Windy Cross House was once a clockmaker's shop, and Furse House, number 42 used to be Singh's clothes shop and general drapers. Before the war, Mr Banta Singh, who opened the shop in 1957, used to take his wares around the countryside on a bicycle. In Calf Street, number 35 was a hairdresser's opened by Margaret Bennett but it has not been a shop for some time and the bay windows were finally removed by a local builder in 2011. In Well Street, the tall house next to the Cavalier pub's car park used to be a clothes shop called Jade and there was a hairdresser next to the launderette called Berenice. On the other side of New Road, number 74 Well Street was Popham's bakers in the mid-20th century. When people had smaller ovens in their houses, they would take their Christmas turkeys to be cooked in the bakery's large ovens. In School Lane, opposite the swimming pool, was Westcountry Crystal – glassware engravers – and years ago the car park alongside used to be a nursery which supplied Sparks' shop in the square.

(For a more detailed list of former shops in the town, see the Appendix at the end of the book).

With thanks to:
Roy Beer
Roger and Sally Cole
John and Jackie Davis
Roger Hickman
John and Tilly Kimber
Derek and Margaret Jewell
Alison Norman
Shaun Roach
John and Diane Rollinson
Rick and Phyllis Smale
Brian Squire
Mike Steer
Margaret Trounson
Owen Warne
Wendy Wigley
Joyce Wooldridge
Pat Wilks

32   Where was the Old Cinema?

The old cinema was a small building in Church Lane which runs from Whites Lane round the back of the old infants' school into the churchyard. It had been converted from a building on the site of an old tannery. After many years of providing entertainment for the people of Torrington, it closed and became used as a bingo hall. Then it stood derelict for a while and was finally knocked down when Tannery Row was built.

Elderly Torrington people who were children in the 1920s and 1930s remember going to see films there. Each year the Mayor and Mayoress used to treat the school-children to a film just before Christmas and, as they came out, they would each be given an orange and a toffee. They particularly remembered Mr Harold Vincent, manager of the glove factory who lived up Villa Road and was Mayor in 1926, being a nice man who 'gived us sweets'.

In the 1930s a Mr Long and his son, Rex, were in charge of the cinema. Rex did the film projection. Possibly, MrsLong was at the cash desk. Prices ranged from 4d to 6d (6d = 2½p) for children and 6d to 1/- (1 shilling = 5p) for adults. Cinema audiences, especially during the day when lots of children enjoyed the films, were generally noisy and, 'if we got too noisy, Mr Long would chuck out the worst offenders.' The seat at the rear of the cinema, which could accommodate about six people, was leather and made from the old back seat of a 'charabanc' and mostly used by courting couples in the evenings.

Inside the old cinema   Photo courtesy of Sue Scrutton

Bingo hall

The black and white films shown included such names as Boris Karloff (horror), Nelson Eddy, Jeanette McDonald and Bing Crosby (musicals), Shirley Temple ('rather sweetly twee'), James Cagney (gangster), Charles Laughton, Joan Crawford, Jean Harlow, Marlene Dietrich, Katharine Hepburn, Spencer Tracy, Mae West, Myrna Loy, Charlie Chaplin, Buster Keaton, Laurel and Hardy (comedies), Greto Garbo, Mary Pickford, early John Wayne and other cowboy films such as Hopalong Cassidy. There were also Micky Mouse and Donald Duck cartoons.

Local people who were children in the 1950s often used to go to the cinema for entertainment (and some remember being thrown out for mucking about!). Two films a week would be shown, one on Monday, Tuesday and Wednesday and a different one on Thursday, Friday and Saturday. At that time it cost 'half a crown' (2/6 = 12½ p) at the back, 1/6 (7½ p) in the middle, 1/- further forward and 7d (seven old pence = about 3p) at the front. Dick Long was in charge and used to make his own ice-lollies with a stick in an egg cup and Fred Stapleton was the projectionist.The films would often break down and Fred would take himself off to the pub!

The cinema closed in May 1964 (the last film to be shown was Elvis Presley in 'GI Blues') and, like so many cinemas across the country, it became a bingo hall. Women in full make-up and wearing their best clothes would be dropped off by their husbands at the end of Church Lane looking forward to their weekly entertainment. When that activity in turn fell out of favour the building remained closed, becoming ever more dilapidated and still advertising 'meat bingo' over the doorway. One of the governors of the Bluecoat school suggested that the building be used as a recreation hall for the children but was unable to get funding for the project. Eventually, it was demolished to make way for the building of Tannery Row which was completed in 2006.

These days films can be seen at the Plough Arts Centre.

With thanks to:
Maurice Cockwill
Dave Kelly
Dulcie and Bryan Leate
John and Diane Rollinson
Cathrine and John Simmons
Michael Street
Barbara Ward
Pat Wilks

33   How long has Torrington been twinned with Roscoff?

Torrington has enjoyed a lively twinning association with Roscoff in Northern Brittany for nearly 40 years.

The earliest cross-Channel links between our two regions were the 'Onion Johnnies', Breton farmers who came over to Britain each year to sell strings of onions. They started making the journey across the Channel to sell their wares in Plymouth in 1828 when Brittany had a bumper crop of the rose-coloured Roscoff onion. One brave farmer from Roscoff decided to go and sell his onions in London carrying a board marked 'The English onion is not good'! Many of them wore traditional striped tops and berets and were called Jean which gave rise to the 'Johnny' nick-name. By the 1930s, more than 1,500 were in Britain. The economic downturn has had an adverse effect on this long tradition and by 2008 there were only 15 Onion Johnnies trading in the UK compared with 160 in 1973. Those that remained said they had noticed a 30% decline in sales and were forced to consider whether their future was financially viable. They travel to Britain in white vans these days, not on bicycles, and those who sell their onions in London find short-term accommodation there so expensive that they sometimes have to sleep in their vans. One Johnnie says young people don't want to be away from home for months at a time and struggle to make a living – 'We're dying out.'[1]

Town twinning began in the UK more than a century ago but it was after the Second World War that the idea of municipal co-operation flourished as a way of promoting reconciliation and healing wartime divisions. Bombed out Coventry was twinned with Stalingrad and Dresden. There are tens of thousands of agreements across Europe with more than 2,000 in the UK.[2]

A lot of twinning between towns in Britain and Europe started in the 1970s. Devon towns mainly twinned with towns in the French département of Normandy but Torrington chose a town in Finistère in Brittany. Legend has it that Clifford Quick and other representatives of Torrington Town Council were on their way via Plymouth and Roscoff to visit a town in Normandy. The ferry boats on the newly-opened Channel crossing were far more uncomfortable than they are today and, after a churning six hour crossing, the Councillors arrived exhausted at Roscoff and couldn't face travelling any further. They decided to choose Roscoff as Torrington's twin town.

Bob Peacock of Torrington secondary school made the initial contacts and, with the help of Frank Claxton, Devon Twinning Secretary, there was an exchange of letters between the Mayors of Torrington and Roscoff in the summer of 1974 accepting, in principle, a twinning arrangement between the two towns.

In October 1974 the first official delegation from Torrington visited Roscoff with a view to getting to know at first hand the proposed twin town. The delegation was led by the Mayor and Mayoress, Mr and Mrs Reubin Cotton, Deputy Mayor, Margaret Pitts, Councillor Jimmy Martin and Town Clerk, David Elliot. They enjoyed a busy, informative and entertaining programme and excellent hospitality at the Hôtel des Bains, courtesy of Mme Cadou. However, the visit was marred somewhat by the cancellation of their scheduled return crossing to Plymouth and a marathon 28 hour return journey via Le Havre.

The first delegation from Roscoff visited Torrington at the beginning of December the same year. It was led by the Mayor, Adrien Stephan, Deputy Mayors Cabioch and Guivarch, Michelle Branellec and Corentin Coic, the Town Clerk. They too endured a frantic two-day stay with an intensive programme of visits and hospitality. Bert Waldron, the award-winning Town Crier, was brought out of retirement to welcome the French guests in traditional fashion.

In early 1975 there was a public meeting in Torrington Town Hall to discuss the formation of a Twinning Committee. In the middle of April a second delegation from Torrington visited Roscoff, this time with the main purpose of signing a Twinning Charter linking the two towns. This was done on 13th April 1975 and repeated in Torrington Town Hall during the May Fair celebrations later that same year. The English and French Mayors signed the charter of friendship in a crowded Town Hall with a French delegation and civic heads from all over North Devon among the witnesses. At the May Fair luncheon local MP, Peter Mills, called not only for many exchange visits but exchange trade as well to cement the new partnership. At the end of the visit the parting advice to all from Monsieur le Maire was, 'You must learn some French, you know. The ferry has put our two towns just a stone's throw from each other.'

By June 1976 Larry Croxford had been elected Secretary of the Twinning Committee and Mike Sampson was appointed as Treasurer and they remained loyal servants of the twinning for several years. Gerry Milnes became Chairman in 1977 and he was followed by Cilla Bangay in 1978. Members of the Twinning Committee at that time included Bob Peacock, Keith Mayhew, Graeme Barber and Bob Gordon.

One of the first visits to Roscoff by members of the general public was made in September 1977 led by the Mayor, Harry Cramp. This was followed in April 1978 by a visit of Torrington Girl Guides at the same time as the mounting of an ambitious exhibition of 'Torrington History, Life and People' at the old port in Roscoff which attracted over 900 visitors. This colourful and informative exhibition was housed in a converted coach which was loaned by Peter Horn, driven across to France by Larry Croxford and staffed by Larry, Gerry Milnes, Jim Bastin, Judy Barber and Diana Hansen.

By 1978 a pattern of twinning visits was beginning to emerge. Torrington visited Roscoff over the Easter weekend and Roscoff made a return visit at August Bank Holiday with junior school exchanges and visits of official delegations to Torrington often coinciding with May Fair. This lasted until 1994 when visits became once a year at Easter, the English going to Roscoff and the French coming to Torrington in alternate years. The Corps of Drums, led by Derek Skinner, visited Roscoff in August 1978 and they were soon followed by the Silver Band, led by Herbert Oke in 1980. At about the same time the Plough hosted a concert by the Roscoff choir, 'Mouez Rosco', and an exhibition of paintings by the Roscoff artist, Jean-Claude Helou. Keenly contested international games of football, table tennis (players of 'le ping-pong' being known as 'les pongistes'), bowls and pétanque were starting to become integral parts of twinning weekends.

At Easter 1979 a street in Roscoff leading down to the port was named 'Rue de Great-Torrington' and in September 1984, as part of the 10th anniversary celebrations of the twinning, the Mayor of Torrington, Dave Davis, and the Mayor of Roscoff, Michel Morvan, joined in a ceremony to name one of Torrington's newest streets on Burwood 'Roscoff Close' which was toasted in champagne. 77 French people had come over to Torrington and, under the heading 'Vive l'Entente!', the North Devon Journal of 6th September 1984 tells us that there were table tennis and football matches, a bowls tournament, a barbecue, a skittles match and a dinner dance.

The second leg of the 10th anniversary celebrations was held in Roscoff at Easter 1985 and 69 Torringtonians took part. The Mayor, Dave Davis, and Torrington Twinning Association Chairman, Mike Whateley, took a commemorative plate made by local potter, Harry Juniper, and decorated by his daughter, Susan, which they presented to Roscoff Town Council. A harvest jug, also made by Harry Juniper and decorated to depict the twinning links which had been established between the towns, was presented to Roscoff Twinning Committee. At the celebration dinner, as a thank you to the people of Roscoff, the Torrington Mayor sang a selection of songs in his rich bass voice including his pièce de résistance, 'Ol' Man River'. Mike Whateley and the Roscoff Twinning Committee Chairman were both interviewed at length on local radio. The North Devon Gazette reported the twinning event on 26th April 1985 under the heading 'Entente was so cordiale'.

At the 20th anniversary celebrations in 1994 the Torrington Mayor, Bill Brook, and the Deputy Roscoff Mayor, Anniek Labat, exchanged a bronze plaque of St Paulette, the Breton saint of friendship, and a large Dartington Crystal goblet. Over 60 Roscovites came over including a group of musicians called 'Les Forbans de Roscoff' who contributed a good deal to the liveliness of the proceedings.

At the 30th anniversary celebrations in 2004 the French twinners were accompanied on their visit to Torrington by François Keriven, a 'Johnnie' who sold strings of onions at the entrance to the pannier market. Marion Gardiner, Chairman of the Torrington Twinning Association at that time, wrote in the anniversary programme:

'Twinning between our two towns began as a formal municipal arrangement, developed as football and table tennis took a lead, was sustained by the regular involvement of the Silver Band and has now become a twinning based on strong and long-standing family ties.'

French connection

Twinning 20th anniversary

Photo courtesy of
Bill Brook

SMILES and commemorative gifts mark the 20th anniversary of the setting-up of the Torrington twinning connection with Roscoff.

The group are pictured at Torrington Town Hall during the French visit. Torrington mayor Bill Brook (pictured right) holds a bronze plaque of St Paulette, the Breton Saint of friendship presented to Torrington, and next to him is Mlle Anniek Labat, deputy mayor of Roscoff, with a Dartington Crystal glassware gift from the North Devon town.

Left is Jean Paul Creignon, Roscoff councillor, alongside Torrington mayoress Janet Brook.

Twinning in Torrington is still healthy rather than thriving as it once was. In the early days it used to be the only foreign holiday for some people but cheap flights and a variety of Channel crossings, including Eurostar, have made it easier to go abroad. However, staying with a family and sharing their everyday life gives someone a far greater insight into a country and its people than the superficial nature of a package holiday. One year an English visitor was reported to have 'drunk so much red wine that his lips were purple' but others maintain that twinning weekends are about more than boozing and eating. Both the French and English have made an effort to arrange visits of historical and cultural interest for their visitors and to show them around their local area. The Torrington Silver Band, choral society and St Michael's church choir have performed in Roscoff, and Roscovites have had a float in the May Fair Carnival and played their unique musical instruments and performed Breton dances here in Torrington.

Jean Tyler, retired doctor and keen supporter and promoter of many community initiatives, was one of the first people to take part in the twinning with her husband – known by the French as 'l'homme avec les favoris' (sideburns) – and four teenage children who all 'benefited from exchange hospitality in Roscoff homes – without their parents!' She has also welcomed a good many French guests into her home over the years. Her younger son and daughter enjoyed trips with the Silver Band, especially playing on the ferry, and her elder daughter who loved the French language as well as the people took advantage of the facilities and hospitality of Roscoff's Station Biologique where she did her A-level biology dissertation. As well as gaining first-hand science knowledge, her French improved no end as no-one in the laboratory spoke English. For youngsters, having to make themselves understood in another country is the best motivation for learning a foreign language and they begin to see the point of those French lessons at school.

Matching of English and French families is done in a fairly random manner and sometimes the relationship works and endures while at others it doesn't last. It is possible to change although, obviously, this can be diplomatically rather tricky. One English couple regret the fact that over the many years that they have been part of the twinning they have been unable to spend Easter with their family but over-all they feel the advantages have greatly outweighed the disadvantages. A local builder says he and his wife find the weekends in France, away from the pressures of work, thoroughly relaxing. Since they have known their twinning family well enough to talk about things like money and personal aspirations, they have realised that their French friends, despite differences in language and traditions, have just the same concerns as they do. They, along with several of the English twinners, have enjoyed so much visiting the country, getting to know the people and experiencing the way of life that they have bought a property in Brittany.

A 40th anniversary celebration of the Torrington/Roscoff twinning is being planned for 2014.

With thanks to:
John Hayes
Paul Tilbury
Jean Tyler

34   Who were the Rolles?

The Rolle family were Lords of the Manor for some 350 years. They lived at Stevenstone (spelt Stephenstone up to 1635) in the adjoining parish of St Giles-in-the-Wood. George Rolle (c1485-1552), who acquired the manor of Torrington from the Fortescue family in Henry VIII's time, was the founder of the dynasty which came to an end with the death of Mark Rolle in 1907.

Amongst George Rolle's descendants were Dennys Rolle (1614-1638) who was known for his intellect and amiability and who made many benefactions to the people of Torrington during his short life, including the foundation of the Blue Coat School.

There was Sir John Rolle (1626-1706) who was knighted by Charles II in 1660. He had remained loyal to the King during the Civil War, had helped Charles II when he was in exile by payments of money and had actively supported the Restoration.

Another Dennys Rolle (1720-1797) was Mayor of Torrington in 1749-50 and again in 1756-57 and was Recorder from 1781 to 1797. He was also MP for Barnstaple from 1761-1774. He was a colourful character who had many interests and adventures. His ambition was to set up a colony in Florida where he bought a vast piece of land and set about its cultivation. He persuaded many Devon farmers and agricultural labourers and tradesmen to accompany him and help his project but, eventually, the enterprise failed. He was very interested in natural history and liked working on the land himself. He provided schools and garden allotments for the poor. He died under a tree in June 1797 while walking, as he often did, between his estates of

Left: The Hon. Mark Rolle
        Photo courtesy of
            Linda Downing

Below: Stevenstone 1906
        Photo courtesy of
            Linda Downing

Stevenstone and Hudscott (near Chittlehampton). He was the first to propose building a canal at Torrington in 1793.

John Lord Rolle (1750-1842) was elected MP for Devonshire in 1780 and retained the seat in the general elections of 1784 and 1790. He was a supporter of Pitt and a staunch Conservative. In June 1796 he was raised to the Peerage, receiving the title of 'Baron Rolle of Stevenstone'. He was Colonel of the South Devon Militia and Royal North Devon Yeomanry, a county magistrate, a good landlord, liberal benefactor and supporter of the church. He commissioned plans for the canal his father had proposed and paid for it to be built. It was started in 1823 and completed in 1827. He died at Bicton, another family estate, on 3rd April 1842.

Although he was married twice, John Lord Rolle had no children and his Torrington estates were left to his nephew, the Hon. Mark George Kerr Trefusis (1835-1907), son of Lord Clinton, on the condition that he changed his name to Rolle. This he did by Royal Licence in 1852 at the age of 17. Mark Rolle sold the canal land for the building of a railway in 1871 and he had the section of the canal which ran from Taddiport along the base of Castle Hill converted into a toll road. He donated land for the cottage hospital, paid for the pannier market to be roofed and for a drinking fountain to be erected in the square which bears the inscription 'Presented to the Town of Torrington by the Honourable Mark Rolle, 1870'. He built an extravagant new manor house at Stevenstone in what was called a 'French Italian' style of architecture. It was started in 1868 when he was only 33, 'an ambitious project for so young a man'[1] and one which took four years to complete but in less than 100 years later the house was in ruins.

Mark was the last of the Rolle dynasty. He died leaving no male heir and his estates then passed to his nephew, Charles John Robert Hepburn Stuart Forbes Trefusis, the 21st Baron Clinton.

The information for this section has been obtained from:
  Alexander and Hooper – 'The History of Great Torrington'
  Rosemary Anne Lauder – 'Vanished Houses of North Devon'
  Sue Scrutton – 'Lord Rolle's Canal'

35   How many Pubs are there in Torrington?

At the beginning of 2011 there were probably fewer pubs in Torrington than ever before. Recent years had seen the closure of the Admiral Vernon in Well Street, the West of England and the Newmarket in South Street, the Torridge Inn at the bottom of Mill Street and, in January, the Globe in Fore Street, which left only five pubs in the town:
  Black Horse, High Street
  Cavalier, Well Street
  Torrington Arms, New Street
  Royal Exchange, New Street
  Puffing Billy, a mile out of town on the Bideford road.

When Cherries are ripe, in July,
This Market-day scene meets the eye,
In Torrington Street,
And with Cream what will beat
A Devonshire Mazzard Pie?

Black Horse   Photo courtesy of Linda Downing and Tilly Kimber

The Black Horse in the town square, of Tudor style with double-gabled frontage, is one of the few remaining ancient houses of half-timbered construction in the towns of North Devon. At the time of the Battle of Torrington in 1646 during the Civil War, it is believed that both Lord Ralph Hopton, the commander of the Royalists who were trying to defend the town, and Sir Thomas Fairfax, who led the victorious Parliamentarian army, used the Black Horse as their headquarters at different times.

The Cavalier in Well Street was formerly called the Hunters Inn. Its name was changed in 1996 when there were celebrations in the town to commemorate the 350th anniversary of the Battle of Torrington.

The Torrington Arms in New Street was previously known as the Railway Hotel and was run by Phyllis and Maurice Smithson from 1967-1981. It was the nearest public house to the railway station before the Puffing Billy opened in the old station building itself.

The Admiral Vernon in Well Street, now a private residence, was called the New Inn until Jack Boyd, landlord from 1973-89 renamed it. (In the 19th century there had been a Vernon Inn in South Street). Admiral Vernon's capture of Porto Bello had been a popular event in the war with Spain in 1739. It was the first pub in town to start selling food in around 1975.

A room in the back of the West of England has been used for many years as changing facilities for the May Queen and her attendants. They process out of the front door of that building, which became Captain Jack's and is now Taylor's restaurant, into the street and up the square amongst the cheering crowds.

Cavalier

Photo by the author

The Newmarket was a lively, somewhat rowdy pub popular with young people (some of whom were too young to be drinking alcohol) and for a time there was a night club called The Shed at the rear of the building. After being closed for a year or so amid rumours of the building being converted into flats, it reopened in time for May Fair 2012 and is to be renamed 'EX38'.

The Torridge Inn, down opposite the old dairy at the bottom end of Mill Street, is an attractive building of cob and thatch which probably dates from the 17th century. It had been closed for quite a while but reopened at the end of October 2011 under the ownership of Robert Collier.

The Globe was a commercial and family hotel and posting house during the 19th century and all coaches, including the 'North Devon' from Plymouth to Barnstaple and the 'Torridge Express' from Exeter to Bideford, called there. In the mid 19th century the Globe was considered a much higher class establishment than the Plough

Newmarket

Inn next door and it has been a fine building. Its bedrooms have been furnished with four-poster beds and it has a large function room and magnificent ballroom, complete with sprung wooden floor and pillars supporting winged cupids! However, it costs a lot to maintain and the last landlord departed in January. The people at the Plough had hopes of buying the property to give them more room for their arts and community events but that plan was shelved. Towards the end of 2011 the Globe was taken over by new people and opened for meals just before Christmas.

The Plough was formerly a public house from about 1750-1910 and this is where the name of the arts centre originated. When the building was converted into a drill hall, fine oak panelling was removed and installed in the Mayor's parlour in the Town Hall. Old photos of the Plough inn show what appears to be a barber's pole to the right of the front entrance indicating that men could have a shave or a haircut there as well as a drink. (See 'What goes on at the Plough?').

Old directories from the 19th century show that there were at least 16 public houses in Torrington at that time. In 1878 a referendum was held to close public houses on Sundays and the result was 505 in favour, 8 against and 22 neutral. In 1880 a 'coffee tavern' was opened in the square under the auspices of the local temperance movement.

Above: Globe and Plough   Photo courtesy of Margaret Trounson, Roy Beer and Dave Kelly

Below: Royal Exchange   Photo courtesy of Dave Kelly

Inns that no longer exist include the following:

Barley Mow, Well Street

Barnstaple and Bideford, New Street

Bell, High Street

Black Swan, Potacre Street

Boot, South Street

Canal Tavern, Mill Street (an article in the *North Devon Journal* of 17th February 1859 announces 'The Old Canal Tavern in Mill Street catches fire.')

Castle, Castle Street

Exeter, Calf Street

Glovers Arms, New Street (from the arms of the Glovers' Company or Guild)

Kings Arms, High Street

Plough, Fore Street (once an ancient house, then a pub, then a drill hall and now the arts centre)

Greyhound, Mill Street

Malt Scoop, Well Street

Market House Inn, South Street

Nelson, Mill Street

New Inn, Well Street

Old Inn, Well Street

Plymouth, Mill Street

Railway Inn, Well Street (in Kelly's Directory of 1866 a Railway Inn is listed in Well Street while seven years later a Railway Inn is in New Street – now the Torrington Arms)

Ring of Bells, New Street

Rising Sun, Cornmarket Street

Rolle Arms, South Street (from the arms of the Rolle family – this was a coaching inn set back from the street alongside Castle Hill Hotel and burnt down in 1886)

Setting Sun, Cornmarket Street

Star, Potacre Street, possibly an old coaching establishment as it had a big yard

Tradesmens Arms, New Street

Vernon Inn, South Street

West Country Inn, New Street

White Hart, New Street (the white hart was the badge of Richard II, 1377-99)

White Swan (location unknown)

It is rather amusing that there was an Old Inn and a New Inn in Well Street and a Rising Sun as well as a Setting Sun in Cornmarket Street. (The Setting Sun was at 24 Cornmarket Street and the Rising Sun was opposite, actually at number 1 South Street, the building with a curved front wall). Terry Finnamore, a Land Girl based in Torrington after the war, describes the interior of the Setting Sun as it was in the late 1940s:

'The main bar was like the sitting room of a house, with long tables and benches across the bay windows and the opposite wall, with a seat fixed to the wall behind the door. The small bar had just enough room for one person serving. There was a hatch at one side where people would bring jugs and bottles to be filled to take home. Anyone who wanted to use the room opposite would go into the corridor and collect their beer from there, as the old landlord rarely left the bar for long. He was too busy most of the night giving orders to his customers to be careful or be quiet. Not, I may add, to the young-sters, but to the old regulars who were real characters.'[1]

In the 1980s and '90s the House of the Setting Sun, on the site of the former pub, was an Aladdin's cave of art and craft gifts with a little café to one side which served light refreshments and excellent coffee. I remember buying a mirror there and being allowed to carry it home to make sure it was the right size for my bathroom before paying for it. Such trust! Many people were sad to see the shop close. It is now a private house.

As well as the pubs, an alcoholic drink and chat can be enjoyed at the Torridge Vale Social Club and the Conservative Club in South Street, at the football and rugby clubs and at the café in the Plough.

With thanks to:
Dave Kelly
Andrea Magarotto
Michael Taverner

36   Where is Mill Street?

Mill Street drops down the hill from the town to the river. It starts from the corner of South Street and Halsdon Terrace and winds down to the site of the old ruined dairy at Taddiport. The Methodist church is at the top and the Torridge Inn is at the bottom.

The road is narrower and steeper at the top where only one-way traffic is allowed coming up from where Warren Lane joins Mill Street, although people have been seen driving down during the snow in 2010, when New Street was closed during road works in 2011 and a complicated diversion was set up, and at other times if the fancy takes them!

Mill Street is a very old street of mainly terraced houses with the odd newer house or bungalow fitted into gaps. Some of the old houses have been divided into two while others are two houses joined into one. Those on the south side have very steep gardens plunging down to the commons by the river while those on the other side of the street have gardens sloping up to the Mill Street common to the north. The hous-es were originally thatched, some of them up until the 1960s, but the only thatched buildings remaining are Rose Cottage and the Torridge Inn down at the bottom.

Mill Street was the escape route taken by Royalist soldiers fleeing to the west after their defeat at the Battle of Torrington in 1646.

The houses are of a variety of styles and, as in any street, some are neatly kept while others are shabby and neglected. There is a tangle of overhead wires and a high pavement (which was known as 'the course') on the north side of the street

Above: Looking up Mill Street

Photo courtesy of Philip and Jill Dixon

Below: Looking down Mill Street

Photo courtesy of Philip and Jill Dixon

which had railings added 20 years or so ago and ramps down to the roadway. There is a 'drangway' up between numbers 84 and 86 leading to Mill Street common and a steep pathway down towards the river between numbers 101 and 103. Gardens are irregular in shape and sometimes access can only be gained through a neighbour's garden.

Some of the houses, mainly on the north side of the street, have a well indoors or in the garden and there used to be wooden doors in the wall under the pavement which led to water supplies of some sort. What looks like an old well can be seen outside number 120, which was once the Canal Inn, down towards the bottom end of the street and there is a square hole nearer the top end outside number 4 where there is the sound of running water. Some houses are still not on main drainage and have septic tanks.

An elderly lady who lives at the junction of Mill Street and Warren Lane gave me the following poem, author unknown, taken from a postcard printed at the end of the 19th century:

MILL STREET, TORRINGTON

Of course you've heard of Torrington,
Or seen it in your rambles –
Where streets are decked with flowers (wild),
And fruit, that grow on brambles!

You've heard about Niagara Falls –
There's gutters here that match it,
The water rushing o'er cascades,
Form lakes, below, to catch it!

You've heard about the Pebble Ridge –
At Westward Ho! you'll strike it,
But why go there? Here is a street
That's absolutely like it!

You've heard there's miles of common land
For sheep and goats to roam through,
But if they want to fill up quick,
This is the street they home to!

You've heard gold-finches seek their food
Where thistledown is plenty –
Bird-catchers, take this tip from me,
You'll cage from ten to twenty.

You've heard the Council has proposed
This lovely scene to mar it –
Root up the flowers, (they call them weeds)
Fill in the trench and tar it.

They've pondered long and carefully,
At last decreed to banish
The bed of watercress! – so germs
That flourished there must vanish.

Were these familiar scenes removed
How Mill Street folks would grieve it –
But I don't think they will – do you?
'No, Fi! We don't believe it!'

There has been a change of usage in many of the buildings over the years. Barns and sheds have been incorporated into houses, and shops and businesses have disappeared. Number 130 used to be a fish and chip shop and the shop at the corner of Sandfords Gardens, number 29, which closed sometime in the 1990s has been converted into a dwelling for a disabled person. It was originally opened by Derek Bidgway, who worked for the *North Devon Journal*, and his wife, Olive (aka Margaret) who ran the shop. They sold groceries and bread and general supplies. If there was something particular that a customer wanted, Olive would phone Derek and he would get it and bring it back when he returned home from work. Old photos show boards fixed to the outside of houses advertising the business carried on inside, such as 'Kingdon – Tanner and Currier' (someone who colours and dresses tanned leather).

A map dated 1430 shows only five houses between Rose Cottage at the bottom of the street and the drangway up to the common. Besides the Torridge Inn down at the bottom, there used to be four other pubs in Mill Street in the 19th century. They were the Canal Inn at number 120 (which burnt down in 1859), the Greyhound, the Nelson and the Plymouth.

Number 129, together with its neighbours 131 and 133, is a very old house and the present owners have traced documentation dating back to 1640. Over the centuries

Canal Inn

Photo by the author

the house has been lived in by people involved in a variety of trades – woollen draper, cordwainer, ropemaker, tallow chandler, weaver, fuller, dyer, carpenter – which
were carried on in outhouses which used to be behind the house. The present owners are themselves occupied with arts and crafts: ceramic restoration, art and design,
spinning, weaving and dyeing. When I visited, beech leaves, stinging nettles and the
like were boiling on the stove to produce natural dye for home-spun skeins of wool.

The solid stone house, number 127, is still known as 'the police house' although it
wasn't built for that purpose and has no old cells or anything exciting like that. It
was used as a police house from 1919 when it was sold by a Mr A. Moore to Devon
County Council until 1961 when the County Council sold it to a Mr K. G. Harrild.

The row of connected houses, numbers 61–67 on the south side of the street, were
known as 'Hoopers Cottages'. Number 63 is still referred to as 'Old Nell's house' and
somewhere amongst the museum's photographs is one of her standing in the front
doorway. In her time the house very likely consisted of only two rooms fronting onto
the street and the people who bought it from her, Ray and Jenny, built onto the back.
There is now a lovely view out across the valley through a floor to ceiling window.
Ray was a carpenter and it was he who installed the front door and the rather distinctive piece of wood over it. At one time the whole row of cottages caught fire
when burning on the commons behind ('swayling') got out of control and the
thatched roofs went up in flames. The houses were left derelict for some time.
Eventually, they were refurbished and the present owners have found a piece of
hardboard engraved with the words 'HOOPERS COTAGES (sic) 1938' and wonder if
this indicates the date when they were restored. They understand that the cottages
were owned at one time by farmers who let them out. Eric, the previous owner to
the present ones, had a lot of children to stay and converted the attic into a room with
skylights on the south side.

Number 49 used to be a religious meeting house, possibly for Quakers or Non-
Conformists – the early Methodists had a 'preaching-room' in a cottage in Mill
Street.[1] Although this isn't apparent from the front, and the inside of the house has
been altered considerably, the back of the house has a roof and upper window
shaped in a pointed arch which gives a clue to its former usage. The present owner
says the property still retains 'a peaceful aura'.

Number 39, a tall property with a room in the roof, is believed to have been built
onto two small cottages which now form the rear part of the house where a recently
installed picture window enables the owners to enjoy the view across the valley. The
house is thought to have belonged to the head gardener at Caynton House, just up
the road, as it has a wide hallway supposed to be to accommodate his wheelbarrow.
Coincidentally, the present owner is a gardener by trade.

Caynton House is a large property which stands back off the road and faces out
over the Torridge valley. It is thought that there was once a pottery on this site as
sherds and the remains of a kiln were found when the three new houses, now
Caynton Court, were built in the grounds. (See 'Which are the notable buildings in
the town?').

Mill House, number 19, is a substantial stone-fronted property with outbuildings
in the rear courtyard. In 1842 there were two cottages on this site and the Plymouth
Inn behind occupied by Thomas Vicary, a carpenter, and others. By 1891, 19 Mill

Street was occupied by Sarah Gunn, a dressmaker aged 40, who had a schoolmaster boarding with her. In 1901 the house was lived in by Thomas Andrews, 42, local photographer whose postcards are collected to this day and his son and assistant, Joseph.

At one time in the early 20th century number 3 Mill Street was known as 'Kilgobbin Cottage'.

Number 1 Mill Street was built in 1808 and is described as a 'terraced centrally heated three bedroomed period gentleman's residence set in an elevated position with magnificent views across the valley' and a walled garden at the rear. In 1843 the house was sold by Thomas Kingdon to a Mary Hemborow. It was known as 'The Retreat' and then in 1903 as 'Revette' and in 1904 a certain Thomas Fowler owned it. Thomas Fowler, the inventor after whom the IT centre formerly at Castle Hill was named, died in 1843 but it seems his descendants had connections with number 1 Mill Street: in 1918 Thomas Fowler, a chemist, bought the house from John Page and in 1949 a Thomas Hugh Fowler owned the house.

The Old Coach House, the first property on the right as you come down from the top of the street, is a tall, three storey building. It was converted in the 1930s out of the stables and coach house belonging to Penhallam next door. There was a barn or stables across the road which now belongs to number 15 and is used as a garage and workshop where, it is said, the horses' feeding rack or trough can still be found. There used to be a strip of land behind this barn that extended behind the cottages from number 3 to number 15 and a lane which led down to the commons.

A list has been compiled by a member of the Torrington History Society of the occupations and trades of people who lived in Mill Street from the 1891 Census:

MEN

Agricultural Labourer	25	Blacksmith	1
Farmer	1	Apprentice Blacksmith	1
Gardener	3	Master Blacksmith	2
Master Gardener	2	Master Mason	1
Garden Labourer	1	Journeyman Mason	7
Former Farmer	3	Grounder*	1
Sawyer	1	Painter	1
Thatcher	2	Limeburner Journeyman	1
Miller	1	Labourers at Limekiln	2
Rail Labourer	1	Retired Limeworker	1
Excavator	1	Retired Grocer	1
Master Tanner	1	Butcher	2
Apprentice Tanner	1	Grocer	2
Glove Cutter	2	Tallow Chandler	1
Cordwainer	3	Victualler	1
Apprentice Cordwainer	1	Tailor	3
Apprentice Saddler	1	Master Tailor	2
Master Hatter	1	Journeyman Tailor	1
Hatter's Apprentice	1	Tailor's Apprentice	2
Shoemaker	1	Former Weaver	1
Shoemaker's Apprentice	2	Errand Boy	1
Bootmaker's Journeyman	1	Porter	1
Pauper Caudwainer	1	Carrier's Labourer	1

Home Carpenter	1		Merchant's Clerk	1
Master Carpenter	2		Gent's Servant	1
Cabinet Maker	3		Retired Butler	1
Apprentice Carpenter	3		Accountant	1
Apprentice Joiner	1		Curate	1
Journeyman Joiner	2		Rector (of High)	1
Journeyman Carpenter	6		Gentleman (Rochester)	1
Proprietor of ...	1		Pensioner	1
Lodging House Keeper	1		Fundholder	1
Captain (unattached)	1		Attorney's Gen.	1

*Grounding was the final operation in production of chamois leather, carried out in the grounder's own home.

WOMEN

Glovers	106 (including girl of 10)		
Dressmakers	8	Grocer and Draper	1
Seamstress	1	Former Schoolmistress	1
Hatter Trimmer	1	Former Governess	1
Worsted Dealer	1	Greenwich Pensioner	1
Housekeeper	1	Invalid	1
House Servants	9	Dependent	1
Servants	2	Annuitants	4
Cook	1	Wife of Porter	1
Laundress	4	Washerwoman	1
Former Washerwoman	1 (aged 92)	Charwoman	1
Nurse	1		

MEN & WOMEN

Paupers	4	Former Paupers	7
Vagrants	3		

CHILDREN

Scholars	78 (one born New York)	School	4
Orphan	1 (name of Leach aged 2 – occupation listed as lodger)		

Betty Norman, who belongs to one of the three unrelated Norman families who live at the lower end of the street, told me how she and her husband used to keep sheep in fields down by the river. They were also able to let them roam on the commons to the north of Mill Street and up by the golf course (grazing was allowed up until 1981). She remembers there being problems with people exercising their dogs where sheep were grazing and, on one occasion, the sheep being driven back onto Station Hill. One year there was a woman who would let her dogs go free while she played golf and a lot of their sheep aborted their lambs that year. The Normans had a shed at the end of their garden adjoining the common where they used to shear their sheep, keeping them in a pen formed by putting up a temporary fence around the shed.

Mill Street 1923

One local man remembers living in Mill Street as a lad in the 1950s and the mischief he and his friends used to get up to. He said people had big families and all the children used to play out in the street as there was hardly any traffic in those days. The boys played football and a game called 'tin can' which involved hitting each other's legs with a ball. They played 'milk tops' with the cardboard tops on milk bottles at that time which they used to collect, propping them up against the wall, and when a boy flicked one and it landed on top of another, he won that one too. They played whist and other card games on the ramps between the pavement and the road and they also played on the commons from a young age. They sneaked into the dairy and ate the milk powder and cheese and drank the milk. They climbed into the coal hoppers and played in there as the coal dropped down into the boilers that powered the dairy. They had wars with other streets – Taddiport or New Street – with stones and bows and arrows. Every street had its own bonfire on Guy Fawkes night and the children from Mill Street would drag 'fuzz' down from the commons at the top of the 'drang'. The Taddiport kids tried to burn down Mill Street's bonfire before the actual night.

To the south of Mill Street and around the factory were orchards and market gardens belonging to the Sandfords (who started up the dairy) and the kids would go scrumping for apples. Access to this area was where there are now two bungalows and later, in the 1960s, Sandfords Gardens was built. Descendants of the Sandford family still own land behind houses at the top of Mill Street.

Apparently, there were some 'real characters' living in Mill Street in the 1950s. People knew each other more than they do now, knew each other's business and helped each other out. They were out in the street a lot more in those days and they also had their arguments out there! I'm sure, in fact I know, there are still a good number of 'real characters' living in the street today. Although people spend less time nowadays chatting to their neighbours as they scrub the front doorstep or watch their children playing in the street because of the nature of modern-day life and traffic, they are still caring and friendly to their neighbours when needed. The snow in the winter of 2010 brought out the younger ones to shop and help the elderly and those who are frail and confused are guided by those who live nearby.

In the past few years there have been some community activities in Mill Street, such as the cycle races up the steep street and the ping-pong ball race down the street, all in aid of charity. Many households have taken part in 'Torrington in Bloom', decking their houses and frontages with pots and troughs and hanging baskets, and some people opened their gardens for the National Gardens Scheme which raised a good sum for Macmillan.

With thanks to:
Maurice Cockwill
Pat Dekker
Philip and Jill Dixon
Rosemary Hutchinson
Maggie Jones
Dulcie Leate
Betty Norman
John and Jackie Paddon
Grahame Rutherford
Chris Tattersall
Michael Taverner
Chris Whitehead
Wendy Wigley

37   Is there a Supermarket in Torrington?

There is a small Co-op in South Street near the town square and a Lidl supermarket in New Street which opened in May 2011.

Local opinion has been divided over the years about the need for a supermarket in the town. Some people felt a supermarket was long overdue to 'bring the town up to date'. They wanted to be able to buy cheaper food than was available in the smaller shops without having to travel to Bideford or Barnstaple, to be able to get everything under one roof and with free parking. A supermarket was particularly popular with young mums and elderly people without transport.

Others felt that most food requirements could be met in the independent, family-run shops around the square and that a supermarket would harm these businesses and destroy the unique character of the town. In February 2011 Torrington received national recognition as one of the UK's top five towns for independent shops (while

Exeter was named the country's third most 'cloned town'). A survey by Torrington's Green Group carried out in 2010 compared the cost of 22 popular food items, including fruit and vegetables, meat, dairy and dry groceries, at the local shops with the prices at a supermarket in Bideford and found that the bill at the local shops (£31.13) was not a lot more than the bill at the supermarket (£28.97) and without the cost of transport. People who have lived in Torrington for many years say there used to be a greater variety of shops in the town than there is now. (See 'What shops are there in Torrington?').

There were plans for a supermarket to be built on South Street car park (now Sydney House car park) in the 1990s but these plans never came to fruition.

The small Gateway supermarket in town was taken over by Somerfield who made a planning application in 2005 to build a new store and some houses down School Lane on Cobbledick's land opposite the swimming pool. There was disagreement about the number of houses to be included in the project, local residents objected to the plans and Somerfield was taken over by the Co-op. Nothing has happened on this site up until now but word around the town is that the Co-op still plan to build a supermarket there.

In 2006 Tesco applied to build a store in Torrington. This would have been on the Vicarage Field football pitch, tennis courts and scout hall area and plans involved road alteration, traffic lights and house demolition. Tesco made promises to build a new swimming pool and provide a new football pitch but there was a lot of local opposition from traders and residents to letting the Tesco juggernaut come sweeping into Torrington. Eventually, the planning application was refused in December 2006 for the following reasons:

a) the Vicarage Field had been left as a bequest to the town to be used for leisure purposes and wasn't, in fact, the Torridge District Council's to sell;

b) the size, scale and dimensions of the proposed building were too large;

c) there was an inability to provide provision for rainwater run-off from the large tarmacked area;

d) the County Council decided that Torrington's infrastructure couldn't cope with the increased volume of traffic that a large supermarket would cause.

Tesco made another application early in 2007 to build a store up on Hatchmoor but this was refused on the same grounds as d) above. There is a rumour at present, however, that the town may not have seen the last of Tesco who hope to build on the Dartington Crystal site when the lease runs out in a couple of years and the glass factory relocates. It would be ironic if within the next five years Torrington, which had been without a supermarket until 2011, were to find itself with three of them. That would certainly sound the death knell for the independent shops around the square.

In 2007 the Torridge District Council proposed selling off the New Street car park to Lidl for a supermarket to be built. This seemed a rather short-sighted move in a town with desperate parking problems and where New Street car park was a pick-up point for coaches and the only car park in Torrington with access and turning space for HGVs. However, despite considerable local opposition, the District Council seemed determined to sell off the car park for short-term financial gain and, although an initial planning application was turned down, it was granted on appeal and a Lidl supermarket opened in May 2011.

Some people have said, 'If we have to have a supermarket, why couldn't we have a decent one?' Others feel that, due to its somewhat random stock of goods, Lidl will not pose as great a threat to local shops as one of the other supermarkets. People who are struggling financially in the present difficult economic situation are pleased to be able to purchase cheap bread and milk and good quality fruit and vegetables. For those who live out of town it is convenient to be able to pop in for items of food without having to drive into town and pay for car parking. Although Lidl altered the plans of the building to leave more space for car parking in order to gain planning permission, there are still unresolved issues about who owns and who will receive revenue from the public section of the car park (it was promised to the Town Council) and there is some doubt about assurances of jobs for local people having been honoured.

With thanks to:
John and Tilly Kimber
Roger Hickman
Danny Ryan

38   What is that large empty building that looks rather like a chapel in Whites Lane?

This building is an imposing Grade II listed Victorian former glove factory built in 1884. It is constructed from local cream-coloured Marland brick with a slate roof. Clues to its former use can be seen in the pair of stone hands at the top of each column flanking the entrance doors and the designs in stone relief of a cutting press above the door on the left and a pair of crossed gauntlets on the right, as well as the sign on the door 'VAUGHAN TAPSCOTT GLOVES LTD'. The building has been on the market for some years and, although planning consent and listed building consent had been granted for conversion to 14 flats, various obstacles (such as access to car parking up the private Villa Road, problems with foundations which don't meet present-day requirements, the need for repairs to the roof, pointing etc.) have prevented development from taking place. From the top floor there are views to Westward Ho! in one direction and Dartmoor in the other.

The factory was built by William Vaughan, a wealthy and influential glove maker, when his business outgrew its original premises in New Street. He was a staunch Methodist and believed that people worked better in pleasant surroundings and he had the factory built in the style of a grand chapel – 'a chapel to industry'[1] – with an impressive decorated frontage. His philosophy was successful for his workers were soon producing 36,000 pairs of gloves a week and his factory was considered to be one of the most efficient in the country.

In 'Industries of North Devon' written in the 1880s, the author tells us that Vaughan employed some 600-700 workers (machine hands, cutters, 'punchers', 'pointers', 'toppers', boxers, box-makers and outdoor hands) whose employment 'heightened the prosperity and the happiness of the community in and about' Torrington. These gloves were packed in huge wooden cases and forwarded by rail to the London

Vaughan's Glove Factory 1904   Photo courtesy of Linda Downing

warehouse of Messrs. Ormes, Upsdale & Co. 'from whence they are dispersed to the markets of the civilised world.'[2]

William Vaughan built a very imposing house for himself and his family in South Street, where the entrance to the car park is now, and they moved there in 1889. It was originally called Enderley but subsequently became known as Sydney House (see 'Where was Sydney House?'). William Vaughan died on the way from his home to his factory in 1903 and his family left the house shortly afterwards.

Gloves had been made in Torrington since the 16th century with up to three-quarters of the population involved in the industry. The earliest mention of gloving in Torrington is in 'Magna Britannia' by Samuel and Nathaniel Lysons: 'There is considerable manufacture of gloves in this town in connection with the trade there of woollen manufacture.' A town warden's accounts of 1689 mention receipt of six shillings from three glovers which was the fee that had to be paid to the authorities to permit traders to carry on their business in Torrington. Gloving was carried out in various premises throughout the town and much of the work was done by out-workers within a radius of 30 miles. By 1850 13 glovers were listed in *White's Gazetteer* including Thomas Vaughan, William's father and founder of Vaughan & Co., and it was about this time the trade organised itself into factories.

Harold Vincent took over the running of the factory in 1912. There was a 'boom' in glove making during the First World War but in an article written in the early 1920s entitled 'Is the fabric glove trade to die out?' Harold Vincent laments the 'serious menace' of foreign competition. However, things picked up during the 1920s and from then until the mid-1950s, when there were over 200 people working for

Thomas Quick, cutter 1953   Photo courtesy of the North Devon Journal Herald

Vaughans in the factory and 'outdoors', was something of a peak period. There had been a great revival of fashion gloves in the 1920s and a demand for pure silk linings for airmen's gloves during the Second World War.

Harold's son, Michael, took over the factory in 1954. New, more streamlined machinery was introduced and five women with their miniature sewing machines were able to do the work that previously required many machinists to carry out. At the end of the 1950s gloving started to decline again because of competition from Asia – Pakistan, Japan, etc. – and Vaughan's were unable to compete. Under the management of Michael Vincent the factory became really depressed and in 1989 there were fewer than twelve people working there. Tapscott's closed its glove factory in New Street and amalgamated with Vaughan's in 1989 and Michael Vincent decided to sell the factory to Bennett Safetywear of Crosby in Lancashire whose great asset was that they were very good at selling things and the company was built up again. Roger Davey, who had worked at Vaughan's since the mid-1950s, became factory manager and within six or seven years the number of workers had increased to well over 50.

The top floor of the building was where patterns were produced and the laying of fabric and cutting out of gloves was done. Silk was lined up in rows of 20 in preparation for making the linings of horse riding gloves and fabric was cut into the hands of gloves with fingers while the thumb was cut separately.

On the first floor was the making room where the fabric shapes were trimmed up and made tidy to be made up into gloves, some by hand on a sewing machine, others automatically using a jig, a kind of press with glove-shaped patterns through which a machine would sew the gloves. Then they were turned inside out to take downstairs to the finishing room on the ground floor. Here each glove was put on an iron model hand in front of a mirror and was checked for any holes, in which case it would be marked with a red spot to be repaired. The gloves were packed into boxes to be sent off to the customer.

In later years, the company diversified into hats, scarves, bags, jumpers, trousers and balaclavas using both man-made and natural fabrics. There was a large customer base for their industrial products including the health service, electronic firms, the nuclear power industry, police and Ministry of Defence. Fashion items were made for high street stores, such as the House of Fraser, John Lewis, Oasis, Accessorize and Harrods. In the 1920s nearly all Vaughan's production was fashion, in the 1980s it was nearly all industrial, and by 2002 it was about 50/50.

Cutting and sewing work of different fabrics such as fleece, faux furs and knitwear was possible because the factory had in-house knitting facilities. Knitwear was produced for the ladies' fashion market in the 18-35 age group and a particularly popular range was the matching set of scarf, pillbox or ski hat and bag. All UK made producers had to be innovative to compete with goods from the Far East and the factory increased its range of knitwear to include a variety of colours, stripes, jacquard, Argyll and jumpers with lettering on. Fleece hats were produced in an American lumberjack style or a pillbox shape and some more 'wacky' items, such as fancy hats in shiny pink material with imitation fur around the brim. Vaughan's operated in different markets. They sold their own brand to smaller independent shops and contract manufactured to larger retailers i.e. they made the article and the House of Fraser, for example, would put their own label on it.

The three surviving glove factories in Torrington were Vaughan's, Tapscott's and Sudbury's and they played an important role in providing employment for women in the town and the local district, both working in the factories and in their own homes as outworkers. Roger Davey said girls who worked as glove makers in the early days could earn more than in service or agriculture, which were the only other options at that time, but in more recent years their wages fell behind in comparison with workers at Dartington Glass and for other employers in the town. He felt they deserved more pay for what was, after all, very skilful work. As a child, Roger used to collect work from outworkers and take it home at 4pm every day for 1/6 (7½p) a week.

Vaughan-Tapscott were bought by Bennett Safetywear and continued in operation until September 2002 when they were bought by Sudbury's and the Whites Lane factory closed for good. Sudbury's, the last remaining glove factory in Torrington, had left its premises behind Vaughan's in around 1980 and moved up to Greenbank in the 1990s but it too closed in 2010. Vaughan's glove factory building has stood empty for years now and looks increasingly forlorn with weeds growing out of its front steps.

The people who live in nearby Ramla, which had been the Methodist manse up until about the 1950s, still remember the background noise of the whirr and clunk of the gloving machinery and a couple of men who, each lunch time, would put a pile of telephone directories on a table by a certain window and lie back for a rest in the sun. When their little boy was learning to ride a two-wheeler bicycle on the concrete apron just inside their front gates and he finally got the hang of it, the gloving women cheered and clapped as they watched from the upper windows of the factory during their break.

Before closing, Vaughan-Tapscott approached 1646, the Civil War centre, to see if it would be possible to run tours round the glove factory if Bennett's would keep a small part of it open, but that plan came to nothing. In 2009 Great Torrington Heritage Museum and Archive was given the opportunity to bid for the old glove factory. Members of the Museum Executive Committee inspected the premises and were enthusiastic about the possibilities of the building as a museum. However, despite the attraction of such a plan, sufficient funding was not available to make it a reality. (See 'Is there a Museum in the town?').

The future of the old glove factory building remains uncertain (March 2012).

With thanks to:
Val Colwill
Roger and Gwen Davey
Dave Kelly
Jay Nicholson
Diane and John Rollinson
Mary Short
Elaine Weeks
Webbers estate agents

39   Where is Rosemoor?

Rosemoor is a mile and a half to the south of Torrington along the road to Exeter. The area was known originally as Rowe's Moor. There has been a garden at Rosemoor since 1931, at first extending over eight acres and now consisting of 65 acres, which attracts 140,000 visitors a year. 16 full-time gardeners are employed aided by around 50 volunteers.

The garden boasts a spectacular display of over 2,000 roses with 200 varieties, colour themed gardens, herb garden and potager. There are woodland walks, a lake, gazebo, numerous attractive shelters (which can be used for weddings), three model gardens – a town garden, a terraced garden and a shade garden – and 'The Brash' which is a family play and picnic area.

The house, dating from the 1780s and originally the property of the Rolle family, local landowners, was bought by Lady Anne Berry's father in 1923 as a family fishing lodge to be used only from March to May. Following the death of her father in 1931, Lady Anne moved to Rosemoor and with the help of her mother began some landscaping of the garden. In 1939 she married Colonel Eric Palmer and her early life was spent 'camp following' the regiment and having two sons. During the Second World War Rosemoor was lent to the Red Cross as a rest home for Londoners from the East End who were suffering the effects of the Blitz. After the war her

Cottage Garden   Photo courtesy of RHS Rosemoor

husband bought more land round Rosemoor and established a dairy farm. Lady Anne's passion in those days was horses.

It wasn't until 1959, while recuperating from measles in Spain, that she met Collingwood 'Cherry' Ingram who suggested that she take up plant collecting and start a garden of her own at Rosemoor. She subsequently travelled widely in South America, Papua New Guinea, New Zealand, the USA and Japan to build up the collection of 4,000 plants in her garden. In 1980 Eric Palmer died and in 1988 Lady Anne donated Rosemoor plus eight acres of pastureland to the Royal Horticultural Society (RHS). In 1990 she married New Zealander Bob Berry and went to live with him at his farm at Tiniroto, Gisborne in North Island and created the Homestead Garden of Hackfalls Arboretum.

The original garden at Rosemoor tucked into the north-eastern corner of the estate included a plantsman's garden and arboretum planted during the 1970s. Landscape architects Elizabeth Banks Associates designed the master plan for the new garden which was carried out under the knowledgeable and creative eye of the newly-appointed curator, Christopher Bailes. The site isn't without its challenges. The local climate is mild but the garden's low-lying location makes it into a frost pocket, with temperatures falling as low as -9 degrees C (16 degrees F), while late spring frosts are also common. RHS Garden Rosemoor lies in a valley on west-facing slopes, enclosed on all sides by sheltering woodland, and cut in two by the A3124 road. The two parts are linked by a dramatically-landscaped underpass, using 500 tonnes of local stone to develop a wild valley, crammed with woodland plants, through which a stream flows, leading to the bog garden and a substantial lake.

Lying at the heart of the new areas developed by the Society is the Formal Garden. This area not only provided Rosemoor with an exciting design but also with structure and focus to attract visitors. It is designed on a grid system around two principal axes: one leads north-south linking Lady Anne's Garden with the new Peter Buckley Learning Centre; the other runs east-west and links to the Robin Herbert Visitor Centre. Within the formal area are rose gardens, a potager and the dramatic Hot Garden which is planted with a range of perennials in predominantly hot colours. Outside this cluster of rather intimate spaces, the garden opens out, becoming more expansive. Across the stream, past the lake, is the impressive Fruit and Vegetable Garden – 'a triumph of artistry, design and productivity'[1] – in its use of colour and texture combined with growing plants to eat.

There is a rich diversity of plants at Rosemoor, including many recent introductions, taking advantage of its warm microclimate. 'It has a charming, traditional "West Country garden" atmosphere, with tender plants thriving within its shelter.'[2] Like all gardens, Rosemoor continues to develop. The South Arboretum and expansion into the woodland margins has provided interesting locations for widening collections of plants, thus maintaining Rosemoor's prominent position as a garden of regional and national importance.

40   What happened in Torrington during the Second World War?

Torrington may not have been near the fighting or suffered any bombing but the people of the town were greatly affected by events during the two world wars. A lot of local men were called up to fight in far off places and many of them didn't come home.One only has to look at the war memorial in the cemetery (unveiled by Col. Radcliffe in 1921) to see how many men gave their lives: 83 in the First World War and 19 in the Second. There are many familiar Torrington names listed so there must be a lot of local families who lost loved ones.

Lisa D'Alberti's grandfather, Leon, was one of those who died during the Second World War eight months after her father, Tony, was born. He was only 23. He was in the 43rd Reconnaissance Regiment and died during the Normandy landings in 1944 when his ship, the 'Derrycunihy', was blown up by a German mine. His name is listed on the Bayeux Memorial in Normandy, France.

Men from Torrington have always fought in wars alongside their countrymen including the Battle of Waterloo in 1815 (see 'What is the significance of the Monument on Castle Hill common?'), the Crimean War of 1854-6 when a sailor, William Friendship, told his parents in Torrington in December 1854, 'We have lost 30, only two have been killed by the enemy, the rest died from exposure on the shore,'[1] two world wars and, more recently, in Iraq and Afghanistan.

This scroll commemorates

Serjeant L. D'Alberti
Reconnaissance Corps

held in honour as one who
served King and Country in
the world war of 1939-1945
and gave his life to save
mankind from tyranny. May
his sacrifice help to bring
the peace and freedom for
which he died.

Leon D'Alberti's scroll
of commendation

Photo courtesy of
the D'Alberti family

Jack Sing was away for most of the Second World War. He married his childhood sweetheart, Gladys, in 1941 before he went abroad and they didn't see each other for years. Jack was sent to many different places in Africa and India and spent three years in Burma. He suffered from malaria on five different occasions. 'It was quite an experience in life, you know,' he said. 'I wouldn't do it again.' Men found it very difficult to settle back into civilian life when they got home.

While he was away, Gladys went to live with her widowed mother in Well Street and worked at the Torridge Vale milk factory on the condensed milk. She also worked in the back of the chapel in South Street (now the Torridge Vale social club) making 'scrim' (camouflage) nets. Then, during the week, she would go up to Castle Hill to do all-night fire service. 'We had to stay awake all night to be alert if the air siren went and on the telephone exchange.' When Exeter and Plymouth were being bombed 'We used to go to Castle Hill, on the mound there opposite the castle, and you could see the fires from Plymouth and Exeter and the air-raids. You could see it quite plain.'

First World War soldiers, New Street   Photo courtesy of Linda Downing

Dulcie Leate and her brother, Bryan, also remember knowing when Exeter and Plymouth were being bombed. 'T'would be a glow in the sky. Sometimes they'd both be on fire at the same time and there'd be a crowd in Rack Park watching.' Dulcie also says, 'From the top of our house in Halsdon Road you could see Bristol burning.' Her other brother, Roy, was fighting out in the Middle East.

Dulcie saw the fire at Sydney House in South Street which burnt down in 1942 and five of the children staying there were killed. (See 'Where was Sydney House?'). Owen Warne also remembers that night. He was living over the Midland Bank and the upstairs of the flat was nearly in line with the steeple of the parish church. The sparks and smoke from Sydney House were drifting past and silhouetting the spire and reflecting in the windows of the gazebo in the garden of Palmer House before landing in what was then a nursery owned by a Mr Sparks, 'our local Captain Mainwaring.'

Owen Warne, who was a child of eight when the Second World War broke out, remembers Torrington being like a ghost town at first. Shops and businesses were only open part-time, a surprising number of people were in the TA (Territorial Army) and went away to fight and, within a few weeks, people were starting to be called up. 'Everyone was on the move.' He remembers lots of evacuees coming from places that had suffered bombing, the first two batches being from Bristol and then there were children from London and all over Kent. They were mainly billeted in farms around Torrington rather than in the town itself. A school log book kept by the first head-master of Great Torrington School during the war mentions the effects on the school of the influx of evacuees – children and staff. School buses had to make double runs and it was quite a problem accommodating all the extra pupils and feeding them.

Local people rallied round sending in food and crockery, and potatoes were planted in the school grounds. The boys at school also used to plant and dig potatoes in other areas, such as Beaford Moor, Potheridge and on Torrington commons, with two masters in charge. Reed's Field, down beyond the station, was dug up to grow vegetables and Mr Copp had a corn and potato patch up on the golf course. Staff were on holiday duties at Great Torrington School and were only excused if they were occupied with work of national importance. Pupils did voluntary war work: gardening, salvage of paper and iron, stripping tin at the milk factory, needlework – mending and making clothes – and fixing lace on the school windows for air-raid protection. Staff and pupils were given a demonstration by Mr Jackson, the Rural District Surveyor, and the Fire Brigade on how to deal with fire bombs.

Owen Warne remembers all the regiments that were stationed in and around Torrington. The first to arrive were the Hampshire Yeomanry and then the Warwicks followed by the Gloucesters and then all went quiet for a short period until the Americans arrived. They made more noise than everybody else! The men of the first regiment that came were mainly from New York State, Virginia and New Hampshire and then there was a lull and the American Airborne came for what seemed like 48 hours. They arrived by train and bus and were billeted in all the big houses in the locality, a surprising number of which stood empty at that time. The owners of Stevenstone House, which was still standing then, received a penny a person for accommodating the soldiers. Joyce Warne remembers some Americans bringing a huge vehicle around where she lived at Kingscott. It ran into trouble in the narrow lanes and one of the men was squashed between the vehicle and the wall and her mother ran out to help him. Owen said when the Americans first came to Torrington they only had big caterpillar tracks. After they had been here for some months, he and his friends saw a collection of large packing cases all over the road near Goose Green garage when they were on their way to school. On the way home they saw men assembling gun towers that had arrived in the boxes and it was the first time the schoolboys had ever seen electric welding being done. The common above Torrington Station was used for training purposes by American army tanks which resulted in a number of potholes appearing in the railway track.[2] They used to dig holes in order that their tanks could stand level for these exercises which resulted in there being a lot of humps left on the commons. The soldiers would trundle their vehicles down to the stream or to the little beach by Rothern Bridge to clean up their equipment, and they would go off to Dartmoor for firing practice. There was an artillery regiment in Torrington with two lots of 'Long Toms' (howitzers) and a searchlight camp out at Kingscott. Local children followed the soldiers around, in awe of their huge anti-tank guns and other equipment, and the Americans would give them sweets and chewing-gum.

Dulcie Leate remembers the Americans being around the town. She worked part-time in the library, when it was upstairs at the entrance to the pannier market, and she didn't like it during war-time because all the windows were blacked out and they had no telephone. She felt rather nervous when she left to go home because the light on the stairs was dim and she could hear soldiers up in the pannier market but wasn't able to see them in the dark. Life wasn't all doom and gloom, however. Dulcie loved dancing and during the war was able to go folk dancing, to keep fit classes and a health and beauty class. 'You can see that, can't you?' she said, with a twinkle in her eye.

There was a prisoner of war camp built opposite the school which housed Italians who worked on the land. After Italy surrendered and changed sides, they were allowed to wander round the town without restrictions when they were free on a Saturday afternoon. They got on well with the local population but not with the German POWs. A few of them worked at the dairy as well as some Greeks, who were under restrictions and had to report regularly to the police station, and other nationalities every so often. It was a new experience for Torrington people to have foreigners in their midst.

Cross House had people billeted there but wasn't able to accommodate large numbers because it had a limited water supply. Water had to be taken there in the water cart. At different times after Dunkirk it was the billet for the Warwicks, the Royal Army Medical Corps and the Americans. Two searchlight batteries near Cross were each manned by up to a dozen soldiers.

John Down, whose family lived at Chapple Farm between High Bullen and Atherington, was at school at Belmont College, Bickington towards the end of the war. It was a school that had evacuated from Streatham in London and they went to Braunton for about six months before they bought Belmont. They called it 'Ellerslie Belmont'. Before going to that school, John had attended Atherington school and walked there and back from Chapple each day – up and down the steep hills – and also on Sundays to Sunday school. While walking to school during the war, he had a few unpleasant experiences and was lucky not to have been injured. The army used to go from place to place with an old tank and one day it 'passed us children when we were a littleways out of Atherington on the way home from school.' The tank ran out of control down the first hill at a place called Brook Hill at Eastacombe – on the old narrow winding road – and it went up over a hedge and capsized on top of a well which provided drinking water for the people who farmed there. John could remember the farmer's wife fetching water from the well. Petrol spilt into the well from the tank, polluting it, so it could no longer be used. Not long afterwards the people moved away from that little farm. On another occasion, coming up from Langridgeford towards Chapple, a steam engine with a thresher behind it ran away down the hill and tipped over. This had just happened as the children came past and the man in the engine was in a real state and said to them, 'Go by very quickly!'

The fires from Plymouth and Exeter could be seen from Chapple and a few stray bombs dropped in the locality. One was jettisoned by a returning German plane (probably to lighten its load) at Sittycleave in Yarnscombe parish between three farms. John and his family went to see where it had landed. It had created a huge crater 'large enough to put a house in' but, fortunately, no-one was hurt although the ceiling (lath and plaster) in one of the farmhouses had come down. The Downs' farm was about a mile and a half away and during the night when the bomb fell his father had heard small stones raining down on their roof.

Prisoners of war were stationed in Nissen huts opposite Great Torrington School and when he went to school John would see them boxing. They worked on his farm, brought out in a lorry to help with 'dropping and picking' potatoes, threshing and harvesting. The Downs had an Italian and a German and, at one time, two Germans.

They found the two races to be 'totally different people' from each other.

The Women's Land Army was first formed in 1917 during the First World War. In June 1939, with the threat of war looming again, the organisation was re-formed so that by September 1939, when the call came, 1,000 volunteers could immediately be sent into employment, many of them already trained. The Women's Land Army was disbanded in 1950.

Thelma Kett, as she was then, was sent to Torrington in February 1944 to join the Land Army. She was 20 years old and came from London where she had seen the first doodlebugs (flying bombs). She arrived by train and, as she emerged from the station with her luggage, it was raining and she looked up the long blank hill in dismay. Tears mingled with raindrops as she wondered, 'Where on earth have I come to?' As she walked into the town she didn't notice a young man standing outside Pope's garage (where Lidl is now) but he noticed her and thought to himself, 'She's the one for me.' This was Derrick Oke and, sure enough, he and Thelma got to know each other and, in the fullness of time, they married and had two children.

Thelma stayed with nine other girls in a hostel in New Street opposite the Royal Exchange pub while some of the girls were billeted in private houses. They came from various parts of the country and were of different ages and backgrounds. Ann Spencely was the oldest at 32 and was in charge of the canteen. Ann de Haviland was a member of the well-known aircraft family and she and Chrissie Snell (married name Ayre) were drivers.

The girls did 'gang work' in a group of 18 and cleared moors and planted them with potatoes or wheat. They were hired out to farmers. They did four months forestry work at Okehampton, lopping off branches, and lived in iron Nissen huts at Moretonhampstead (where a carpark is now). They slept in bunks and it was so cold that snow piled up inside the huts.

At other times they would do re-stooking work, picking up the sheaves and putting them in stooks of eight, leaning them against each other to finish drying off. One day on Hollacombe Moor, their boss reckoned they had walked 17 miles on the stubble which was hard work but the feeling of camaraderie between the girls kept them going. It was so hot they took off their jumpers and shirts and tied their headscarves bikini-style around their tops. On another occasion they were re-stooking corn all morning in the pouring rain over towards Dartmoor and, returning at lunchtime, the girls took their wet clothes off and hung them on the lorry rafters to dry. At Sampford Courtenay the lorry broke down so they all had to get out wearing nothing but their satin underwear to give the lorry a push to get it going!

They went down to Sidmouth and Countesswear to dismantle barbed wire coils. Thelma says the men wouldn't do the job, as there were no gloves to wear, so the women did it! They had to wind the barbed wire around 'grannies' (granary sticks).

Their foreman was an Austrian (possibly Jewish) by the name of Rehburger who lived at the Old Rectory, Beaford. He made the girls work hard but was very proud of them, saying they could do better than anyone else. They worked with other gangs of boys and 'conchies' (conscientious objectors) who were a mixed bunch of about 30-40 who were billeted down near South Drive. They also worked with the Italian POWs from the hutments by the senior school who were 'lovely', pleasant and courteous, although 'they would tread spuds back into the ground rather than pick them up.' They also worked with German POWs who were billeted somewhere out of town and driven to work by lorry. The Germans were good workers but, unlike the Italians, weren't allowed to talk to anyone and not even permitted to go out of sight to the lavatory but would line up against the hedge.

Every day the girls had spam, jam or cheese in their sandwiches. Rationing wasn't as hard in Torrington as in London and although food was restricted no-one went hungry. Land girls were allowed 12 oz of cheese a week whereas it was 2 oz for other people. In the country chickens were kept to supply eggs and milk was available, although no-one was allowed to make cream. Occasionally, it was possible to obtain a lemon from the greengrocer's which, with a hole pierced in it, could be sucked during the day for refreshment.

3,000 Americans came to Torrington, virtually doubling the population at the time, and they were good fun although they sometimes used up all the water which had to be carted back to the hostel in buckets from the butcher, 'Captain (Stan) Kelly'. The Americans had lots of food and supplies from their quartermaster's stores which seemed to stock just about everything. They were billeted at Porch House and at number 88 New Street where rough-spun servicemen's shirts have been found in the attic by the present owners of the house. Thelma was billeted opposite number 88 and could see a 'Red Indian' who sat in his window gazing out and smoking a pipe but he never went out drinking or to dances with the others. There were lots of pubs in Torrington during the war and the West of England run by the Misses Doe was the last place to have a spittoon. A Mr Sweet used to sit by the fire with the spittoon next to him. The land girls cried when the Americans departed and later wondered if they had been involved in the disastrous operation at Slapton Sands which happened soon after they left Torrington.

I asked Thelma Harper, as she is now, if she looked back on her time as a land girl as having been fun or a difficult and unpleasant experience. She said it had been 'bloomin' hard work' but none of them would have changed it. They liked the life even though they were often muddy, soaked or sunburnt. It had been the first time away from home for all of them which was wonderful! Of those in Thelma's group who stayed in the area, only she, Ivy Quick and Maggie Stacey are still living in Torrington.

Terry Finnamore was a land girl after Thelma, between 1946 and 1950, and spent a good part of that time in Torrington. She tells her story in her book, 'Petticoats to Pitchforks'. She stayed in a hostel which was a large L-shaped corrugated building with a low wall surrounding it fronting onto the road. Terry says it was 'really nice inside' with two sets of bunks and lockers in each cubicle in the sleeping quarters and a communal lounge and dining room. Hot baths were always available and the hostel was lucky to have an excellent maintenance man. There were about 40 girls who came from all over the country – London, Liverpool and even as far away as Newcastle.

Work included potato picking, muck spreading which Terry describes as 'good fun', digging out muddy ditches and threading wires through a baler all day in high open fields. One of the jobs she liked best was threshing corn and other jobs included pulling mangolds, sorting potatoes, working with carthorses, haymaking and harvesting. They also cleaned out the cow shippen and other animal houses. The

1	2	3	4	5	6	7	8	9	10	11	12	13	14	15	16
Chrissie Ayre (Snell)	Margaret Stacey (Thornton)	Ann Spenceley	Edna?	Ivy Quick (Stuart)	Ruby Spragg	Edna?	Mary Pike	Ruth Snell	Rene Coombes	Doris Davie	Fay Mars	Winnie Braun	Thelma Harper (Kett)	Phyllis Baker (De Haviland)	Ann Needham

Land Girls

Photo courtesy of Sally and Roger Cole

farmer's wife would give them a hot meal at the end of the day's work. Tasks became more difficult as the weather turned colder. If any farms were less than three miles away, the land girls walked or went by bike – there were no bicycles in Torrington and it was too hilly anyway – otherwise, they were taken by lorry.

'No matter how tired we were at the end of the day, we always managed to sing. As the lorry did the rounds picking up each gang from different farms, they automatically joined in.'[3]

The only entertainment in town was the Saturday night dance in the drill hall (now the Plough) and the pubs. The place that was to become their local was the Setting Sun in Cornmarket Street. The Saturday night dance 'appeared to be attended by every able person in the town, including people from the outlying farms and villages.' There was a three piece band – drums and cymbals, an accordion and a well used piano – and there were very few tunes that the band were unable to play. Terry says they appeared to enjoy singing and playing as much as the people enjoyed dancing to their music.[4] On Tuesday nights the girls would go to Bideford by lorry to see a film and have chips on the way home.[5]

Terry and the other girls were split up and transferred to other hostels as the Torrington hostel was going to be used to house displaced persons from Poland who would take over their jobs on the farms.[6] Farmers were not too happy as they had become used to having the girls working for them and would have to start training the Poles, who possibly knew nothing about farming, which could be difficult because of the language barrier. After being billeted in Barnstaple and Crediton, Terry spent her final months back near Torrington living and working with the Easterbrooks at Belle View Farm. Like Thelma, she seems to have found her time as a land girl a tough but, at the same time, enjoyable experience and was sad to learn that the Land Army was to be disbanded.

Ron Juniper was evacuated to Torrington from London in early 1940 at the age of five. He travelled by train with his older brother, Harry, who was seven, and they were brought up to the Old Bowling Green where people selected which children they would take. Ron and Harry stayed with a Mr and Mrs Lock in Well Street who were distant relatives. Unfortunately, they weren't accustomed to children, having none of their own, and the boys were not very happy living with them. However, despite this, Ron came to like the small town he found himself in and didn't want to go back to London after the war. From the age of seven he used to do paper rounds and got to know a lot of people. He said that during the war the population was around 2,500 and he described Torrington as being 'a bit like the Wild West.' He thought the Americans who came to Torrington were like the Yanks in the films, rather larger than life, and would fetch fish and chips for 30 soldiers out at Stevenstone camp from Nicholls fish shop in Calf Street. They would practise manoeuvres on the Old Bowling Green and the neighbouring commons and churned the place up with tanks. They offered to carry out repairs but the Town Council refused. As an adult, Ron had a business in Torrington for 12 years. He also gave guided tours, meeting coach parties at the back of the Globe and walking them around the town telling them about his experiences as an evacuee and pointing out places of historical interest. He did this until 1646 came into being and operated on a larger scale. He also taught ballroom dancing lessons in Taddiport village hall, the Globe (which has a nice sprung dance floor upstairs) and the former Castle Hill Hotel. He says his father who, although not a countryman, started up a smallholding owned two of the leper strips where he kept cows and pigs and is buried there. Although he now lives in Bideford, Ron says, 'There's no place like Torrington for me.'

With thanks to:
Tony, Pauline and Lisa D'Alberti
John Down
Thelma Harper
Ron Juniper
Dulcie and Bryan Leate
Gladys and Jack Sing
Owen and Joyce Warne

41   What Sports are played in Torrington?

Torrington has rugby and football teams, tennis, bowls, golf and athletics but no cricket club. There is a swimming pool which has a variety of activities and a competitive swimming club. There is a sports hall with a programme of activities on the site of the senior school which has been a sports college since 2002. There is no netball club (the nearest is Langtree Reunites) or hockey which can be found in Barnstaple. There is a rambling club (Torridge Ramblers), a Torridge 'Walk and Talk' group and a variety of exercise classes, including yoga, aerobics and pilates, held in different venues around the town.

Rugby in Torrington is played at Donnacroft up on Hatchmoor Road on the edge of town. There are two pitches, a flood-lit training area, a clubhouse with a bar and function room as well as spacious new changing rooms. Torrington is currently (2011) in the Cornwall and Devon League and hosts two senior teams, occasionally a veterans' side and a large junior section with colts right down to Under 12s and minis. This has proved to be a great strength to the club in the last few years.

Rugby had been played in Torrington in the past but the present club started in 1985. There had been some 'semi-serious' games of rugby between the athletics club and Exeter Harriers. Local lads, who hadn't played before, and some ageing retired players decided they enjoyed it so much that a meeting was called and training was started. One young lad, new to the game, asked if he should wear boots and, when told this would be a good idea, he turned up in Wellingtons! In the late summer of 1985 Torrington Rugby Club played their first game. It was against RAF Chivenor and to everyone's amazement Torrington won.

Before the clubhouse was built, home games involved changing at the comprehensive school, a walk up to the pitch at Hatchmoor and then the hospitality of Judd and Josie Bond at the Newmarket Inn. This trekking came to an end on 15th December 1996 when the clubhouse was opened next to the Donnacroft pitch.

Since 1985 the club has progressed steadily. In 1985 Torrington played the third teams of clubs such as Bideford, Crediton, Exeter Saracens and Teignmouth. Nowadays they play the first teams.

Football is played at the Vicarage Field. Torrington are known as 'the Super

Torrington rugby team 1898/99

Photo courtesy of Dave Glover

Greens' (because of the colour of their home shirts – green with white hoops) or simply 'Torrie'. Torrington FC was established in 1908 and, after spending several decades in local North Devon football, they stepped up and joined the South Western League in 1978. After five years they were elected to the Western League Division One in 1984 and were immediately successful as Champions, earning promotion to the Premier Division. That 1984-85 season also saw their best ever run in the FA Vase when they reached the last 16 (5th round). Despite being based in one of the smaller towns represented in the league, and having some of the longest distances to travel, the club has often finished in a respectable position with the undoubted highlight coming in the 1990-91 season when the club finished in the runner-up position under former Plymouth Argyle boss, Johnny Hore. They have been unable to repeat that feat since and dropped down to the lower division for a five-season spell around the turn of the century but returned to the Premier Division in 2003. Gates at the Vicarage Field (capacity 500) dropped to an average of 44 in the 2006-07 season and the club decided in June 2007 to withdraw from the Western League and return to the North Devon League taking over the position previously occupied by their reserve side. In 2009-10 they were 9th in the Premier Division.[1]

The rise of Torridgeside football club is one of the sporting success stories of North Devon in recent times. Started in the late 1980s for juniors by dads, Paul Nicholls and Fred Sussex, their home pitch is at Donnacroft and they train on the all-weather pitch at the senior school. When the lads were over 16, they wanted to carry on playing and so a men's team was started in 2004/5. There are now two men's teams. The first team play in the North Devon Premier League and are currently the most successful Torrington town team. The Reserves play in the North Devon Intermediate One Division. There are Under 9, 10, 11, 12, 13, 14, 15 and 16 teams and at least one women's team. Consequently, Torridgeside FC provide soccer for over 100 young people from the locality.

The club was put on the right track by 'the two Mikes' (Harding and Sealey) who were able to give advice on how to get grants and pitches, and so on. Hundreds of boys and girls have been coached over the years by local men such as Paul Callaghan, Steve Ware, Bill Pyke, Paul Stacey, Mark Lewis, Steve Jones, Paul Hutchings, Nigel Cockwill (now President), Tony Copp, Geoff Huxtable, 'Mac' McConnachie, Sean Kenneally, Andy Stevens among others, and coaching courses have been held to train parents and others to carry on the teams. Various cups and leagues have been won. There are also five and six-a-side tournaments for youngsters. Having three sons who played for Torridgeside, Geoff Huxtable's interest in the club extended over some 12-15 years and he was Secretary as well as helping with coaching. Barry Paine started when his son was a junior and then took on the men's side. He trains and coaches the men's first team and has helped a lot of lads progress in their football careers. The club has raised its own finances, including money for new changing rooms, and the players' kit is sponsored by local people. Parents have transported youngsters all over the county and without them the club wouldn't have managed to continue. Mums, such as Jackie Cockwill, have been involved, too, as members of the Committee as well as washing copious amounts of muddy kit! Former youth players have become league referees and UEFA qualified coaches and have run the football academy at the local FE college.

In the 1920s football teams representing different streets in Torrington used to play on the commons with the annual inter-street finals played on the Old Bowling Green. (See 'How far do the Commons extend and for how long have they existed?').

The tennis club meets on Monday and Wednesday evenings down Gas Lane by the Scout Hut where there are three tarmacadam all-weather courts with floodlights. Home matches are played on Tuesday and Thursday evenings. There are currently two men's teams (playing in divisions two and four of the North Devon League). The ladies have only one team but that currently plays in division one and in 2011 they were runners-up, a remarkable achievement for a small town playing against much bigger clubs from places such as Barnstaple and Ilfracombe. Two internal club mixed doubles tournaments are held each year as well as club singles competitions. Adult membership is currently £65 and the visitor's fee £4. The running of the courts is currently (December 2011) being passed from Torridge District Council into the hands of Torrington Town Council. When the handover of the courts is complete, the arrangements by which other members of the public can obtain the key to the courts will be reviewed. (It will not be from the swimming pool but alternative arrangements have not yet been finalised). Up till now, facilities for tennis haven't kept abreast of the times and the pavilion is an old shed with no toilets which has been embarrassing when hosting matches with other clubs. It was an old concrete garage erected by members of the club in the early 1980s when the original wooden hut fell down. However, things are about to change. The Town Council, now that they will be looking after the courts, are determined to improve the tennis facilities available to residents of the town and this includes providing a more suitable clubhouse, with toilets. It is understood that funding has already been put aside for this and that the plans are to complete this upgrade within the next two years, earlier if possible.

Tennis club records go back to the 1950s but an elderly lady who lived in Torrington during the 1930s says she belonged to the junior section of the tennis club and played on the two grass courts which were in the same location down by the gasworks. 'Uncle' Bruce Blatchford, who had a saddler's and sports shop in Potacre Street, was the juniors' coach. Arrangements for an hour's evening coaching were made at evensong where Bruce was a sidesman at church. As he passed the collection tray amongst the youngsters, he would whisper 'See you Tuesday at the club?' and a nod and smile was sufficient reply. The club has provided coaching for youngsters for many years but, sadly, this has recently stopped because there was not enough support to make it financially viable. It is hoped that, once the upgrade of the facilities is complete, the playing experience will be more enjoyable and that the club will be able to attract enough youngsters to make the coaching viable again.

The Great Torrington bowling club was founded in 1645 and is the third oldest in England. The bowling green is on the site of the old castle looking down over the valley of the River Torridge. Presumably, bowls was formerly played on the part of the commons down beyond the cemetery which is still known as the 'Old Bowling Green' but it is not known when it transferred to its present site. The old wooden clubhouse was demolished in 1987 and a new brick-built clubhouse was opened in 1988. The gazebo in the corner of the bowling green, where bowls equipment is kept, dates from the 1850s. (See 'Is the Bowling Club really as old as the date on its clubhouse?').

Bowling green with gazebo but no clubhouse   Photo courtesy of Linda Downing

In a letter to the Commons Conservators in 1895 a proposal was made to form a Torrington Golf Club. This proposal was accepted and a nine hole golf course was established on the Old Bowling Green where play continued until the First World War. There were a few problems with the site: it was rather hazardous for passers-by; one hole was considered rather too near to the workhouse (where Woodland Vale care home is today); horse drawn traffic on the way down the hill to the station had to stop if golf was in progress and one of the players wished to drive across the road! In June 1921 a meeting was held at the Town Hall to consider the idea of restarting the golf club and 30 people expressed an interest. A new course was made and opened at Darracott. The club moved to its present site at Furzebeam in 1932. As the course is part of the commons (the golf club pay rent to the Conservators) there have always been problems with protecting the greens from grazing animals (up to 1981 when grazing stopped) and from walkers (and their dogs) but, on the whole, the club and the Commons Conservators have managed to work together. During the Second World War the central part of the course was ploughed up to grow corn and pota-toes. Some players from other clubs find the Torrington course shorter than they would like and its layout rather tight but this is compensated for by the immaculate-ly kept greens and the magnificent views over the surrounding countryside.

Torrington Amateur Athletic Club was started in the late 1970s by Maurice Cockwill and Roger Davey when their children showed ability and an interest in run-ning. Over the years members have taken part in many local athletics events and have achieved considerable success, even reaching the National Championships. The club meets at the Sports College on Wednesday nights.

Torrington sports 1913   Photo courtesy of John Down

There used to be a Torrington cricket club but it folded in the early 1990s because no-one would look after the wicket. The team played on the school pitch but the school wouldn't tend the wicket either and the drainage was poor. Villages such as Weare Giffard, Newton Tracey and Westleigh had strong sides and Bideford and Barnstaple had numerous teams so Torrington couldn't compete.

Torrington swimming pool was built in 1972 and many Torringtonians have learnt to swim in its warm waters and held birthday swimming parties there as children. Torridgeside Amateur Swimming Club relies on volunteers to run the club. It holds swimming sessions for all ages and competitive swimming from age nine. The club meets at Torrington pool on Monday, Wednesday and Friday and at Northam pool on Sunday and Monday. Head coach is Laura Bennett, senior coach is Larry Hill and there are six general coaches. The pool is three metres at the deep end and one metre at the shallow end with steps leading down into the water in the corner of the shallow end. Activities, apart from regular swimming for the public and schools at specified times, include parent and toddler sessions, water movement, aqua aerobics, mood swimming with music and a free sauna, flipper and snorkel sessions and, once a month, a naturist swim (though I gather that particular club is not meeting now through lack of membership).

The building is old now and constantly in need of repair. It has been closed for almost a year as the roof, which contained asbestos, needed replacing at a cost of around £300,000. Torridge District Council, which owns the pool, says it has earmarked £550,000 for the project which includes grants of £100,000 from the Amateur Swimming Association and £50,000 (over five years) from Torrington Town Council.

Torridgeside Swimming Club has suffered from the closure and seen its membership fall by more than half as a result. The swimmers have been using West Buckland in the interim but, because of the long distance involved, training hours have been limited. In February 2012 head coach, Laura Bennett said, 'We survived, but we were pushed to our limits. We have the talent and are still competing in national leagues. We can't wait to get back into Torrington Pool.'[2] The general public has had to go to Northam or Holsworthy for a swim as Barnstaple pool has also been closed for refurbishment.

Torrington pool reopened in April 2012 with a smart new roof. The swimming club 'made a spectacular comeback with a 24-hour swim' to try and raise funds to give the club a boost. Laura Bennett swam every other hour for a total of 12 hours to support the 68 other swimmers who were mainly children. Laura, who has been head coach for four years, was nominated by several members of the club to carry the Olympic Torch on its route through her home town and said, 'I am really excited to be carrying the torch.'[3]

In the late 1990s there were plans for a new swimming pool on the school site but, because of delays and price rises, that never came about and now there is no space available at the school.

There used to be a plaque at the swimming pool bearing the inscription

'Provided by the Women of Great Torrington
During the Mayoralty of Austin R. O'Flaherty 1927-1928'.

This referred to the Ladies' Pool down on the river where townspeople used to go swimming. A concrete platform was made on the river bank and a shed was built for the swimmers which was divided into two, one side for women and the other side for men. (Boys used to punch holes through the dividing wall to look at the girls!).[4]

Various activities are held at the sports hall up next to the comprehensive school, such as gym for adults and for OAPs, under eights' football, adult and junior badminton and table tennis, roller blading, five-a-side football, other junior activities and, like the swimming pool, it can be hired for birthday parties. There is also a climbing wall.

There is Motocross out at Waggadon Farm, about two miles out of Torrington, where there is an excellent championship circuit and racing can be seen there several times each year.

There is fishing available in the locality. Coarse fishing is permitted for 12 months of the year with many locations within easy reach and, if you are a game fisherman, then there is the River Torridge just below the town as well as a number of local fish farms.

Torrington is an ideal centre for walking because of the 20 miles of footpaths on the commons around the town and access to the Tarka Trail which comprises some 180 miles extending to both Dartmoor and Exmoor and is ideal for both walking and cycling. (See 'What is the Tarka Trail and where is it?'). The Torridge Ramblers meet at least once a month for walks of between three and ten miles. They have brought out a leaflet featuring a Millennium Path which they have created of about 20 miles which encircles the town using existing rights of way and permissive paths and passes through varied countryside including riverside, woodland, farmland, part of the commons and the Tarka Trail.

There are pub teams for skittles and darts, snooker is played at the Conservative club and the Torridge Vale club and there is a 'walking league' for pool played in the pubs in the town so no-one has to drink and drive. Some teams have had to move venue as several of the pubs have closed in recent years.

Older women in the community remember playing hockey and the similar game of shinty on the Old Bowling Green. 'We went down there once a week with Miss Woodley. Time I got out there I was worn out, talk about playing blessed shinty. . . 'twas a long way, at the end of the day, every Friday.' The country sports of hunting and shooting continue to be carried out in the locality and huntsmen still meet in the town square on Boxing Day. Otter hunting used to take place on the River Torridge, as described in Henry Williamson's 'Tarka the Otter' and shown in the film of the book made in the 1970s which featured Torrington folk. The horrible 'entertainment' of bull baiting used to take place in the Bullring Tannery behind the High Street in past centuries, but ceased at the end of the 18th century, and cock fighting (some-times called 'cock cubbiting') was banned by law in 1849. 'Outhurling', an early form of football with lots of players on each side and goals a long way apart, used to be played on the commons.

The 'round the tree race' at May Fair is a long-held tradition. Runners start from the square and race up through the pannier market to Barley Grove, down the com-mons paths, across the river via Taddiport bridge and along to a field where there used to be an old oak tree and back by a different route. In the past, when there were fewer trees and bushes on the commons because of grazing, the runners used to plunge straight down over Castle Hill and wade through the river. There were breaks when young men were away at war and, in fact, the race hadn't taken place for some years until it was revived in 1981 and the new route was introduced. Townspeople gather at the top of Castle Hill to watch the progress of the runners and cheer them on as they return, exhausted, at the end of the race.

With thanks to:
John Baker
Nicola Brend
Bob Brewer
Maurice Cockwill
Roger Davey
Dave Glover
John Hayes
Geoff Huxtable
Dulcie Leate
John Norman
Andy Stevens
Pat Wilks

A sign on Torrington bowling club's pavilion says the club was founded in 1645. According to the club's archive, evidence for this comes from mention in a paper written about events in Torrington at the time of the Civil War[1], that the 'Prince's Guards were in the Castle Green' before the battle of Torrington.[2] It seems to be assumed that this was a bowling green although it could simply have referred to an area of grass.

Another piece of evidence is that John Howe, chaplain to the Parliamentary army and perpetual curate at Torrington, referred to a game of bowls in a sermon in 1654 on 'Thoughtfulness for the future' while he was resident in Torrington implying that his parishioners would be familiar with the game and understand the metaphor employed.

Elsewhere in the bowling club archive, alongside the date 1717, it says 'Castle Green was laid out for recreation – the summer house was built for £3 7s 4d in the Castle Green' and afterwards, in brackets, the compiler of the archive has written ('was this the gazebo?'), the small six-sided building in the corner of the bowling ground overlooking the valley which is now used for storing bowling equipment.

In 1741 a certain John Squire was paid five shillings for laying turf on the bowling green and the Town Wardens' Accounts show two payments regarding the bowling club in the 1750s:

'Received by subscriptions for repair the Bowling House   £10s 10d
George Towle for Repairing the Bowl House   £1 14s 10d.[3]

Bowls must have been played at one time on the part of the commons just beyond the cemetery which is still called 'the Old Bowling Green' but no-one seems to know when it transferred to the Castle Hill site.

The archive states that in 1837 Lord John Rolle of Stevenstone granted a 25 year lease of the Castle Green to the Great Torrington Town Council – 'specifically for the purpose of a bowling green' – at a rent of two shillings and sixpence per quarter. In 1883 the bailey of the castle – now known as Barley Grove – was conveyed to the Town Council. It refers to the bowling green as already held by the Council. Assuming the lease of 1837 ran until 1862, some time between 1862 and 1883 the green was conveyed by either purchase or gift to the Town Council.

In 1992 A. F. Fitzjohn, Honorary Secretary of the bowling club, suggested setting up an archive using 'the large amount of memorabilia relating to the Club's history which, if not carefully preserved, would soon become lost for ever.' He proposed that such an archive should be kept in the pavilion and not hidden away in the Secretary's possession. He gathered as much information as he could from the old Minute books but found there was a large gap of details between 1920 and 1950 and asked if any member knew their whereabouts. It seems they have never come to light.

The earliest photograph dates from 1862 and shows a group of men, all wearing either top hats or bowler hats, playing bowls on the 'Annual Day' with a marquee set up on the south side of the green with the hill across the valley in the background and the gazebo, its bricks unpainted, in the left of the picture.

In 1888 the bowling club was invited to send a team to Plymouth for the Tercentenary celebrations of the Armada as Torrington was considered the most

Players early 1900s   Photo courtesy of Torrington Bowling Club

active bowling club in Devon. Their opponents would be a team from Leeds and the Torrington club wrote to them insisting that they would only play with a 'non-biased jack'. Crown Green bowlers still play with a biased jack which is much larger than the one played with today. The Armada cup from this match played on Plymouth Hoe is the club's oldest possession. Lawn tennis jacket and white trousers were suggested for the match but in the end Elizabethan costumes were provided by the Plymouth Celebration Committee. The members of the Torrington club whose names were drawn out of a hat to play in that game were: John Jackson, Joseph Bower, John Bower, John Adams, C. R. Doe, H. Blatchford, Joseph Slee, William Werry and Henry Bangham.

1890 saw the first match with Barnstaple at Torrington which Torrington won by 66 points.

In 1892 the archive states,

> 'The Greenkeeper was instructed to roll the green three times and cut it twice a week. He was paid £11 for 22 weeks work during the season. There were 10 Honorary and 75 Members. The Annual Subscription was five shillings (this was equivalent to a week's wage)'.

On 8th June 1892 there was the first recorded match against Bideford.

In 1903 the English Bowling Association was formed. Dr W. G. Grace of cricketing fame was instrumental in setting it up. In 1908 the Devon County Bowling Association (DCBA) was founded and in 1911 a North Devon Division of the DCBA was proposed. In this year the Torrington green was re-laid.

Above: Torrington v Leeds at Plymouth 1888   Photo courtesy of Torrington Bowling Club

Below: Torrington v Torquay 1903   Photo courtesy of Torrington Bowling Club

In 1912 Torrington bowling club won the Devon County Trophy. The team consisted of F. W. Hodge, W. J. Slee, F. R. Hodge, F. Tucker, Dr J. G. Macindoe, C. H. Slee, C. R. Doe, J. Bowden, H. Blatchford, L. Ashton, J. Short and R. M. Doe. They beat Ilfracombe at Barnstaple by 32 points, Barnstaple at Cowick by 35 points, Exonia at Tiverton by 76 points and Tiverton at Heavitree by 36 points. Their final match was against Torquay at Barnfield which was a drawn game but, after five extra ends, Torrington won by 13 points.

The Hodge family feature prominently in the club's successes over the years. In 1914 F. W. Hodge was made President of the DCBA and an Honorary Member of the club. In 1920 and 1922 his son, Reg Hodge, won the County Singles Title and in 1924

Bowling green with old clubhouse   Photo courtesy of Linda Downing

he won the National Singles Title at Denmark Hill in London as well as the County Singles Title. In 1927 and 1928 Reg Hodge won the County Pairs Title with W. J. Slee. In 1931 and 1932 he won the County Secretaries' Competition and in 1953 he was skipper when the club won the County Triples Title. In 1955 H. Hodge was the team skipper when they won the County Fours. When he died in 1969 Reg Hodge had been Honorary Secretary for 25 years and a member of the club for over 60 years.

Pat Wilks, a child in Torrington in the 1930s, remembers most members of the bowling club as being young and middle-aged men although 'there were a few devoted ladies.' Her father, S. R. Webb, Manager of the Midland Bank, was an enthusiastic player. She said play could be watched from the 'Barley Grove tump', as she called the hump of ground between the bowling green and the car park.

In 1972 the North Devon Triples League was formed.

On 19th July 1988 a Commemorative Armada Bowls Match at the Armada 400 celebrations was played on Plymouth Hoe, once again between Torrington and a team from Leeds. In 1888 the Original Oak Bowling Team from Leeds had beaten Torrington by two shots but this time (again dressed in 16th century costume) the Devon team had its revenge beating the Northerners 99-63. After the game a civic tea was held at the Council House and the Torrington team found themselves presented with a trophy, a plate, a set of engraved bowls and medals for all.

In 1987 the old bowling pavilion – a wooden building painted green with a tin roof – was demolished. Excavations were made at this time to see if any remains of the old castle could be found. 'The masonry foundations of part of a domestic building were discovered, the tail of a rampart of clay and stone was located and considerable quantities of medieval pottery were recovered.'[4] The smart new clubhouse, brick built with a tiled roof, was opened in 1988.

With thanks to:
Roy Kent and the Great Torrington Bowling Club for allowing me access to the club archive
Pat Wilks

The square and the roads leading into it are a conservation area and there are many Grade II listed buildings worthy of notice.

'Fore Street and High Street have a certain degree of Georgian feeling, and the Market Place is Georgian in scale and atmosphere.'[1]

Standing by the drinking fountain looking up the square you can see, on your left, the Black Horse Inn which is believed to date from the 15th century but whose frontage was rebuilt in 1681. There is a stud-and-panel screen in the passageway. This inn was headquarters, at different times, to both Royalists and Parliamentarians during the Civil War.

Further up on the left, the NatWest Bank is formal 19th century Italianate with alternating window pediments.[2]

At the far end of the square, at number 7 Fore Street, is the Globe Inn, formerly a hotel. The present building dates from 1830 with a three storey front with very tall first floor windows with round-headed arched recesses which used to have an iron balcony along in front of them. The Globe closed in June 2011 but opened its doors once again in time for Christmas of that year. (See 'How many Pubs are there in Torrington?').

Next door to the Globe is the Plough Arts Centre, a red brick neo-Georgian building of 1913 (see 'What goes on at the Plough?') and across the road is 'the cheerfully eclectic'[3] former Post Office built in 1903.

Black Horse   Photo courtesy of Roy Beer and Margaret Trounson

Town Hall

Back at Mark Rolle's drinking fountain, looking up the square, on the right about half way along is the colonnaded Town Hall, once called the Guild Hall, which dates from the 16th century. There have been additions and restorations made over the years and now it houses the fine oak-panelled Council Chamber and a large hall which was once the town's principal meeting hall and court room. A group of build-ings including the Town Hall, Leather Hall, Cordwainers' Chamber, Yarn Hall and the Shambles occupied the site of the present Town Hall (built in 1861) and the yard at the rear. The building is in the classical style with a rusticated limestone lower storey and red brick with stone dressings above. The pedimented centre reaches out into the square and has arched openings leading on to a cobbled and paved area beneath the large assembly room. From this area two doors lead to imposing stair-cases: one goes directly into the assembly hall and the other leads to an impressive landing outside the Council Chamber.

In 2003 a Music and Arts Festival in Torrington culminated with the opening of the Shambles project which aimed at decorating the passage between the Town Hall and Cornmarket Street with murals depicting life in the 17th century when this area was the old slaughter house and meat market and also held the ancient lock-ups and stocks. It was opened by then Mayor, Margaret Brown, and Town Crier, Al Mitchell, gave a special proclamation. These murals can be seen if you walk under the Town Hall and out under the arches at the back on the right.

There is an ongoing project for a £1 million redevelopment to create a new community venue in the Town Hall but this has been held up due to a lack of available funding. The building needs major structural change to make it fully accessible, notably to people with disabilities, and plans include a glass front, a lift between floors, a 150 person function room, and kitchen and toilet block. From October 2007 a mysterious benefactor calling himself 'The Viper' sent £1 coins in aid of the Town Hall project from all over the world, accompanied by short notes or poems. By February 2011 the total received had reached £100 and in the *North Devon Journal* of 9th June 2011 the Viper signed off with a poem entitled 'Retirement Time'.[4] General restoration work on the building has had to be carried out by the Town Lands who currently own the building. These works became urgent before other project-delaying problems could be solved. Roof work had to begin straight away to ensure preservation of the fabric of the building, rather than wait and risk further expense in the future.

Dr Harry Cramp who has chaired the committee of the Great Torrington Buildings Preservation Trust, led the project and written regular articles in *The Crier* over the past few years has handed over to Richard Phillips, though he (Harry) will remain as Vice Chair. Richard Phillips wrote in *The Crier* of February 2012:

> 'I hope that the many pitfalls and problems encountered over the years will soon be at an end and we will finally see our Town Hall firmly back as a civic and social centre for Great Torrington.'

The Great Torrington Heritage Museum and Archive which was housed in the Town Hall assembly room (free entrance and run by volunteers) had to vacate the building in 2007 and has been unable to find new affordable premises. (See 'Is there a Museum in Torrington?'). Many of the archives including the old lock-up, cell doors and stocks, together with a fine collection of photographs illustrating many aspects of the town's social and industrial past, have been in store. At the end of 2011 there were hopes that part of the old Board School in Whites Lane could be used for the museum but that has not been possible. Chairman of the museum trustees, Val Morris, said in *The Crier* of February 2012, 'Great Torrington Heritage Museum and Archive is alive, but still homeless. We are hoping to have good news to pass on in the Spring.' It has been a long and frustrating process.

Looking back down the square to the lower end is the Market House in South Street which was built in 1842. The upper floor of this building has had many uses including the Town Assembly Room (prior to the rebuilding of the Town Hall in 1861), the public library from 1936-2000, a sale room for Little John's Charity in aid of a Romanian orphanage and an art workshop and gallery. The archway under the Market House gives access to the pannier market. (See 'How long has there been a Pannier Market in Torrington?')

Corner House, number 18 Potacre Street, was built by a member of the Glubb family, six generations of whom lived in or near Torrington for two centuries and were very active in the life of the town and district as mayors, vicars and Town Clerk. John Warren Glubb (c1760s-1804) built Corner House. He was a banker and lawyer and was Town Clerk from 1796-1802. He had two sons, John Warren, who was killed in action during the Peninsular War, and Thomas, who died young. His sister, Sarah Susanna, married the Rev. Joshua Le-Marchant and their youngest daughter, Sophia, married Thomas Stevens of Cross, Little Torrington (the manor house on the hill

Corner House

Photo by the author

opposite Torrington). Their elder daughter married the Rev. George de Carteret Guille, Rector of Little Torrington. John Warren's youngest brother, William, held many public offices in Torrington and when he died in 1850 was the last person to be buried in the parish churchyard. One of William's sons, William Frederick, was a great benefactor to the town. He donated five painted glass windows to the parish church and he endowed the Torrington Cottage Hospital with the residue of his fortune. He remained a bachelor and lived with his unmarried sisters in Corner House and died there in 1901. They were the last of the Torrington Glubb family.

In the 1930s Corner House was a small private school called St George's. The author Rosemary Sutcliff attended the school when she lived just outside Torrington. In 'Blue Remembered Hills' she remembers:

> 'We wore panama hats with red-and-white ribbon round them, and were expected to behave ourselves in the street in a way which would not bring dishonour upon the school, the United Kingdom including Church and Crown, or the British Empire. Beside Miss Davies the Headmistress, there was an assistant who took the juniors in another classroom, and various visiting staff including Miss Wright who taught us music and the curate who taught us Latin.'[5]

Rosemary Sutcliff said Miss Davies was 'a nice, conscientious, well-meaning woman and a properly qualified teacher; but she lacked the natural gift for teaching. . .' and held beliefs that 'raised the devil in me'. Miss Davies was

'. . .a devout high churchwoman and tried hard to make us over in her own image, though without much success. Most of us were Wesleyan or United Methodist; I had been brought up in the lowest possible layer of the Church of England.'

Miss Davies was also 'an ardent Royalist in the Stuart sense of the word' while Rosemary Sutcliff 'had been brought up ardently Cromwellian. . . and this did not make for harmony between us.' Most of the pupils were happy enough to follow Miss Davies's lead and turned up wearing sprigs of oak leaves on Oak Apple Day but Rosemary and a boy called Michael Vincent 'formed a two-man Cromwellian faction in an otherwise Royalist school, and very much enjoyed being an oppressed and rebellious minority.'[6]

Doctors John and Gwen Searle, he a GP, she an optician, lived and worked from Corner House for over half a century. After they both died the house was sold, part of the back garden was sold off by the new owners and in 2009 local builders, Tolley, built a row of houses behind the property's high wall not realising it was listed and couldn't be demolished. It must be a very dark and gloomy existence in those new homes. How do these planning applications ever get passed?

Castle Street is an attractive street off the main square consisting of old cottages and substantial houses. At the top of the street on the left is the Castle House nursing home which offers accommodation for 33 'providing quality nursing and residential care in a relaxed, friendly atmosphere and traditional home cooking.'[7] (See 'Are there any Care Homes for the elderly in Torrington?). This grand, late 18th century house with its recessed Greek Doric porch (now closed in) and deep balcony with iron balustrade and canopy was once the home of Mrs Elizabeth Deane (née Johnson), one of the nieces of the artist, Sir Joshua Reynolds. She modelled for him as 'Fortitude', one of the Virtues in his memorial window at New College Chapel, Oxford.

Opposite the nursing home is a Grade II listed building known locally as the Eric Palmer Centre. It is believed to be on the site of the chapel of the medieval castle which, when the rest of the castle had disappeared, remained as a schoolhouse. On the wall of the building is a plaque which states:

'This BUILDING was Erected by the
RIGHT HONble JOHN LORD ROLLE
of STEVENSTONE in this COUNTY
as a SCHOOL HOUSE for the Education
of the Poor Children of this Parish in
the Principles of the Established
CHURCH.
ANNO DOMINI 1834.'

This was the Blue Coat School, also known as the Barley Grove School, which occupied the building until 1978 when it joined the Board School in Whites Lane.

The building had been given to the town in 1940 and, when it ceased to be used as a school, it reverted to the trustees of the Denys Yonge Educational Foundation who leased it at a peppercorn rent of £1 a year to Devon County Council to be used as a youth and community centre. Eric Palmer, husband of Lady Anne of Rosemoor, was one of the trustees and the chairman of the Devon County Council. He died in 1980. When the building re-opened it was thought appropriate to name it after Eric Palmer who had been a conscientious worker on its behalf, firm but fair, always there, and Lady Anne opened the centre in 1981. A plaque referring to that event is in the museum. The Eric Palmer Centre (or EPC as it was often known) was used by a variety of community groups and organisations and generations of Torrington people have taken part in activities there. Then came the day when this building, one of the largest and oldest community buildings in the town, was forced to close its doors. The Torrington-based Denys Yonge Trust, which owned the building couldn't afford its £24,000 annual upkeep. (The Denys Yonge Educational Foundation was formed in December 1939 for the upkeep and maintenance of the school buildings when Lord Clinton conveyed the freehold to the vicar and churchwardens. Denys Yonge died in 1834 only a few months after the upper storey of the school was opened. His son, Rev. Francis Yonge, died in 1841. Both have grave slabs in the centre aisle of the parish church).[8]

Devon County Council, who had leased the EPC and consequently took care of the maintenance costs, had given notice to leave the building which closed in 2008. The trustees tried to find other groups or individuals willing to take on the lease but were unsuccessful. 'It does seem like the curtain is coming down on this piece of Torrington's history', said trustee, Mike Sampson. The EPC was sold at public auction at the Plough Arts Centre on 10th September 2009. Bidding started at £100,000 and the property was eventually sold for £205,000 to a local businessman who started to renovate the run-down building with the intention of opening it as a children's nursery. However, these plans didn't come to fruition and for a time the future of the building seemed uncertain until, in January 2012 under the title 'New Lease of Life for the Eric Palmer Centre', it was announced in *The Crier* that a local couple, Paul and Louise Banfield, together with their son Charlie, were taking over the building to run it as a health and fitness centre available for use by the whole community.

Walking up South Street from the square you come to number 28 on your left. This fine house was built in 1701 and completely restored by the Landmark Trust in 1996 using authentic materials, such as lead for rainwater pipes and sash window weights, and retaining historic window glass wherever possible. The house is of a similar architectural style to Palmer House in New Street with its red brick, sashed windows, wooden cornice and alternating dormer pediments. One of the finest features inside is the ornamental plasterwork in the principal staircase and main rooms which are heavily embellished with natural motifs such as acanthus leaves and branches, and there is also some rope work. In one of the ground floor rooms there is a plaster ceiling with lobed centre with an exquisitely modelled group of musical instruments. Outside there is a very attractive porch head with trophies in relief inside the hood. This house can be rented by holidaymakers from the Landmark Trust and can sleep up to seven people.

28 South Street

Photo by the author

Next to number 28 and set back off the road is a large building that used to be the Castle Hill Hotel. Built in around 1820 as Castle Hill House, it was a grand private residence with 'a nice cantilevered curving top-lit staircase inside and romantically battlemented garden walls.'[9] It became a hotel but gradually fell into disrepair before it was acquired by the Landmark Trust. Now refurbished and leased to the CDT (Community Development Trust) it houses a variety of bodies – the town's library, District Council and Town Council offices, the Tourist Information Centre and Torrington 1646.

Between the entrance to the old Castle Hill Hotel and the Conservative club (where the entrance to the car park is now) once stood Sydney House built by William Vaughan who owned the glove factory in Whites Lane. This building burnt down in 1942 when it was being used as a Devon County Council School for Delicate Children and, tragically, five young boys lost their lives. There is a memorial slab of slate from the building bearing the boys' names at the entrance to the car park. (See 'Where was Sydney House?')

Further up South Street, on the same side, is number 42, Furse House, built in about 1810 for Charles William Johnson. The son of a Torrington apothecary, Johnson was orphaned at the age of ten and brought up by relations who sent him to India at the age of 17 to become an indigo planter. There he made his fortune and

Furse House

returned to marry a cousin, Theresa Furse, of Halsdon, Dolton. His hobby was designing and renovating houses and this property eventually extended up to the Londis shop and the family cow was kept in the paddock that is now part of the car park. Although the front elevations of numbers 42 and 44 are radically different, it is obvious, when looking at the two houses from the rear, that there was a single mind involved in the design and build of the balcony and verandah spanning the back. Charles William Johnson was Mayor five times and his name appears on the Market Hall. He was one of the people who encouraged Thomas Fowler with his inventions. One of his sons was the classical poet, William Cory (he took his grand-mother's name), a master at Eton and composer of the Eton Boating Song who spent his childhood in this house.

After the death of Charles William Johnson the property was split into individual houses. Furse House (so called from the mid 19th century onwards after the Johnson family changed their name to Furse) was acquired by Samuel Doidge and for about 40 years housed the Middle Class School, a day and boarding school for boys.

A builder, Henry Grant, lived in the house for a while and then during the First World War the house was occupied by an artist, Francis Edward James, who leased it from the Torrington Town Lands who owned the property. He was a flower painter, a widower who was crippled. To Torrington's amazement he painted the house peacock blue and white, furnished it exquisitely and created a formal, flowery garden out of the vegetable patch at the back which stretched into the fields. He was well read, an amusing and sophisticated talker and very popular with children with whom he played card games and for whom he bought ingenious creeping, crawling, tumbling 'pavement toys' and gave 'lavish and original children's parties at his house.'[10]

In 1920 the Town Lands leased the house to a Mrs Isabella Van Wisselingh, a widow whose address was 3 Hyde Park Mansions, London. She bought it from the charity a year later in 1921. In 1926 she sold it to a Mrs Sandford (whose husband ran the creamery) who also bought a further piece of garden which stretched across the back of numbers 40 and 42, according to a plan attached to the deed of sale from the Misses Grant (three sisters). Furse House remained in the Sandford family until it was sold to Mr Banta Singh in 1957 who turned the ground floor into a drapery shop. A dumb waiter used in the shop exists to this day. Mr Singh eventually sold the property and it returned after some 40 years to being a family house.

Number 50 South Street, known as Windy Cross House, is a large four-storey house which dates from the 1820s and may have been built as a boarding house. It is situated where South Street, Mill Street and Halsdon Terrace meet and from the back of the house there are lovely views across the Torridge valley. The sash windows on the front of the house are the original windows and each one has the very unusual feature of an acorn under each side of the upper part of the window. Does this denote that they were made by someone called Oke? There is a dumb waiter which passes through the corner of the kitchen and extends from the first floor to the basement where there is a larder with slate shelves and meat hooks. There are fireplaces in many of the rooms and it would seem to be a house that needed plenty of domestic staff to run it. The garage probably dates from the 1750s with its thick cob walls, fireplace and steps to the upper floor. A room at the farthest end wasn't opened up for some 10-15 years during the tenure of the present owners until it was converted into a pottery.

In February 1904 the house was sold by a Major William Thomas Furse (who lived in Salisbury) to a Mrs E. F. Medland. Major Furse also owned the property next door

Acorns under the sash windows

Photo by the author

Windy Cross House and Halsdon House   Photo courtesy of the Beaford Archive

but one down South Street (recently CAT computer shop) which he let to a Mr Doidge. In July 1920 Windy Cross House was sold by William Cock Medland to Charles Cocks who sold it only two years later to Dr V. Blacker Kyle. The room to the right of the front door could well have been a doctor's consulting room as there is a door with a knocker on it immediately inside the front door which would have enabled patients to enter the room without going through the inner door into the main house. There is also a washbasin in this room. In a photo of the house in the Beaford Archive there appears to be a plaque on the wall of the house which could well be a doctor's name-plate. In 1926 Dr Kyle sold the house to a Mr Arthur Bailey Pugh, 'Physician and Surgeon of 28 Barons Court, West Kensington,' for £1,200 with stamp duty of £12! It is not known if he actually lived in the house and only two years later he sold it to Arthur Henry Heaman and his wife, Alice Mary. The house was owned by the Heaman family from 1928 until 1983. At one time during this period the house was divided into flats and the front door bell still rings on the top floor. A local couple started their married life in the 1960s in the basement flat which has its own entrance. In 1983 Clive and Patricia Richards (a furniture decorator) bought the house from the Heamans and sold it to the present owners in 1989.

Turning right at the top of South Street, and opposite Windy Cross House, you find Halsdon Terrace on the right. This row of large, rather elegant houses was a more symmetrical terrace before a double-gabled building on the right-hand end (which mirrored the dental practice premises on the left-hand end) was demolished in the late 1960s to make the turn into South Street easier for traffic.

On the other side of Whites Lane is the old glove factory which has lain empty for some years waiting for a buyer to convert it into a building with a present-day use. (See 'What is that large empty building that looks rather like a chapel in Whites Lane?').

Just down Church Lane, opposite the old glove factory, leading to the parish church is a property called The Old Smithy. The smithy was where the integral garage is now, which still has a cobbled floor, and the smith lived in the adjoining cottage. An elderly local man remembers the smithy in operation and said it used to make the equipment for the glove factory over the road. The smithy was converted into the present house in 1951 and this date is etched into a pane of the leaded window in the door to the garden from the living room. Mrs Christine Williams, who lived in the house for many years, told the present owners that the walled garden is where the horses were tied up ready for shoeing, or after they had been shod, and there is a rectangular brick structure, which she used as a sand pit for her children, which had been the manure heap for the smithy. There was a large carriage house at the end of the garden, where the four garages are now, which used to block the light from her garden so she was pleased when it came down. The house created in the 1950s had a galleried landing and three bedrooms and seems to have had an Aga for heating and cooking. In 2002 it was converted further by the Kesslers, who lived in the house at the time, and the gallery was blocked in to create a four bedroom family house. (Number 12 Calf Street near the roundabout was also a smithy at one time).

On the south side of the church, in Church Walk, is the Sexton's House, white plastered with black paintwork, low with Gothic windows. The rather unusual and attractive Tannery Row set behind the high stone wall was completed in 2006 and stands on the site of the former bullring, where bull-baiting took place up until 1753, which then became the site of a tannery. The large bark shed which fronted onto Church Lane was converted into a cinema which, in turn, became used as a bingo hall and was finally demolished to make way for Tannery Row. On the corner of the churchyard and New Street are two houses which used to be the old police station and are now called, appropriately enough, 'Peel Cottage' and 'Peel House'.

The vicarage opposite the parish church dates from 1841 (see 'How old is the Parish Church?') although it stands on the site of a much older manor house. In the garden was one of the few remaining examples of the Turkey oak which was imported to replace the native variety felled in their hundreds to build ships of the line. Many parishioners were dismayed to see this felled in October 2011 but it had been examined by more than one arborist who found it to have a large area of rot and decay and was considered to present a potential hazard to users of the highway.[11]

Palmer House in New Street opposite the western entrance to the parish church is one of Torrington's most historic buildings and has been called a 'house of style and consequence'.[12] It was built in 1752 by John Palmer, an attorney who was several times Mayor and whose wife, Mary, was the eldest sister of Sir Joshua Reynolds. The artist visited her occasionally at Torrington and on one visit in 1762 he was accompanied by Dr Johnson. Reynolds's portrait of Mary is in the Cottonian Library, Plymouth. Mary Palmer was the author of 'A Devonshire Dialogue' between two country people written to illustrate the characteristics of the Devonshire dialect. She died in Torrington in 1794 aged 76. John Palmer had died in 1770 aged 61. Successive generations of the Palmer family lived in Palmer House until 1870.

Palmer House   Photo by the author

In its description of this Grade II listed house, when it was on the market in 2003, the *Gazette & Advertiser* says the Palmer coat of arms can still be seen in the main staircase window. The drawing room is reputedly modelled on the Cabinet Room at Number 10 Downing Street. It has four bedrooms plus two separate and self-contained units offering income potential or home for a dependant relative. The building retains many original features and architecture of the period including panelled doors, ornate ceiling mouldings, shuttered sash windows at the front and a number of open fireplaces. There is also a magnificent split-level galleried landing and a 23ft (7m) master bedroom which was the original drawing room. Palmer Mews is a self-contained, single storey dwelling attached to Palmer House which is believed to have been converted from former outbuildings. The present railings at the front of the property belong to the early 19th century. The gazebo which used to be in the back garden fell into disrepair and was dismantled at great expense and re-erected at Rosemoor gardens, a couple of miles out of town. (See 'Where was the Gazebo, now at Rosemoor, originally situated?'). It can be seen in its new situation from Castle Hill.

The Town or Rolle Almshouses, numbers 90 and 92 New Street, were built in 1843 of a symmetrical design with Gothic doorways in two gabled projections.

Between the almshouses and the Royal Exchange pub is number 88 New Street, a substantial stone house built in around 1860, possibly by John Long who was a glover and died in 1865. The house extends a long way out to the back and part of the building was once used as a small glove factory. A horse used to be brought through the side passageway behind the double doors and stabled in a bothy. There's a variety of old outhouses and chickens now live in the outside lavatory. The rear garden extends some 200ft (61.5m) and includes an attractive cobbled yard together with a lawned area, separate vegetable garden and a small wooded copse with a pond and timber decking. A parking area at the very bottom can be accessed from Town Park.

Local people have said that the house was known as The Hermitage or The Retreat at some time in the past. During the Second World War American soldiers were billeted there including a Native American who used to sit at an upstairs window looking out at the street smoking a pipe. The present owners of the house have found old rough-spun shirts in the attic which may well have belonged to the soldiers.

In 1946 the Town Trustees, who owned the house at that time, sold it to Audrey Sharpe for £2,200 and she lived there for 50 years. She is remembered as a kindly woman who liked a drink and had a little car which she used to park in the passageway. When she was elderly she lived in only a couple of the downstairs rooms. She let the large room at the back (the former glove factory) to the Catholics for their services and for a Sunday school before a new church was built in Gas Lane in 1964. A bell hanging on an outside wall in the yard would summon the worshippers. They would come in from the street through the double wooden doors, down the passageway and out across the yard to a door into the place of worship without having to go through the main house. A local man who attended the Sunday school remembers having to negotiate layers of curtains which hung over the doorways, presumably to keep out the draughts. The town band also used to use this room for practice.

A Mr Gilbert who used to be caretaker at the Borough Road junior school attended the Bluecoat school when he was a lad. The headmaster of the school at that time lived in number 88 and Mr Gilbert was one of a group of boys who used to work in the garden. Several years ago the present owners of the house invited him round and he was delighted to see the garden he used to tend full of fruit and vegetables and not built on. There were plans drawn up by the Baptist Housing Association in the early 1990s for a development of sheltered flats behind the house and the Royal Exchange next door and the church and number 80 with a pedestrian access to New Street through number 88's passageway but these plans came to nought.

As well as the shirts in the attic, the present owners have found love letters hidden away in the roof, under the stairs and fireplace addressed to 'Darling' and 'My Own Dearest' dating from the 1930s. We'll never know who the participants in this correspondence were and what became of their romance.

Porch House, number 83 New Street, dates from around 1700 but has been altered over the years. It was possibly built originally onto two existing cottages which were on either side of the main house. It is a two storey house of an early Georgian style with a seven-bay front with the early 18th century type of flush-frame sash windows

88 New Street   Photo courtesy of Pat and Nigel Stark

with glazing bars. One ground floor window on the left is a splayed bay with altered glazing. The front is of dark red brick and a Tuscan porch which has been filled in. This was done by Mr Marshall who lived in the house, probably before the First World War or at the end of the 19th century. He owned Marshall's Yard further down the street on the other side and he had narrow windows built into the sides of the porch so he could check on the times of the comings and goings of the horses and carriages in and out of his yard. The roof beams of the house are tree trunks and there is an extensive attic. The Darches rented a flat at the top of the house in the early 1920s which was reached by an outside staircase which must have been at the back somewhere. Americans were billeted in the house during the Second World War and after they had gone it was found they had burnt all the wood in the house because, with its exceptionally high windows and ceilings, it was very cold inside. The Darch family of builders owned the house from 1938 until 1965 and after the war they worked on the house and paid their employees' wages in the front room. The house was divided into two in 1946 and the smaller half was rented to a policeman known as 'Trigger'. Strangely, a door connected one of the upstairs rooms of the main house with a room in the other house where one of the Darch family had a bedroom. A local man who lived in the house when he was newly married with his wife's parents who were connected to the Darches said it was his job to dust the chandelier in the back room and the ceiling was so high he had to stand on a chair on the table to be able to reach it. He also remembers that the bath was 7ft (about 2.10m) long and he could float in it.

Amongst the deeds of the house, there is a handwritten note by a certain John Bird regarding the 'East Wall of Porch House'. In it he states:

'I the undersigned do hereby declare and assert that in the year of our Lord one thousand eight hundred and twenty-four: I made mortar and tended masons for building the east wall of a flower garden belonging to a house in New Street, Great Torrington for Mr Francis Kingdon Attorney in whose possession and occupation it then was: and I hereby further declare and assert that I have from time to time during the last twenty years repaired the said wall for the late Richard L. Hole Surgeon, and since his death I have repaired it for his daughter Ann L. Hole.'

Since 1984 a potter and his wife, a jeweller, have lived in Porch House.

In an old aerial photograph of Torrington, taken probably in the 1930s, there are very few houses in Warren Lane: Culver House (opposite where Warren Close is now), Uplands and Rock Mount (two 'gentlemen's residences' overlooking the valley on the corner of Rack Park path), Enfield, The Warren (now called Warren House), Hillcrest (which my six year old son used to say was given that name because it was 'on a hill and overlooked Dairy Crest'), Torridge House and Penhallam (down on the corner with Mill Street). A map of Torrington in 1843 shows the street was called Warren Lane until just past Uplands and from then on until it meets Mill Street it was called Rack Park Lane. It seems to have had a variety of names at different times.

It is not known exactly when The Warren was built but it may have been over 250 years ago according to the type of red brick used on the building. The magnificent holm oak by the front gate is believed to be much older than that. The castellated walls in front of the property are similar to those at Castle Hill and Town Mills erected by the Rolles in the 1840s. It is thought that the house was called The Warren because the owners kept rabbits which were a welcome addition to the diet of impoverished townsfolk.

Existing documentation dates back to the 1860s when the house was part of the Town Lands of Great Torrington. In a document of 1901 it is described as a

'Dwellinghouse with the Coach House Stabling and Garden and one close of land thereto belonging called by the name of the Warren All which said premises were situate near New Street in Great Torrington aforesaid and were bounded by a Lane formerly called Fare's Lane but then Warren Lane on the West side the land of the said Trustees on the North and East and Mill Street Common on the South.'

From the front of the house there is a wonderful view over the Torridge valley.

In September 1864 a Mr White applied to rent 'the Warren House'. At a meeting of the Trustees of the Town Lands it was proposed that it would be advantageous to the town generally that Mr White's offer to take Warren House for a term of three, eight or fourteen years should be accepted from the half quarter between Michaelmas and Christmas at a rent of £27 per annum which was carried unanimously. Numerous repairs were needed on the house: a new kitchen stove and water closet were required, the staircase and passage were in want of repair and repainting. In 1865 Mr White was allowed the sum of 35 shillings towards the expense of raising the wall at the north end of the Warren field. In 1867 Mr White applied to purchase the freehold of the premises but this was refused. In the late 1860s and early 1870s the Trustees and Town Council had problems with non-payment of outstanding bills from the tenants at the Warren.

In April 1872 the following letter was sent to the Steward of the Town Lands from the Town Clerk:

'My dear Sir,

'After you left the Council Meeting this evening it was resolved that application be made to the Trustees of the Town Lands for the use of the Warren as a smallpox hospital, and that an early reply be requested to enable the Council to take action at the adjournment of the meeting. As the adjournment meeting is to take place at six tomorrow evening it is hoped that the Trustees will be able to meet in the course of the day to consider the application.

'It was unanimously resolved that it will not be advisable to allow the Warren to be used as a smallpox hospital, owing to the great loss of rent which must be sustained in consequence but the Trustees will contribute any reasonable portion of the expense of obtaining other premises or erecting a temporary building for the purpose.'

The present owner wonders whether the house was, in fact, used as an isolation hospital for a time as he found during renovations that the outside walls had been painted red at some period, perhaps as a warning to keep people away from the building.

A Mr James Balsdon took on the house in 1874 and then it passed to a Mrs Mary Annie Reading Banks for the sum of £350. Whenever The Warren changed hands a proviso was included in the legal paperwork to allow Mr George Doe, local historian, Town Clerk and twice Mayor, who lived next door at Enfield, to view and inspect and, if necessary, repair the drain from his house and his cesspit which was in the garden of The Warren.

In 1892 an indenture was drawn up in large copperplate handwriting between the 'Honorable Mark George Kerr Rolle (signed by him and sealed in red wax) and James Jackson Banks Esq. for Lease of Stabling and premises adjoining "the Warren" at Great Torrington in the County of Devon' from 25th December 1889 for a term of 90 years expiring 25th December 1979 at a rent of £1 10s 0d and insurance (by Lessee) of £100. Mr Banks had put a coach house and stable (and 'dung pit') on Rolle land north of The Warren (which would eventually become part of the garden of the property).

After Mrs Mary Banks, the property passed on in 1896 to a Mrs Annie Barnes. In 1901 a Mrs Elizabeth Mary Williamson conveyed the premises to Mr Henry Slee, auctioneer of Great Torrington, for the sum of £925.

In 1923 the Charity Commission obtained the authority to sell real estate and sold 'Dwellinghouse and garden known as "The Warren" situate in Warren Road, Great Torrington subject to and with the benefit of the existing lease expiring at Ladyday 1983.'

Captain Walter Bayntun Starky purchased the Warren from Walter John Slee (son of Henry) in 1923 for the sum of £1,450. He had worked as a civilian engineer for the government in India and had been given an honorary title. He was three times Mayor of Torrington in 1930, 1931 and 1933. His wife retained some of her colonial ways and a local man remembers calling at the house and, when he rang at the front door, Mrs Starky's face appeared at an upstairs window and told him to go round to the tradesmen's entrance at the back. This he duly did only to be told, 'Not today, thank you!' Mrs Starky had been to the Slade school of art in London and painted in pastels. She kept all her art materials in what had been the groom's cottage behind the main house. She stayed on in the house after her husband died with a lady companion, Miss Pickering, and tenants.

Margaret and Emlyn Williams lived in The Warren for some 50 years and brought up their family there. The present owner of the house spent his boyhood in the house next door and always dreamed of living in The Warren. When it was up for sale, his house was also on the market and he and his wife exchanged houses with the Williams (with certain adjustments of price) in 2006. They lived in the cottage for three years while extensive renovations were carried out on The Warren. The front door used to be on the front of the house where there are now French doors instead of on the side and, while digging up the floor near the original entrance to install heating, he discovered an underground priest hole. He has added a verandah around two sides of the house and has made the inside into a beautiful property. He and his wife and family moved into the renovated house, now renamed 'Warren House', in June 2009.

Torridge House, a 'late Victorian gentleman's residence', was built in around 1870 and the house was originally square with the front door facing east. The property commands a lovely view over the Torridge valley. An extension was added in 1907 by Mr Boatfield who was a bank manager in the town. The garden stretched down the hill to Mill Street where there was access, and west to the commons where a house, Hillside, was built on the old tennis court. The building was turned into two flats after the war and many original features were damaged. In 1968 the whole house was bought by Theo Page, an eccentric graphic artist, who set about returning the flats to one residence again. He made a studio in the attic where he worked on graphic designs including the 'blown up' drawing of Concorde that was printed in the *Sunday Times* in 1968. He also drew a brilliant cartoon of the Torrington Cavaliers dressed as Vikings and signed by them which can be found in Torrington museum. Theo Page became ill in 1972 and the rather haphazard work on the house stopped so that when the present owners bought it in 1976 the interior was virtually derelict. Since that time they have slowly put the house back together. It has an extensive cellar which used to be the kitchen at ground level on the south side, wine and coal cellars and various larders. There is a deep well with a very worn pump that moved water up three flights to a big tank in the attic through a large lead pipe. When the present owner was a local doctor an old patient called Mrs Dymond told him that as a teenager she was a maid in the house and lived in the attic. Her worst job was pumping water.

Penhallam, at the end of Warren Lane where it meets Mill Street, is a large three storey building divided up since the 1940s into interlocking apartments with 'flying freeholds'. It has fine high-ceilinged rooms and lovely westward views. My children used to call it 'the haunted house', I suppose because of its tall, unusual shape, including a square turret, and its dark-coloured rendering. Penhallam was formerly known as Rack Park House and was renamed by George Stawell, a solicitor, who came from Cornwall in late Victorian times.

Sometime between 1824 and 1840 three Rack Park cottages were converted into one house which was in front of a wall which separated it and the adjoining coach house from the field above. The old wall was partly altered at the western end to allow for the first of two extensions to the main house. The newer outer wall was constructed by Lt Col John Palmer in around 1862. The original address of the main house was number 2 Mill Street but it is now addressed as Warren Lane, formerly Dedalls Lane.

The property had the use of Rack Park field and also a field on the other side of Warren Lane which is now the entrance area to Rack Park Close built in the early 1960s.

Opposite the end of Warren Lane, in Mill Street, is Caynton House, a Grade II listed property built in 1725. It is set back off the road and looks out over the Torridge valley. The Yonge family, who came from Caynton in Shropshire, hence the name of the house, lived there for many years. Before that it seems to have been known as Castle Hill Cottage.

Henry Yonge was vicar of Morwenstowe and on 22nd April 1746 was appointed as perpetual curate, or vicar, of Torrington. His son, William, married Francis, daughter of Samuel Johnson the previous vicar, and became Chancellor and Archdeacon of Norwich. Two other sons married nieces of Sir Joshua Reynolds. Henry's daughter, Sarah, married the Rev. James William Nelson, brother of Horatio, who became the first Earl Nelson in October 1805 after his brother's death at Trafalgar. The Rev. Denys Yonge, Henry's fifth son, was treasurer of the school at Barley Grove. He was assistant curate for 54 years from 1780 until his death and taught at the school.[13]

In 1891 Col. Charles William Yonge, aged 57, was living in the house with his sister, Fanny. A piece from the *Edinburgh Gazette* of 1st October 1897 listing people under the heading 'Bankrupts – from the *London Gazette*, Receiving Orders' includes Charles William Yonge of Caynton House, Torrington, colonel on the retired list, Bombay Staff Corps.

The Jenner Parsons owned the house for some 15 years in the 1970s-80s and sold part of its grounds to a developer who built the three houses in Caynton Court. The present owners, a local GP and his wife, bought the property in 1987.

Mill Street is a fascinating old street winding down from the town to the river at Taddiport with mainly terraced houses of different sizes which were all thatched originally. Escaping Royalists fled down the street, their horses' hooves clattering and echoing between the houses, after the Battle of Torrington in 1646. The Torridge Inn, number 136 at the bottom of the street, is one of only two thatched buildings remaining and dates from the early 18th century. (See 'Where is Mill Street?').

Cross House (or simply 'Cross') can be seen from Torrington up on the opposite hill standing in its own parkland. It is in the parish of Little Torrington and faces north with extensive views across the countryside including glimpses of the sea in the distance. I look out at the house across the valley from my study and I used it as the model for 'North Hill House', home of a Royalist General de Bere and his family, in my first novel, 'Torrington Burning'.

Cross stands on the site of a Tudor manor house and this far older structure was acquired by Henry Stevens and his wife Christiana (daughter of Lord Rolle) in 1733 and he turned it into a fashionable residence. In 1739 Stowe Barton, a great Cornish mansion built in the 1680s for John Grenville was demolished and Henry Stevens was able to snap up all sorts of treasures for his own house including a solid elm staircase in the style of Grinling Gibbons, a stone-pillared Venetian window and roomfuls of panelling.

Henry Stevens was a local magistrate who had several run-ins with Methodist preachers in the 1780s/90s towards whom he displayed violent and intolerant behaviour. He was reported to Wesley who wrote to him protesting about his conduct.

Cross House with third storey   Photo courtesy of Linda Downing

This exasperated Squire Stevens who threatened to drive the Methodists out of the county. Wesley cited the magistrate before the Court of King's Bench and, process having twice been served and treated with contempt, two officers of the Court came to Torrington and took Stevens in charge. He was so humiliated by this that he left the neighbourhood and Cross remained unoccupied for some 30 years.

At the beginning of the 19th century a third storey was added to the house and later, at the cost of £220, the great north-facing granite portico. In 1937, when the roof was in dire need of repair, the top floor was removed for the sake of economy.

Captain George Frederick Stevens-Guille (1898-1966) and his wife lived in Cross during the first half of the 20th century. In her book Judy Barber called them 'Country Squires in the truest tradition, as their lives revolved around the estate, parish affairs and country pursuits.'[14] Capt. Stevens-Guille spent much of his leisure time writing a book on the family and parish.

Lady Fisher lived at Cross in the second half of the 20th century. After she died the house was empty for some years, occasionally occupied by squatters, falling into disrepair, and there were various rumours about pop groups (Pink Floyd, Ah Ha) wanting to buy it.

The present owner has lived at Cross since 1994 and with the help of architect Jonathan Rhind and working from old drawings she has managed to restore much of the interior to its original state. The elegant saloon immediately inside the south entrance, which was two separate rooms for years, has been reinstated and the panelling which had been ripped out has been replaced. Niches either side of the door leading into the hall which had been hidden for years were uncovered and carefully reconstructed, using plaster and lath and painted a soft blue to contrast with the saloon's pale topaz walls. To the west of the saloon is a bright north-and west-facing drawing room, to the east a large kitchen furnished in French walnut. The downstairs cloakroom has a large square wooden toilet seat and blue and white-patterned porcelain echoed in a large ornamental plant holder and dishes.

The saloon leads out into the central hall with its new limestone floor, magnificent staircase and Bath stone Venetian window surround. To the right of the hall is a morning room with panelling also imported from Stowe.

Upstairs everything centres on the landing, each bedroom having a panelled closet or anteroom of its own. Although large and elegant, the interior of the house feels homely and friendly.

Much of the interior is painted in greys, blues, cool peppermints and pale jades and, as you move from room to room, the colours harmonise well with each other in an interesting way but without being bland. The drawing room is papered in a startling but successful fuchsia pink.

Outside, the house has also seen many improvements. Dusty pink brickwork was revealed beneath crumbling stucco when it was about to be restored and was considered too fine to cover again. The south front of the house has a rather cosy informality while the north front has a porticoed grandeur.

The walls on either side of the building were once part of two, single-storey wings. The east wing contained kitchens and domestic offices, while the west wing connected with stables and brew house. By the time the present owner took over, nothing remained but an overgrown garden and a ruined yard. Now a new potager lies beyond the drawing room windows and the east wall shelters a smart paved enclosure with oak and bronze gates. The brew house was demolished and all that remains of the kitchens is a copper which now stands in the larder and provides, along with many other features of the house, a strong link with the past.[15]

This is my personal selection of notable buildings in Torrington and there may well be others which I have not included, and for this I apologise. People have cited the Castle Gardens Surgery, built in the early 1990s and opened in June 1991, as a building worthy of note with its glass dome lighting the waiting room which is surrounded by doctors' surgeries and treatment rooms. The refurbishments carried out in the Methodist church in 2000/01 which provide a variety of spaces for use by the community are also considered worth a mention. There are some fine houses in Villa Road (a road of villas) including Ramla, the original Methodist manse, and Blenheim which had belonged to the Vincent family who owned the glove factory at the end of the road. There are some large properties at the Bideford end of New Street, including two former manses and the rather elegant Rolle Terrace, as well as in Warren Lane, Rack Park path, South Street and Castle Street. You will have to walk round the town and judge for yourselves.

With thanks to:
Paul and Cilla Bangay
Pat Dekker
Nick Chapman and Charmian Harris
Dave Kelly
Nikki and Andy Kennelly

Brian Nash
John and Mary Paddon
Trish Partner
Marjet and Ben Patterson
Mike Sampson
Paul Seed
Chris and Eileen Sing
Alan Stacey
Becky Staines
Pat and Nigel Stark
Emlyn and Margaret Williams

44   Who was Thomas Fowler?

Thomas Fowler was an inventor of a calculating machine which was a forerunner to today's computers and the Information Technology centre at Castle Hill was named after him.

He was born in Torrington in 1777, son of a cooper, and at 13 was apprenticed to a fellmonger (dealer in hides and skins, especially sheep, who removes the wool or hair from the hides in preparation for tanning). In his spare time he began to study mathematics. He was entirely self-taught as money was short and he had no opportunity to study at university.

He built himself a printing press from a plan of his own invention and set up as a printer and book seller. He did well in this business and subsequently became a clerk and then a partner and finally manager of the only bank in town which was where the NatWest is now. He was also organist at the parish church.

In 1828 he patented a device known as a thermosiphon which was the basis of the modern system of central heating using radiators. However, patent laws were very weak in those days and his invention was pirated and, as he couldn't afford legal proceedings, he received no royalties or recognition for his invention.

His talents were recognised by some prominent people in and around Torrington (including Lord Clinton) who did everything they could to encourage him in his work and bring his inventions to public notice.

In 1838 he published his 'Tables for Facilitating Arithmetical Calculations' and in 1840, when he was 63, he constructed his first calculating machine. He himself considered this to be his greatest achievement. It was made of wood and measured 5ft high, 4ft wide and 4ft long (1.5m x 1.2m x 1.2m) and was capable of working out complex multiplications and divisions. He had been advised to make his machine out of metal but couldn't afford to do so. He took his machine to King's College at London University where many leading scientists were impressed with its efficiency and it was exhibited for some time in the college museum.

Although this calculating machine was a direct forerunner of the pocket calculators and home computers we have today, the only result of this experiment for Thomas Fowler was loss of money and health and final disappointment. Like many inventions, his calculating machine was used by others to their own advantage but he wasn't able to make any money out of it.

While his machine was at King's College, Thomas Fowler died in 1843 and the machine was taken apart and sent back to his son, Hugh, in pieces. Hugh admitted that he didn't know how to put it back together again despite having some written instructions dictated by his father on his death bed.

Thomas Fowler is remembered in a stained glass window in the south transept of the parish church installed in his memory by the townspeople and others who recognised his talents.

His name also lived on in the Thomas Fowler IT Centre at Castle Hill. As part of the Genesis project – a multi-million pound scheme to bring about the economic regeneration of Torrington – the former Castle Hill Hotel was converted into a modern day communications centre including library, Tourist Information Centre, authentic Civil War museum, and a computer centre offering training and services for businesses and individuals. This new telematics centre was named after Thomas Fowler as a tribute to this son of Torrington and his previously unheralded work. (It subsequently became the Pathfinder Thomas Fowler Centre which has recently merged with the Westward Ho! IT centre and is now in Mill Street, Bideford).

45   Where is Windy Cross?

The place known as Windy Cross is not a crossroads but a four-armed cross which sits on top of a stone structure that used to be a pump house and, before that, an ancient well.

It is situated at the top of Mill Street where it joins South Street and Halsdon Terrace, on the corner between the Methodist chapel and a bungalow called Windy Ridge. It is now rather overgrown by ivy and berberis and hidden by trees and shrubs so it is easy to pass by without noticing it or seeing the cross high above. It has an old road sign pointing to Bideford attached to it as well as a sign marking a water hydrant.

The name Windy Cross is appropriate as, according to George Doe in 'Old Torrington Landmarks', it marks the highest point in the town. The 19th century pump house which, presumably, was built over the original well was mostly of local stone but in the south porch the entrance step was a large slab of Purbeck marble.

The shaft and circular base of the cross are believed to be ancient but have been re-cut. The large stone disc which supported the shaft would have formed a suitable coping stone over an ancient well.

In his poem 'Marmion' Walter Scott writes about a well marked by a cross:

> 'Where shall she turn! - behold her mark
> A little fountain cell,
> Where water, clear as diamond spark,
> In a stone basin fell.
> Above, some half-worn letters say,
> Drink.weary.pilgrim.drink.and.pray.
> For.the.kind.soul.of.Sybil.Grey.
> Who.built.this.cross.and.well.'

Windy Cross

Photo courtesy of
Dr Ann Allen

By the 1930s there was no longer any use made of the pump or the old well.

'It is indeed sad to think how this ancient land-mark has been desecrated and mutilated out of almost all knowledge and a portion of it even cast away and lost, probably for ever',

wrote George Doe, local historian who was Mayor of Torrington in 1923 and 1924. Until its restoration in the 1930s, the original base and shaft of the cross used to lie on the hedge of an old field which had been built on. The restoration of the cross consisted of re-cutting the whole of the original circular base and shaft and surmounting them with four arms and the upper portion of a new cross.

I don't know when the old pump house was blocked up but a local man can remember climbing inside to shelter from the rain many years ago.

This old local landmark was given a Grade II listing in 1973 and reminds us of former times before we all had the luxury of running water in our homes.

With thanks to:
Roy Drew

46   What is the Care Forum?

The Care Forum is a networking forum for those working in health, welfare, caring and religious areas in Torrington and 23 surrounding parishes. Group membership has been between 30 and 40 over the years and earlier this year (2011) the Forum celebrated its 25th birthday.

Keith Hughes, who was the Devon County Council's Community Education Tutor at the Eric Palmer Community Centre responsible for Youth, Adult and Community development, perceived a need to develop greater communications within the town and its neighbouring parishes, especially in the area of local care groups and organisations. His views were shared by the Rev. John Bradley who helped Keith set up the Forum in February 1986 when 15 people took part in its first meeting.

The proposal was to bring together representatives from any caring, welfare, educative, religious, health, social group or organisation, either from within the town and district or serving the town but based elsewhere. The representatives might be full or part-time professionals, full or part-time voluntary workers. They would meet over lunch where one-to-one contacts and introductions could be made. There followed an hour's informal yet structured meeting, with members sitting in a circle – no hierarchy here! The idea was that members should come either with specific needs or ideas they wished to share with others or to listen and learn of other agencies' work or issues.

At first, they met at the Eric Palmer Centre but now they meet at the Bluecoat Early Years Centre with a snack lunch provided. Apart from paying a small membership subscription each year, the general monthly meetings manage themselves without the need for a committee. Members come, representing their group, organisation or area of work, and both give and receive information. Ideas are floated, areas of general concern to all in the community are voiced, as well as individual requests for help, advice, or suggestions to run a project jointly, and are all thrown into the general and open discussion. Time is allowed after the meeting for one-to-one contacts and for follow-up points raised earlier in the meeting. The Forum can also act as a pressure group.

Since the Forum began it has played a part in establishing a variety of projects, for example, setting up *The Crier*, the Torrington newsletter, and getting a zebra crossing which had been campaigned for by young mothers in the town. It also helped to create the Community Development Trust which redeveloped the pannier market and established the Castle Hill Centre with library, ITC, council offices and Torrington 1646.

Keith Hughes is still a member of the Forum which continues to meet and function much as it did a quarter of a century ago. It has met the needs of community care workers and proved invaluable for them in making personal contacts and affecting outcomes in their respective groups or areas of work. Keith says members are extremely enthusiastic about networking and the transfer of information and feels sure the Forum will be around for another 25 years and beyond. He says thanks are due to all those Forum members who have worked for and with the Forum over the past 25 years and made it such a great success and asset to the town's community.

The Forum meets on the second Wednesday of every month at the Bluecoat Children's Centre.

With thanks to:
Keith Hughes

47   Are there any old Toll-Houses left around Torrington?

The Rothern Bridge Toll-house, Frithelstock is a very good example of a traditional angle-fronted toll-house which stands in the fork where a steep minor road goes uphill to Frithelstock off the main A386 to Bideford about a mile from Torrington just past Rothern Bridge. The tall two storey house has a projecting ground floor window overlooking the road and retains its porch on the south side, above either of which there was sufficient space for a toll-board. Occupied in 1871 by 'toll collector' John Tucker and his wife, it was sold off by the trust in 1880 to Mr T. Keaney. After some years of neglect it was bought in 2006 for £169,950 and has since been renovated.

Rosemoor Toll-house, St Giles in the Wood stood near the junction of the present-day A386 with the B3220 at the eastern end of the New or 'Town Mills' Bridge. Probably built around the time of the new road into the town here in 1835, it was used to catch travellers coming from the direction of Morchard Road and Exeter.Although the area is now well-known as 'Rosemoor', in 1871 it is recorded as the 'Row's Moor Toll-Gate' with 71 year old Chelsea Pensioner Joseph Hammon in residence.

Town Bridge Toll-house is an elegant Grade II listed square built classically inspired toll-house next to Taddiport Bridge over the River Torridge. Stone built with ashlar pilasters either side on the ground floor, it has a high parapet wall hiding the slate roof and has been extended to the rear. It was built by the Great Torrington Trust in around 1830 alongside the town's Canal Offices that in 1874 became the Torridge Vale Butter Factory. This company, by then known as Dairy Crest, closed down in 1993 and the house faces the dilapidated remains of the factory buildings. The toll-house controlled a section of the road from Hatherleigh to the south, coming in via Taddiport across the bridge and up the steep Mill Street before the main road was diverted from Little Torrington via New Bridge further upstream. The toll-house stands on the east side of the road at the foot of Limers Hill at the junction with 'Rolle Road', a now filled-in section of canal bed. Census returns of 1871 show 33 year old 'Farmer's labourer and toll-collector' Robert Mitchell living at the house with his wife and daughter nine years before the trust sold it to the Trustees of Lord Rolle. The house has been on the market a number of times in recent years, probably because it is liable to flooding if the river rises and breaks its banks.

A new bridge over the River Torridge was constructed in 1843 to carry the new main road into the town from Okehampton and Hatherleigh and New Bridge Toll-house was built on the west side of the bridge near to the old Town Mills. In 1871 the 'turnpike gate toll-collector' is recorded as 44 year old Sarah Hammet in residence with her four children.

An unusual two storey house which stands in Calf Street opposite East Street at the eastern end of Torrington where the roads from Barnstaple (B3232) and South

Taddiport toll-house

Photo by the author

Molton (B3227) enter the town was probably the Calf Street East Toll-house. It is in the right position for a toll-house and possesses a blanked out window suitable for a toll-board on its tall projecting front gable. In 1841 the 'Toll-gate keeper' is recorded as 55 year old John Hill. Still recorded as the 'Calf Street Toll Bar' in the Census of 1871 it was then occupied by 53 year old Rebecca Copp and her family.

The all-important build of the new road into Torrington from the direction of Okehampton was completed about 1843. Along with the toll-houses at New Bridge and Castle Garden Lane, this necessitated the construction of another turnpike gate at the west end of Calf Street, which probably also had a toll-house.

Travellers entering Torrington from the direction of South Molton sometimes attempted to evade tolls in Calf Street by passing into Watery Lane. After the construction of New Road into the town a toll-bar operated at the western end of the lane at its junction with New Road, near the present day Dick Hills Lane just below Well Street. Although retaining the name of 'Castle Garden Lane Toll Bar' in 1871, the house was occupied at that time by 71 year old 'Master Shoemaker' Richard Hill and his family and may by then have stopped being used by the trust for collecting tolls on this road.

Calf Street East toll-house   Photo by the author

A Torrington toll-house is recorded in the 1861 census returns at 'Clogs Hill' in the village of Alverdiscott. 55 year old 'Toll collector and agricultural labourer' Robert Baker was then living at the house with his wife Sarah and their three children. The toll-house was on the road from Torrington to Barnstaple, the present day B3232, about two miles to the north of the Huntshaw Cross Turnpike Gate. Recorded in Great Torrington Turnpike Trust records as the 'Bartridges', it was probably built at the junction of a minor road leading westward into Bideford.

The Great Torrington Trust made use of eight toll-houses around the town. One was built at the junction of the road into the town from Weare Giffard at a point where School Lane joins New Street. The toll-house is long since demolished, no doubt a victim of road widening, but was occupied in 1871 by 'Glover and Toll-collector' Fanny Piper and her two children.

Another Torrington toll-house was built at Huntshaw Cross in the parish of Yarnscombe, on the Barnstaple road. In 1871 'Blacksmith and toll-collector' George Priscott was living at the house with his wife and grandson and two boarders, Eliza Matthews and her son William. The toll-house was sold by the trust in 1880 to the Trustees of Lord Rolle.

In 1880 toll gates throughout North Devon were sold off as the old toll road system had come to an end.

With thanks to:
Tim Jenkinson and Patrick Taylor from whose book 'The Toll-houses of North Devon' this section is taken.

For many years the museum was housed in the Town Hall building but since 2007 it has been looking for a new home.

The museum is run entirely by volunteers 'who would like to share with you their interest in our past' and used to open between May Fair and the end of September with free admission. Displays included archeological finds, documents, costumes, portraits of some of the town's benefactors, the old stocks once used as punishment for miscreants, the doors of the old 'lock-up' which was behind the Town Hall and reminders of the town's industrial past. In 1994 the town free guide announced, 'Latest acquisition: a fine collection of old postcards.' These included pictures of people at work in the glove factories, the dairy, Castle House nursing home and the Castle Hill Hotel. In addition, there were regular changes of exhibit and the hosting of touring exhibitions. In 2004 there was a selection of 'Home Front' memorabilia on display for people to see just what it was like during World War II in a small Devon town. A small archive run by the museum's honorary 'archivist' has helped people for many years in seeking their ancestors.

Since having to leave the Town Hall in 2007, the museum has been seeking new premises in the town. There is no shortage of empty buildings but the problem is always a lack of the necessary funding. At first there were hopes of a new build next to 28 South Street on land only to be built on by organisations with charitable status but that came to nothing. Then Palmer House in New Street was on the market and would have been suitable but funding was not available.

In 2009 Great Torrington Heritage Museum and Archive was given the opportunity to bid for the old glove factory. Members of the Museum Executive Committee inspected the premises and were enthusiastic about the possibilities of the building as a museum. The three floors would allow for bigger and more comprehensive displays than the Town Hall but could also fulfil the plans to have a fully-equipped education room and a lecture/conference room with the possibility of hiring out for local functions. The first floor is an impressive area which could be divided up to make artists' studios or let as office space. The second floor, which resembles the interior of a tithe barn, would be for specialist exhibitions and would house the busy Archive department. One of the most enthusiastic suggestions came from local people who said they would like to see a 'cottage-style' glove making industry re-started in the old factory as one of the major exhibits in the town's new Heritage Museum. However, despite the attraction of such a plan, sufficient funding was not available to make it a reality.

Then a plan was put forward to use part of the old Board School building which stands empty in Whites Lane with starter homes built on another part of the site. In an article in the *North Devon Journal* of 1st December 2011 entitled 'New hope for homeless museum', Chairman of the Museum Trustees, Val Morris, wanted to stress to the public that the museum would be making a full comeback.

> 'The museum is still alive and kicking, albeit packed up and in storage. It will definitely re-open but councils take time to make decisions and in the current economic climate they have to make the right decision for the community.'

Planning permission for this project was refused.

In *The Crier* of February 2012, Val Morris writes,

'Great Torrington Heritage Museum and Archive is alive, but still homeless. We are hoping to have good news to pass on in the Spring. Work is going on behind the scenes and we have secured some marvellous agricultural implements. We are continuing the sorting of artefacts and archive material, all of which will be of great benefit when we do open.'

We hope the museum will find a new home soon (April 2012).

49   How long has Torrington had a Silver Band?

Torrington Silver Band has been in existence for 60 years and, according to their website, 'whether we're taking part in national competitions, playing in local carnivals or holding concerts, our combination of fun, enthusiasm and hard work shine through for all to enjoy.'

The band welcomes experienced players but equally welcome are those who want to come and learn. They have a thriving junior section made up of both children and adults and, when a player is good enough, he or she can graduate as a fully-fledged member of the senior band.

There are at present a number of new 'trainee' members who have been taught by Nick Megson and Sylvia Bradley. As well as learning to play an instrument, they have taken part in theory lessons using a fun workbook. They have enjoyed working their way through to a third theory book and have been awarded their certificates during recent band concerts. They also get the chance at these concerts to come together to play a few pieces of music as a beginners' band and have made good progress.

The website continues: 'If rhythm is more your thing, we have a thriving corps of drums, of which we are very proud. We are unique in the region for having such a drum section and they are always an attraction at concerts, carnivals and other events.' The corps of drums practise at Howe Concert Hall on Wednesday evenings from 7 – 8pm.

The band features at local annual events such as the May Fair ceremony and carnival and the Remembrance Day commemoration. The players put on concerts during the year and play for weddings and birthday celebrations and take part in civic parades, fêtes, competitions and festivals all over the South West. There have been some memorable trips to Roscoff with the twinning association and every other year the band welcomes the French visitors, entertaining them at various twinning events. In 2011 they played carols in the square for three Saturdays before Christmas and received donations from the public totalling over £500.

The band started back in 1952 when members of Fred Karno's Band and former members of the Town Band had a meeting at a café in the town and decided to form a band together and thus the Torrington Voluntary Silver Band was born. Permission was granted to use the instruments that had been put into trust at the start of the Second World War. This band continued to play under the direction of Len Short, who trained so many young people to play an instrument, and had many successes

Silver Band at Carnival   Photo courtesy of Bob Brewer

culminating in playing at the Royal Albert Hall in the National Finals. In 2002 the band came together to celebrate 50 years and recorded a CD 'In the Mood'.

The band purchased the former Howe Church building in Castle Street in February 1996 with funding through an Arts Council Grant for £91,000 and additional monies from various local donations and band funds. In total, the entire project to provide the Torrington Silver Band with its own permanent premises in which to practise and perform cost in the region of £120,000. After extensive renovations it was officially opened during May Fair in 1998. The hall can be hired for groups of up to 150 people and the kitchen can also be hired at an additional cost which is decided on by the committee at the time of the request.

Many generations of Torrington youngsters have taken the opportunity of learning to play a musical instrument (with free use of an instrument) which they may not have had the chance to do at home or at school. There are a number of local families who have found that playing in the band has been a happy activity that all members of the family have been able to enjoy.

The Metherells are one such family and they have been involved with Torrington Silver Band for over 30 years. They say that it is like belonging to an extended family. They first became involved when the boys, Russell and Brandon, followed the band on May Fair day while they were marching around the town. They were invited to attend practices by the band master, Terry Hutchings (who is still a vital member as musical director). Bill soon started to learn to play as well and a few years

Silver Band at May Fair c1953   Photo courtesy of Paul Hadley

later Daphne decided 'If you can't beat them, join them!' Over the years they have enjoyed many happy hours practising and performing and meeting people from other bands and they have been to Roscoff three times. A particular highlight was qualifying to play in the 4th section final at the Royal Albert Hall in 1984.

The band is a group of people of all ages who love playing music and they put a lot of hard work into learning and preparing for public performance. They are proud to represent Torrington wherever they go and feel they are lucky to receive so much support from the people of Torrington. Young members move away for university or work but if they return here to live they often come back to the band. Daphne says 'May Fair day is the highlight of the year when many ex-band members come back and join in the music-making and merriment.'

With thanks to:
Bill and Daphne Metherell

50   Are there any Care Homes for the elderly in Torrington?

Less than a century ago, the only institution that catered for the elderly and infirm who didn't have families to support them was the workhouse. Now there is a variety of provision for the elderly in the community.

Abbeyfield Glen Tor in Villa Road offers supported housing for older people with the opportunity to have a full life with independence, privacy, security and in safety. This housing service is intended for older people who no longer feel happy coping alone at home and who wish to remain as independent as possible. The cost of a room (2012) ranges from £210 per week including full meals each day and all housing costs.

Abbeyfield is a national charity providing Supported Independent Housing for older people. There are over 700 houses across the UK. Volunteers manage the Societies and the houses and offer friendship and support to the residents. Paid staff provide all meals and support to residents and organise the day-to-day running of the house.

Glen Tor is a pleasant house with a lovely view over the Torridge valley. It has 10 flats built in 1986 and renovated in 2008. There are stairlifts, lounge, dining room, laundry, guest facilities and a garden. It is situated near Torrington town centre with easy access to shops, post office, bus stops, doctors and a social centre. There is resident management staff available seven days a week and a community alarm service. New residents are accepted from 55 years of age.

Castle House Nursing and Residential Home is in Castle Street and is a privately owned care home with nursing. It has 17 single rooms, eight shared rooms and two rooms with WC en suite. There are 33 residents. Charges for nursing care are currently £522-£600 a week. Castle House offers respite care, convalescent care, the residents' own GP, if required, and own furniture, if desired. Pets can be accepted by arrangement. There is a lift, a stairlift, wheelchair access, a television point in each room and gardens for residents. Shops and local transport are only a short distance away.

Woodland Vale in New Street at the western end of town is a local authority owned residential care home with 23 residents. It is a modern building on the site of the old workhouse and Torridge View nursing home. Only patients referred by Social Services are admitted and the registered care categories include dementia, mental health excluding learning disability or dementia, old age and physical disability. The specialist care category of Alzheimer's is also catered for. There are 17 single rooms and three shared rooms and all rooms have WC en suite and a television point. Woodland Vale offers day care, respite care, patients' own furniture, if required, wheelchair access, ground floor accommodation only, gardens for residents and a minibus or other transport.

Hatchmoor Nursing Home up at the eastern end of town in Hatchmoor Common Lane is a new privately run, purpose-built residential nursing home which aims to offer '21st century care with traditional family values' providing a safe, warm and comfortable environment – 'a home from home.' Living accommodation is on two floors with bedrooms arranged in groups of eight on each floor. There are 32 bedrooms and each group of eight bedrooms has its own lounge and dining room with quiet areas where residents can eat, relax and spend time together. Kitchens are available for residents' supervised use on each floor for making tea, coffee and light snacks. Each floor has a bathroom with hoists where residents can take baths with or without assistance. Main meals are served in each dining room or in residents' rooms. The library on the ground floor provides a quiet refuge overlooking the sensory garden. The building has two lifts and the corridors are wide and spacious with handrails. All doors are wide enough to accommodate hospital beds and the safe and easy delivery of furniture.

All the bedrooms at Hatchmoor are spacious and enjoy views over the countryside or of the sensory garden, or both. They all have en suite 'wet' rooms with showers, WC and basin, as well as nurse call systems. The windows in all the bedrooms are low so that residents can see out and enjoy the view even when in bed or sitting in an armchair. The bedrooms have their own furniture although residents are welcome to bring some of their own favourite pieces. Each room contains a bed, bedside table, chest of drawers, wardrobe, dining table and chairs. Beds are fully adjustable with push button controls and air mattresses with memory foam. All the bedrooms have nurse call systems and high electrical sockets and facilities for residents to have their own telephone line and number. Wifi internet access is also available. Activities co-ordinators organise activities every day to keep residents busy ranging from card making and crafts to dancing and entertainment. The clinical room plays host to a variety of healthcare professionals who visit regularly, including chiropodist, optician, audiologist and dentist. Hatchmoor Nursing Home accepts residents over 65 years of age.

With thanks to:
Margaret Harland

51   What goes on at the Plough?

The Plough Arts Centre situated in Fore Street in the centre of Torrington is a great cultural asset to the town and to North Devon. It hosts live events, films, workshops and art exhibitions and there is a café in the foyer. The Plough is home to the Torrington Players, the Plough Youth Theatre, Ploughcappella singers, the First Thursday Writers' Group, and there is an annual poetry competition. The official staff are helped in the running of the arts centre by a team of volunteers and Plough supporters help to keep the venue afloat by their financial contributions and receive price concessions for events in return. The Plough celebrated 35 years as an arts centre in 2010.

Different areas of the Plough are available for hire by local groups or individuals – theatre, gallery, dance studio, meeting room, wet workshop – and refreshments and catering are available from the Plough Café.

It is thought that the original building where the Plough now stands may have been the town house of a wealthy merchant or, possibly, a building with some municipal purpose as a fine large iron fireback dated 1618 – now in the museum – bears the Royal Coat of Arms and the site has always belonged to the town. There was an elaborate strapwork plaster ceiling and wood panelling typical of the 1580-1620 period.

In around 1750 the building became the Plough Inn run by a William Waldon – 'a Maltster' – and his wife Judith who are both buried in the churchyard. There are

Plough Inn

Photo courtesy of
Dave Kelly

mentions of the inn over the years in the Council Minutes such as in 1855 when the Mayor, Silas Snell, invited the Town Council to a grand dinner at the Globe Inn. Meanwhile, the beadles and constables dined at the Plough. Evidently, the neighbouring inns catered for a different class of clientele. A photo from the Beaford Archive shows the regulars of the Plough all in hats and flat caps with their lurchers, banjo and barrel of beer. Another entry in the Minutes of 1875 mentions:

> 'complaints having been made of the bad state of the closets and dung pit behind the Plough premises adjoining Potacre Street. Resolved: that notice be given for the daily removal of the contents and the prevention of any nuisance therefrom.'

It remained as a public house until 1910 by which time the building was evidently in a shocking state of repair. The chairman of the Town Lands charity, the Rev. Emlyn Jones, reported that 'the Leasing and Repairing Committee had visited this property but owing to its condition, they could not see their way to let the same.' The final indignity was a letter from Mr Parnell of the Globe, dated July 1911:

'Sirs – If you can allow me to put a cow in the Plough premises for a week, I will undertake all risks. . .'

It was resolved that permission be granted.

In 1912 the Plough inn, with its many stables and outhouses, was demolished and a drill hall for the use of the Territorials and Yeomanry was built on the site and completed in 1914. The fine oak panelling was installed in the Council Chambers of the Town Hall. By August war had been declared and the hall became the base for the departure of the Yeomanry. 'The townspeople of Torrington assembled in large numbers on Thursday to give the "D" squadron of the R.N.D. Hussars (some 150 strong) a fitting send off'.[1]

The drill hall was built as a base for the Devonshire Regiment of the North Devon Yeomanry and was uncompromisingly military and Spartan. It had a lobby, a 30 yard shooting range down the right hand side, storage for a large 25 pound field gun and lots of space besides. Its purpose was to train men and women who drilled with the army there. However, a music and dancing licence had been granted in July 1914 and, when not performing its military function, the drill hall was a venue for a variety of social activities such as badminton, concerts, jumble sales, coffee mornings, children's fancy dress parties and dances, especially during the Second World War when the Americans were based nearby.

The Territorial Army gave up the lease in 1968 but the drill hall continued to be used for Cavalier Bonfire dances, Christmas parties, hunt balls and the May Ball where some well-known musicians of the time appeared, such as Nat Temple and his band from London and The Fourmost from Liverpool. The hall was painted dark green and was rather drab so the Cavaliers brightened the place up with a series of murals reflecting the theme of an event. One year they painted shields with rather tongue-in-cheek coats of arms depicting local dignitaries and tradespeople. Monthly auctions were held there as well as other events including a wrestling match modelled on the somewhat stage-managed wrestling shown on Saturday afternoons on ITV at the time.

John Lane from Beaford was one of a small band of movers and shakers who helped establish the Plough Arts Centre. He set up Beaford Arts in August 1966 and later heard that a group of people in Torrington had a vision of creating a community theatre. The late Clifford Quick, former Mayor and Town Councillor, was one of the leading spirits among this group who wanted to convert the drill hall into a theatre. John Lane linked with the working group which eventually became Torridge Arts Recreation Association, of which he became chairman, and they bought the lease of the building from the Town Council in 1974. Work on the building took about six months and the centre was opened on 11th April 1975 by Col. J. E. Palmer who was thanked by the Mayor, R. H. Cotton. This was followed by a concert featuring the famous actress Edith Evans – 'not so much an actress as a presence'[2] – who performed a number of poems and amusing pieces, and the North Devon Music Centre Quartet, a group of the area's most promising young musicians who played Mozart's 'Quartet in G Major'. According to the late Joan Long, Edith Evans was very nervous about the projecting stage and the acoustics of 'acting in the round' and said, 'You will have to do something about it; how can I be expected to face three ways at once?' There followed a month long festival of amateur and professional events culminating in May Fair. People turned up in droves to see George Melly and the Footwarmers and the first film night was so successful that a queue of 200 had formed by opening time and two consecutive showings were put on: the film was 'King Kong'. One of the highlights of the 1970s was when the Royal Shakespeare Company came in 1978 and played to packed houses for three nights.

Not everyone in Torrington was supportive of the idea of an arts centre at first and there was some resentment when the drill hall was taken over by 'luvvies'. There were people in the close-knit community with its entrenched traditions and insular attitudes who felt the whole project was alien and unnecessary and would cost money which would be better used for other more essential causes. However, as time passes and outlooks are broadened by easier travel, the media and the internet, suspicions have lessened and local people have realised that the Plough provides a variety of events to appeal to a wide range of tastes and is a hub of local activity.

Richard Wolfenden-Brown joined the Plough in December 1999 as Arts Development Officer and Programmer and became Director in April 2002. A Council of Management runs the centre and looks after finances, artistic policies, marketing and the employees. The twelve-strong board is made up of people who are members of the Plough Supporters' scheme. People can be nominated for election either by fellow supporters or themselves. Following a ballot, ten members are voted on and another two are co-opted and brought on to the board at any time. It meets quarterly to discuss any issues surrounding the arts centre and each person has a specific section to look after, such as marketing or the volunteers.

Like most arts venues, the Plough has had to fight for its existence over the years and suffered funding reduction and cuts. In 1991 it was threatened with closure but was saved by a merger with the Beaford Centre which lasted until 2002. During this time the Plough benefited from substantial public and private grants and loans for major refurbishment and alterations to the building which modernised and greatly enhanced the facilities. Following a further period of uncertainty and a threat of closure, in 2002 the Plough was re-established as a new independent company and charity. The strength of feeling locally plus the huge support and financial commitment from the local community was instrumental in making sure the Plough survived.

Since 2002 the organic growth of the Plough has been strong under the leadership of the new Council of Management, Director, loyal members of staff, volunteers and audiences. Public funding has been replaced by new lines of income generated from business supporters, fundraising events, individual donations, legacies, gift aid and successful funding bids for arts projects. In 2009 over 65,000 people entered the Plough for all purposes. Turnover, including catering, increased from £85,000 in 2001/2 to £460,000 in 2008/9.

In 2011 the Plough was the winner of the NatWest Community Force Challenge the North Devon area, beating off stiff competition from other charitable organisations across the region. A cheque for £6,275 is on its way and will help to keep the Plough up and running throughout 2012. Director Richard Wolfenden-Brown said:

'It was a fantastic team effort and involved hundreds of people who were keen to demonstrate how much they value the Plough by kindly giving us their vote. Hats off to NatWest for making this significant contribution to local charities and communities across the country. We hope the other banks all follow suit!'

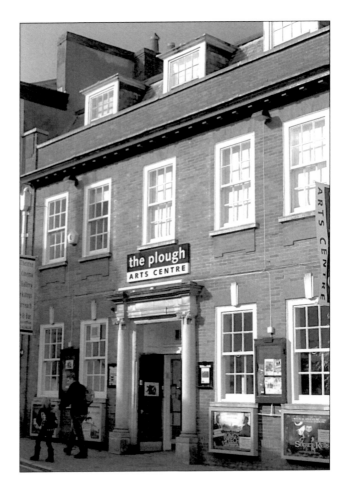

Plough Arts Centre

Photo courtesy of
the Plough

The money will be used to offer some free taster sessions. The venue's thriving out-reach programme will also be expanded.[3]

The North Devon Community Mural in the auditorium was painted by Ken Sprague who lived and worked in North Devon between 1971 and 2004. It is intend-ed as a celebration of the local people, their history and culture.[4]

The Torrington Players dramatic society was founded in 1980 by a small group of enthusiasts in Torrington and currently stages two productions a year. New mem-bers, with or without previous experience, are always warmly welcomed. A list of their productions from 1980 – 2011 can be found at www.torringtonplayers.com.

The annual Plough Prize for Poetry which started in 2003 helps to support and encourage poets as well as raise funds for the Plough. Judges of the competition have included Helena Nelson, Alison Brackenbury, Ian McMillan, U. A. Fanthorpe and Andrew Motion who was judge in 2007 while he was Poet Laureate. As well as awarding the prizes, he read from his own work and took questions from the audi-ence. (He appeared again in March 2012). The Plough receives entries from over 2,000 aspiring poets from around the world and the standard of the poetry is high. Hearing the winners read their poems and the comments of the judge makes for an inspiring and enjoyable evening.

Since opening in 1975 thousands of performers, artists, workshop leaders, speakers and teachers have shared their work at the Plough. Caroline de Groot who has worked there for many years remembers when she was living away from Torrington in the 1970s receiving a letter from her mother telling her that the Russian poet Yevgeny Yevtushenko was appearing at the newly-opened Plough. Caroline was amazed that such a famous person was coming to the small backwater, as she regarded it, where she had grown up. The Plough has been instrumental in opening up the cultural life of Torrington and providing its inhabitants with a wider view of the world. Mind you, there are still some local people who have never crossed its threshold!

With thanks to:
Caroline de Groot
Pippa Jenkins
Margaret Jewell
Richard Wolfenden Brown

52   What is the long cobble-covered hump in the churchyard?

Sometimes referred to as the 'Giant's Grave', it is believed that this hump is the final resting place of Royalist prisoners who were killed when parts of the church blew up in February 1646 during the Civil War.

During the Battle of Torrington, after the defeat of the Royalist forces by Sir Thomas Fairfax and his army, the triumphant Parliamentarians used the tower of the parish church, with its thick impregnable walls, as a prison. The Royalists had already used the tower as an arsenal and had stored 80 barrels of gunpowder there. This was not sacrilege. Arms and armour for local defence were often stored in church towers which acted as strongholds.

In 1996 there was a series of events in and around the town arranged by an organisation of local people calling themselves 'Fire and Steel 350' to commemorate what happened in Torrington in 1646. On Saturday 17th February a group of Devon Dowsers gathered around the mysterious cobble-covered hump in the churchyard. Their aim was to find out once and for all whether this was the burial place of the Royalist prisoners killed in the church explosion.

'They believe there are 67 bodies buried there,' said Fire and Steel chairman, Roy Foster. 'Who am I to dispute that?'[1]

The Parish Register records the burial of 63 soldiers so this discovery indicated there were four more bodies buried than had been recorded and that they were lying in a pit some seven feet deep. One of the dowsers later persuaded a friend who is a clairvoyant privately to examine the mound. Intriguingly, she told him that there were in fact 68 bodies buried there, 63 that were a few hundred years old and five very old ones, probably Neolithic, that had been buried in a barrow.[2]

A wreath is laid on this mass grave each year during the events that commemorate the Battle of Torrington.[3]

'Giant's Grave'   Photo by the author

53   When was the Torrington Canal in operation and where was it?

The Torrington Canal, also known as the Rolle Canal, was in use between 1827 and
1871 when it was replaced by the railway which was built over sections of the same
route. It was seven miles long from Sea Lock to Torrington and canal workers would
have made up to two return trips a day as well as helping to load and unload cargo,
caring for the horse and carrying out various other maintenance tasks.

The idea of a canal as a means to bring heavy goods such as lime, coal, clay, sand
and timber inland from the port of Bideford was first suggested in 1793 by Dennys
Rolle, Lord of the Manor, but it was not until 1823 that his son, John Lord Rolle, set
about having one built. He commissioned civil engineer, James Green, to survey the
land and he designed a canal similar to the one at Bude that he had recently constructed using inclined planes instead of locks and along which square tub boats
would be hauled by horses.

The canal was dug by 200 – 300 men using picks and shovels and barrows. It was
13ft (4m) wide and had a depth of 3ft 6ins (1.1m) of water. Every so often there were
wider passing places and assembly basins. The towpath was always on the outer
bank of a hillside. The canal bed was lined with a thick layer of 'puddled' clay to
keep it water-tight and the banks were strengthened with stones from local quarries.

Thomas Allom's 1830 engraving of Beam aqueduct
Photo courtesy of Linda Downing and Tilly Kimber

The access afforded by this means of transport had an important effect upon Torrington. As Sue Scrutton says in the Introduction to her book, 'Lord Rolle's Canal':

'From being an isolated market town, reached only by a circuitous route on narrow unmade-up lanes, Great Torrington simultaneously gained a canal and turnpike roads, making it possible not only to travel further but also enabling the transport of goods with much greater ease. Torrington was on the map.'[1]

The canal started with a tidal lock on a bend of the Torridge in the small parish of Landcross and ran in pretty much a straight line to Annery Kilns, across the river from Weare Giffard, where there were three large lime kilns and a shipyard nearby where the tub boats for the canal were most likely built. These boats were of the same design as those on the Bude canal, made of oak, elm and pine and fitted with four cast iron wheels to enable the boats to run in the rails set into the inclined plane at Ridd. They were square-ended, except for the leading boat, and were 20ft (6.1m) long, 5ft 6ins (1.7m) wide and 2ft 9ins (0.8m) deep. They were chained together in strings of up to six and

'looked like a row of open-topped boxes[2] drawn by a single horse led by a boy and with one man, armed with a pole, who normally stood in the second boat ready to fend off from the banks.'[3]

Curved accommodation bridge and canal bed   Photo by the author

From Annery Kilns the canal curved in a gentle arc to a wide basin at the foot of the inclined plane at Ridd where the boats were hauled up singly some 40ft by means of a continuous chain worked by a massive wooden wheel. Once they reached the upper basin, the boats continued along the canal which ran along the western bank of the Torridge on a ledge cut into the steep hillside about 50ft above the river. (The railway was built over this section in 1871 and it is now the Tarka Trail walking and cycle track). The canal followed the Torrington to Bideford toll road, which was built at much the same time, and then turned sharp left over an aqueduct which is now the entrance drive to Beam House. It was built from stone taken from a quarry just 50 yards from the western end of the aqueduct where there is now a lay-by on the main road. 'It is possible that the canal was contained by an elm-wood or cast-iron trough set into a thick layer of clay between the dressed stone towpaths of the aqueduct.'[4]

'The original carriageway to Beam House had linked up with the old pack-horse road from Torrington to Weare Giffard on the eastern side of the Torridge. The canal cutting sliced through this carriageway, providing Green with the opportunity to construct one of his elegantly curved accommodation bridges over the canal. This bridge has recently been restored (by Lord Clinton) together with a short section of the canal and towpath. The canal channel is still dry, and provides an excellent illustration of how narrow and shallow the canal was. It also demonstrates the economical construction of tub boat canals in comparison to the larger and better-known canals found in other parts of the country.'[5]

Canal and swing bridges

Photo courtesy of Margaret Trounson, Roy Beer and Dave Kelly

The next section of the canal curved for about 500 yards around the steep slope of Furzebeam Hill high above the River Torridge where settlement and subsidence of the embankment walls caused regular problems. It then crossed open fields to Staple Vale at the foot of Torrington commons, under the road leading to Rothern Bridge and alongside the river to the bottom of Mill Street by the bridge at Taddiport.

The canal basin at Taddiport was the main centre for the canal and its various enterprises. The company offices where the Clerk of Works managed operations were located there as well as numerous warehouses, sheds, a barge repair yard, a foundry and a sawmill. The whole wharf area was a hive of activity. The Taddiport/Town Bridge was nearby on what was then the main road to Okehampton and Plymouth and, in the other direction, the steep Mill Street led up into the centre of Torrington. The old corn mills, after which the street was named, had burnt down in the early 1820s and were then demolished by Lord Rolle during the building of the canal basin.

It was originally intended that the canal should only extend as far as Taddiport but lobbying from farmers further inland persuaded Lord Rolle to extend the canal under Castle Hill alongside the Torridge to the New Town Mills (now Orford Mill holiday apartments) at Woodland Ford. There was some controversy about constructing the canal on common land without permission which led to the Torrington Commons Act of 1835 under which Lord Rolle was obliged to pay compensation to the commoners. The canal cut through several footpaths between the commons and the river bank and wooden swing bridges were installed over the canal in a couple of places to restore these rights of way. The section of the canal between the railway

New Town Mills c1865   Photo courtesy North Devon Maritime Trust

station and Town Mills was made into a road in 1875 after the canal closed and a toll-house was built by Taddiport Bridge but the 'puddling' wasn't removed properly and, even now, Rolle Road, a pleasant commons path along by the river, still becomes waterlogged.

The New Town Mills had their own wharf on a large canal basin which also served as a mill pond for the water-powered corn mill and saw mill. The mills were built in 1826 in a flamboyant, rather military style with gables, mock towers topped by battlements and with false arrow slits. Beyond the mill basin the leat was extended and widened to take the canal a further 200 yards to the site of five new lime kilns completed in July 1827 at Rowe's Moor. These were the largest group of kilns in North Devon and are situated in the RHS garden of Rosemoor.

Eventually, the canal extended beyond Rosemoor through Darkham Wood to the weir on the Torridge. The weir was rebuilt in 1837 and this ensured a reliable flow of water in the canal at all seasons. A stone quay was constructed at the end of the canal next to the weir which was known as Healand Docks.

Sue Scrutton says,

'. . . the prime purpose of building the canal was to make the inland farms more productive, thereby making them worth a higher rent.'[6]

Certainly, it enabled easier transportation of lime and coal inland and agricultural produce, bricks, clay, pipes and oak bark out to the port at Bideford. Ball clay from Peters Marland, which was an important raw material for the 19th century ceramics industry, had at first been transported to the riverside quays at Weare Giffard by

Healand Docks and weir   Photo by the author

pack-horse trains and from there taken down the river by barge to Bideford. The construction of the canal meant a shorter journey from the clay pits to Taddiport wharf from where it was shipped in tub boats.

In 1842 Lord Rolle financed the construction of a new bridge over the Torridge at New Town Mills (with an arch to accommodate the canal) connected to a new road which joined the old Okehampton road at Little Torrington. This route avoided the steep narrow lanes down to Taddiport and enabled wagons to carry clay directly to New Town Mills wharves without the need for pack-horses.

In 1835 Lord Rolle decided to lease the canal to a group of businessmen with a total of 14 shares: six to George Braginton, six to William Tardrew – both local men – and one each to two Arthur brothers who were businessmen from South Wales (who sold their shares to Braginton in 1839).They appear to have made good profits up until 1846 but after that the relationship between Braginton and Tardrew seems to have become more difficult as profits declined and maintenance costs increased. Tardrew died in 1853 which led to a complex court case between his widow and Braginton in which she lost a lot of money. Braginton, who was manager of the Agricultural and Commercial Bank in Torrington, took on two new partners but in the mid-1860s his bank failed and he was made bankrupt. The canal company reverted back to the Hon. Mark Rolle (heir of Lord Rolle who had died in 1842) whose agents managed it until it closed in 1871.

Mark Rolle was enthusiastic about the railway and could see its advantages over a canal (which was becoming ever more expensive to maintain) and was happy to sell. A railway could transport people as well as goods and having a modern railway terminus at Torrington would further enhance the value of his properties in the district by linking them to the rapidly growing towns and opening up more profitable markets for the produce of his estates. The Bideford to Torrington railway line was opened on 18th July 1872.

With thanks to the following two authors on whose books I have based this section:

Barry D. Hughes – 'Rolle Canal and The North Devon Limestone Trade'
Susan Scrutton – 'Lord Rolle's Canal'

54 How long has the building in South Street that looks like a church been a Social Club?

Torridge Vale Social Club celebrated its 60th anniversary on 13th June 2009. An open day was held from noon until late and over 200 former dairy workers came along to look at a display of old photographs and to reminisce over a pint with former colleagues. Evening entertainment was provided by the band 'Morpheous'.

Once a chapel, the building was bought by the dairy down at Taddiport for its workers and was known as the Unigate and Torridge Vale Dairy social club. After the dairy closed, the building remained as a social club used for various functions.

The building originally had a smokers' room but no bar or function room. Jim Thacker, who worked at the dairy from 1957 until its closure in 1993 and is still on the committee which runs the social club, said, 'In the 1960s a licence to run a bar was applied for but, because it was a former chapel, the licence was difficult to get – we had to go to court a few times.' Eventually, the club got its licence and a bar and skittle alley were put into the building.

In the early 1970s a lounge bar was built and, as with the skittle alley, the work was done mainly by volunteers.

When the dairy closed, Jim Thacker, together with other local men Graham Martin, Chris Stacey and Roy Lee, bought the club for the members.

People who were not former dairy employees were invited to join the club, a function room was built and the club has continued to grow.

In 2009 the club had over 1,100 members and a turnover of £100,000. Jim Thacker said, 'It is a vital part of the town and we are very proud of what we have done to turn it into a thriving club that serves the community.' Profits made go back into the club and decisions are made democratically.

55 How long has the Library been at Castle Hill?

A small branch of the County Library was established in Torrington in 1928 when some 200 books were placed in the Board School, in Whites Lane. The teachers took turns to act as librarian and books were issued mainly to children although some were issued to the general public.

When new schools were built in Torrington the County Library Committee worked together with the Town Council and it was decided to offer the market hall in the square for use as a library and this opened in 1936. It was reached by means of a winding staircase on the right under the archway leading into the pannier market. The library had 2,500 volumes comprising reference, non-fiction, fiction and juvenile sections, 'the books being in the custody of Miss W. M. Moseley, the capable and

Torridge Vale
Social Club

Photo by the author

courteous librarian, with Miss Enid Hookway as assistant.'[1] The library is remembered as being at that time 'a slightly fusty, dusty room but full of wonderful books.'

Dulcie Leate remembers working in the library part-time during the war as a young woman. The windows were blacked out, there was no telephone and after the library closed there would sometimes be the heavy footsteps of soldiers on the stairs, 'Tramp, tramp, tramp, coming up and trying the door. I used to be petrified!' The light was dim as she went downstairs on her way home and, although she could hear the voices of American soldiers down in the pannier market, she couldn't see anyone in the darkness. She used to beg Miss Burrow, who was in charge at the library in those days, to come downstairs with her but she would always refuse, saying, 'Oh no, dear, you go on out.' Miss Burrow was a large woman and Dulcie says, 'There was a bit of a job for the two of us to get in the little place behind the counter – we kept bumping into each other!'

The present library opened at Castle Hill in January 2000 as part of the Community Development Trust's refurbishment of the old hotel.

Libraries are at the hub of a community and offer a wide variety of services. As well as books – 'best sellers, classics, all-time favourites, travel guides, reference, specialist, the latest must-reads, books with larger print'[2] – libraries now provide computers and help with using them, music and films on CDs and DVDs, audio books, loans from other libraries, author visits and book launches and reading groups. There is a section for teenagers and children and a variety of activities in which they can take part. The mobile library takes books out into country areas.

Torrington library is well used and the staff are friendly and helpful. Sadly, in the present time of government funding cuts to local authorities (2011), it has lost seven and a half hours of opening time and staff have suffered a reduction in their working hours. The library is now open Tuesday 10am-6pm, Thursday 10am-5pm, Friday 10am-1pm and Saturday 10am-1pm. The reading group has had to find a new place to meet on a Monday morning so returning and collecting books is now more complicated, especially for those members who have come in from the villages. Library Supervisor, Kate Greaves, no longer has the time to edit *The Crier*, the community newspaper. Fortunately, recognising its popularity and usefulness as a local forum and source of information, the Town Council has given an honorarium to help *The Crier* keep going and Kate's duties as editor have been taken over by Becky Huxtable, one of the other librarians.

With thanks to:
Kate Greaves
Dulcie Leate
Pat Wilks

56   What is the CDT?

The Great Torrington and District Community Development Trust (CDT) is a registered charity and company limited by guarantee, wholly owned and managed by local people.

The CDT's area of benefit is comprised of over 15,000 beneficiaries and represents one third of Torridge District including 26 parishes surrounding Torrington.

The CDT is not a political organisation and works together with many groups, including the private and public sectors, to ensure as many benefits as possible are delivered for local people.

The CDT exists to:
> create employment
> improve the local economy
> encourage environmental and community sustainability
> help individuals develop their skills and interests
> support local businesses.

The CDT Fundraising Initiative Team (FIT) also organises many events throughout the year including bingo, tabletop sales and open garden days.

1993 saw the closure of two key employers within Torrington which resulted in major job losses. Following these events, in 1995 the local community formed a Regeneration Forum and, together with local agencies and funders, commissioned a comprehensive study of local needs in the area. The principal recommendation of this study was to form a Community Development Trust and on 1st April 1996 the Great Torrington and District CDT was established to act as a catalyst for regeneration.

In November of the same year the CDT was successful in winning £1 million from the Rural Challenge competition sponsored by the Rural Developments Commission and, with a further £1,400,000 backing from other organisations, the CDT and its partners set up the Genesis Project to oversee the dramatic refurbishment of Castle Hill Hotel and the Victorian pannier market. The Genesis Project has now become Genesis (Great Torrington) Ltd and acts as the trading arm of the CDT charity.

Castle Hill was converted from a derelict hotel into a buzzing community building which became home to the Torrington Tourist Information Centre (TIC), the Thomas Fowler ICT Training Centre, the library, Town Council, Torridge District Council's local office, the Citizen's Advice Bureau, the Torridge Volunteer and Friends Bureau, the CDT and Genesis offices and the Torrington 1646 family visitor attraction.

The second refurbishment was the run-down Victorian pannier market. Torridge District Council contributed the majority of the capital costs of this project and it has been transformed into a thriving market with 12 trading units, a café, toilets and a market hall which is used on Thursdays, Fridays and Saturdays for a variety of stalls, monthly auctions and at Christmas time the 'Big Sing', amongst other activities. Like Castle Hill, the pannier market is now a centre of much activity for the town. The Genesis Project became a model of rural regeneration both locally and nationally, culminating in the official opening of Castle Hill by HRH Duke of Kent in 2000.

When the refurbishments were finished, the Genesis Project became Genesis (Great Torrington) Ltd, the trading arm of the Community Development Trust. The Torrington 1646 visitor attraction is owned by Genesis (Great Torrington) Ltd, is now almost entirely self-sustaining and in 2004 posted its first significant profit. The Thomas Fowler ICT Training Centre became part of a successful joint venture with the Pathfinder Trust which provides IT training in four other North Devon towns and has now merged with the Westward Ho! centre and moved to Mill Street, Bideford. Genesis (Great Torrington) Ltd is also responsible for the management of the Castle Hill building and the pannier market.

Robert Eades, original Vice Chairman of the CDT described its aims in the first annual report:

> 'The CDT was born out of a direct response to negative change, as an attempt to alter the balance away from being victimised by events and as a counter to the helplessness and apathy that negative change can produce. Because it is non-discriminatory (political, religious etc.) the CDT has the opportunity to be relatively free of ideology and act inclusively, for everyone, as a conductor of ideas and solutions, hopes and ambitions – to deal with change by working with the established mechanisms (central and local government, town and parish councils, government agencies, Europe and, vitally, the population). It is a way, hopefully utterly transparent, of absorbing and creating change in a consensual manner; of adding to what already exists, to have an input that allows a sense of contribution and participation that is available to all.'

He said the CDT should not wish nor attempt to replace existing democratic structures but rather to act as 'an additional conductor of people's aspirations and as a builder of bridges and of assisting existing mechanisms to be more effective.' He thought the organisation's success depended 'on being seen and trusted as a tool to be used by both people and authorities to take on the challenge of inevitable change and to construct positive responses. To be, in essence, creative.'

The CDT was keen to raise the profile of the Torrington area. In 1996 this was achieved very effectively by Fire & Steel 350 Ltd and the Torrington Cavaliers who organised a series of spectacular commemorative events based on the concluding battle of the Civil War. The Trust played a minor supporting role but subsequently co-ordinated the 351st anniversary commemoration and drew together a group to plan the Torrington Revels to be held in August 1997.

By teaming up with the Chamber of Commerce, encouragement to the business community flowed from a Trading Seminar, attended by 60 people, with publication of a local Business and Trade Directory and the organisation of a 'Build a Better Business' series of courses with the Open University. Also the Trust was represented at a variety of business meetings, including a satellite conference on the theme of sustainable tourism. Steps were taken to create a range of attractive information signs for Torrington commons and town centre. Also the Trust linked up with the Town Council, Commons Conservators and Torridge Ramblers to introduce a Parish Paths Partnership project.

Support was given to two well-established schemes, the Under Eights Project and Crocus 'n' Toads (a teenage drop-in centre) allowing both schemes to develop their work, offering longer opening hours. The CDT also co-operated with the Great Torrington and District Play Council to provide a computer for use during a range of sessions. The Monkleigh Parent and Toddler Group was helped to get on its feet with some essential equipment. Improved outdoor play opportunities were provided at Merton and the Blue Coat School (when it was at Whites Lane) which were much appreciated. Also, at the Blue Coat School, the Trust helped with the completion of a Mosaic Mural project.

Other projects have included:

-Transforming the Vicarage Garden from a plot of wasteland into a working community garden with the help of BBC's Charlie's Garden Army (with Charlie Dimmock) and a lot of local people.

-The Secret Memorial Garden to the rear of Castle Hill – the creation of a tranquil and beautiful green space for both the community and visitors.

-Torrington 1646 Outreach Education – visiting schools and bringing history to life using song, story-telling, role-play, displays and dialect.

Unfortunately, the contraction of public services due to government cuts in recent years has led to a fading of this regeneration. The library has had its hours cut and the Thomas Fowler IT Centre has moved elsewhere so the Castle Hill building is quite empty at times which has a knock-on effect on the 1646 café and the Tourist Information Centre. The trouble is that when services are withdrawn, they are rarely replaced.

With thanks to:
Kate Greaves

There are three schools in Torrington: infant, junior and senior.

The Great Torrington Church of England Infant and Nursery School shares a site with the junior school in Borough Road. The new eco-building, featuring plenty of wood and lots of light, opened in September 2005. 'We are an early years specialist school with a Christian ethos offering a wide range of experiences to children of nursery age through to Year 2 of the national curriculum.'[1] Every child at the infant school has five or six sessions a year of Forest School when, with the guidance of trained leaders, it is hoped they will become familiar with the woodland world and gain an interest in caring for the outdoors. They create objects using natural materials from the woods and learn how to safely use tools such as secateurs and saws under close supervision and how to cook on a real fire. It is felt that Forest School is 'a powerful and welcome addition to life at school' which adds to pupils' confidence and self-esteem. After Year 2 the children transfer to the junior school. The current headmistress is Angela Fleming (2011).

There is also a Children's Centre at the school, built in 2002, which offers a wide range of services for children of four years old and under and their families. There is a café where parents can meet with friends or make contact with staff who will provide information about the services available through the centre. It won praise in its first Ofsted report in July 2011 for being 'outstanding' and 'best in the county.'[2]

Outside the building there is a Multi Use Games Area (MUGA) for PE and playtime and a bit of grass alongside. If there is a criticism of this new building and its location, I think it would be the lack of outdoor space it has resulted in for both the infant and junior schools.

Before being at Borough Road the infant school was situated in Whites Lane. For the past seven years the building has stood empty, forlorn and deteriorating while it is decided who owns it, who might buy it and what it could be used for. The museum and various community groups would have been glad to use it but didn't have the funds to purchase it. The building originally opened in 1872 as a Board School and, a century later, was amalgamated with the Blue Coat School (aka the Barley Grove School) which had been housed in what became the Eric Palmer Centre.

Jean Shorters began her teaching career at the Blue Coat School in 1958. Mr Hicks was the headmaster at the time. There was a free-standing swimming pool where the memorial garden is and the caretaker, a Mrs Nichols, lived in the cottage adjoining the school. When the town swimming pool was built the pool was given to East Anstey School on the edge of Exmoor. Jean says there was no particular reason why parents chose one of the two schools rather than the other but families tended to send their children to the same school, generation after generation. On occasion, a family fell out with the school and sent their child to the other one but Mr Hicks used to say, 'Schools are the same, you know' (i.e. 'You're the awkward one!'). Sometimes, if a family had two children close in age, they would send them to the Board School because it was larger and had year groups whereas the Blue Coat School only had three classes and mixed ages so siblings of different ages could be in the same class. Jean remembers that she and one of her colleagues, Joan Bowyer, had to teach in temporary classrooms in the car park.

Blue Coat School pupils 1929   Photo courtesy of John and Tilly Kimber

She says that people on holiday who had parked in the Barley Grove car park used to think they were a nursery and young mothers would come in with bottles of milk for them to heat up for their babies. At one time Jo Sampson had a class in the Howe Church Hall down the road in Castle Street (now the silver band practice hall).

The Torrington primary schools grew in size with the closure of some of the village schools. Little Torrington school closed in July 1958 and the children came to the Blue Coat School. The Blue Coat and the Board schools amalgamated in the building in Whites Lane in 1978 when the new junior school was built down at Borough Road. Before that, the two schools had taken it in turn to choose the queen at May Fair: she would be from the Blue Coat School one year and from the Board School the next. Jean worked under Mr Hicks, Mr Barker, Mrs Coombs (who was headmistress at the time of the move), Marjorie Palin and Mary Pearson. She became Deputy Head in 1963. Mr Hicks had a tradition at the Christmas concert where the Boar's Head carol was sung and a boar's head was carried in on a platter. At Christmas dinner everyone sang for some Christmas pudding and, when you were given some, you stopped singing. There were usually two sittings for lunch but only one at Christmas time. A set of hand bells was kept on the cupboard in the hall and Mr Hicks would take hand bell ringing after school. Marjorie Palin was head from 1982-1993 and Jean said she was a 'people person', always laughing, interested in people rather than paperwork, who would take the time to ask you about your holiday. She had a certain presence and had good relations with parents.

Lunchtime, Barley Grove c1970   Photo courtesy of Jean Shorters

Blue Coat School pupils c1976   Photo courtesy of Jean Shorters

Staff at Blue Coat School, Whites Lane 1992   Photo courtesy of Jean Shorters

Great Torrington Junior School shares a campus with the Blue Coat Infant School, the Children's Centre, the Family Centre and Forest School. Jim Cobbett, the headmaster who retired in 2009, was originally appointed to be an interim head while working as an adviser for Devon County Council when the school was put on special measures by Ofsted but ended up remaining in the position for ten years. It was he who introduced Forest School in which pupils take part with a trained ranger when their teacher has his or her planning and assessment time each week. 'Forest schools are based on the simple idea that children flourish emotionally and educationally if they take part in constructive activities outdoors.'[3] Some activities take place on the commons.

Nine classes are organised into lower and upper school teams. In the middle is a library and music area. Children can also use the digital system to borrow books. The 'Digital Creativity Zone' can be used to access the latest technology. All classes have access to wireless laptops and net-books in order to enhance and raise standards of attainment across all the curriculum areas. There are three group rooms which are set up to enhance the children's learning and to ensure that quality resources can be accessed. The sports hall doubles as dining room at lunch time and whole school assembly. The school grounds have an upper and lower playground with football and basketball goals and a MUGA. There is a Forest School area and small grass areas and a very large tepee. According to the website, the Parent Teachers and Friends Association is looking into developing the school grounds in order to provide the children with more play and sporting opportunities during the play and lunch breaks. Ironically, this was available until the infant school was built on the site. Many people in the town who were pupils when Leigh Cullen was head-master will remember him playing football and cricket out on the field with the lads at lunch times in the summer when it was dry. Sports Day was held on the field as well as inter-school football and cricket matches and there was a lot more room for children to let off steam at play time. In the middle of the school there is a small quiet garden area and pond which is home to a number of frogs, toads and a rare great crested newt where children can learn about growing plants and which they have decorated with a mosaic. There are cloakrooms for coats and competitions between classes to keep coats tidy and turn off the lights. After school clubs include drama, dancing, band and choir. In recent years the school has undergone many changes. There is an Acting Headteacher, Sandy Brown, who is also a National Leader of Education and Headteacher of Woolacombe Primary School.[4] Government budget cuts meant that three teachers (two full-time, one part-time) were made redundant in July 2011 and three teaching assistants who had reached the end of their contract weren't replaced. Early in 2012 there are plans for merging the junior, infant and nursery schools to form a new 3-11 primary school sometime in the next year or so.

Great Torrington Community School describes itself on its website as 'a vibrant and exciting mixed 11-16 school'[5] The school was awarded Sports Specialist status in September 2003 and was re-designated as a Specialist Sports College in 2007. Because of its success in this specialist area, the school was given the opportunity to apply for a second specialism and in 2008 was duly awarded Applied Learning to develop new 'pathways to success' for pupils in vocational subjects. In the same year the school also acquired foundation status. The school became an academy in September 2011. Unfortunately, the present coalition government's cuts in sports provision have adversely affected the situation at the school.

The majority of pupils who continue their education on leaving Great Torrington Community School follow courses at Petroc (formerly North Devon College), a tertiary college in Barnstaple.

The school is situated in Calvesford Road where the Barnstaple and South Molton roads join at a roundabout. The buildings are of variable quality, for the most part dating from 1939 when the school was opened. A substantial extension was added in the 1970s and a newer seven classroom building was completed in February 2003. A £2 million major building project has also recently been opened which provided a new performing arts department (complete with auditorium) and art block, togeth-er with new offices, and some existing areas were refurbished. In addition to this there are six science labs, five maths rooms, three food/textile technology rooms, a purpose-built CDT area and classrooms for English, humanities and special needs, a language department, four large computer rooms and a library/resources area. There is a community sports hall on the site, a gymnasium and adjacent playing fields with an all-weather sports pitch.

The school's population has grown steadily and by early 2011 had over 900 pupils and about 55 permanent teaching staff with the backing of a committed support staff team. The school serves a very large catchment area of more than 20 parishes with the majority of pupils travelling to school daily by bus.

The Torrington Army Cadet Force which meets at the school is highly thought of and was one of the first to include girls. Youngsters between 12 and 18 years of age meet at the cadet hut every Friday evening and are able to take part in a wide variety of activities. On their website the cadets describe their instructors as 'dedicated', 'trained', 'great' and 'a good laugh'.

A fascinating archive exists at the school: a Log Book hand-written by the first four headmasters from 1939 when the school opened (built at a cost of £25,582) until it became a comprehensive in 1974. Especially interesting are the first entries which record life at the school during the Second World War.

Written in ink in large, bold handwriting, the first headmaster, Thomas Nancekievill, records the opening of the Great Torrington Senior Council School on 13th September 1939. There were five men and five women members of staff together with a woman from the Agricultural Department who was to teach two lessons a week, a cook, a kitchen maid and a caretaker. Pupils came from 17 contributory primary schools – many of which no longer exist, such as Roborough, St Giles in the Wood, Weare Giffard, Frithelstock, Alverdiscott, Yarnscombe – travelling in seven buses and two cars with prefects 'appointed to each conveyance'. At the end of the first week, 15th September, there were 296 pupils. By 22nd September there were 303 because of the admission of evacuees.

By 13th October attendance was down to 60% because of an outbreak of measles. This epidemic continued into 1940 which caused a lot of staff and pupil absence and this, together with the call-up of several male members of staff for military duties and harsh winter weather which prevented the buses from running, prompted Mr Nancekievill to write, on 21st February, 'It is most difficult to carry on.'

Activities at the school were necessarily of a practical nature to ensure survival during this period and treats were few except around Christmas time when there might be a concert by pupils in school or an outing to the cinema (which was down Church Lane leading from Whites Lane to the parish church, where Tannery Row is now). The Mayor, Mr Lampard Vachell, and his wife often put on entertainment for the pupils of the senior school together with the children from both the Torrington primary schools and Weare Gifford (sic) and on 10th January 1940 Mr Nancekievill writes, 'A conjuring display was enjoyed and oranges were distributed to the children. Nearly 500 children were present.' May Fair didn't take place during the war but on 31st May 1941 it is noted that 'School took part in Folk Dancing on Old Bowling Green at 7pm.' School sports are mentioned from 1942 onwards between the four houses, Drake, Kingsley, Raleigh and Walpole.

By 9th September 1940 the number of pupils had risen to 620, including evacuees mainly from London, and by 28th November there were 645. School buses had to make double journeys and it was difficult to accommodate everyone in the canteen. At first, a double shift was impossible owing to lack of equipment until plates were received from the Bovey Tracey Pottery Company. Everyone rallied round. Gifts of apples, rhubarb, vegetables, jam and, on one occasion, two gallons of ice-cream were sent into school by local people for use in the canteen. Potatoes were planted in the school garden and at the end of the football pitch. 30 chicks were put in the garden shed in March 1940 and poultry houses were set up in April. On 9th October 1940 a 'Mr C. Popham gave the school a swarm of bees and installed them'. In the summer

1

1939.

G. Torrington Senior Council School. 201. changed to. 579.

13th Sept. This new School was opened today On the Staff Mr. Archie Claude Parker. Harry Colwell. Horace Arthur Holley. Norman John Harf. Alfred Geoffrey Chivers Miss Ellie Blatchford Judd Woodley Florence Joan Bellringer " Hazel Boston Pindray. " Ethel Mary Vickery. · Frances Johnston Miss Shotton from the Agricultural Dept. visits the school for two lessons a week. Myself. Thomas Hunckievill is in charge. Mrs Edith Mary Pearse is the appointed Cook and Miss Molly Quick Kitchen Maid. Mr Robert John Pearse is the Caretaker.

First page of GTS Log Book   Courtesy of Great Torrington Community School

holidays the school was unofficially opened for the voluntary attendance of children engaged on work of National Service which consisted of gardening, salvage of paper and iron, stripping tin at a milk factory, mending and making clothes and fixing lace on the school windows for air raid protection. Staff took it in turns to be on duty during the holiday. Groups of boys were employed 'potato dropping' in the locality in March and 'potato picking' in October.

Doctors and nurses regularly visited the school for nutrition surveys, psychiatric tests, examinations for cleanliness (sometimes children had to be re-examined or were sent home), inoculation against diphtheria, eye tests and dental inspection and treatment.

On 24th May 1940 the school held 'a Special Service in Commemoration of Empire Day. Children contributed the sum of £2 7s 9d to the Over-Seas League Tobacco Fund.'

Several male members of staff were called up for military duty including Mr Pearse, the caretaker. Women teachers were allowed days off if their husbands were home on leave. Staff who had come from London with the evacuees were often called away because relatives had died or their houses were destroyed. Other teachers obtained jobs elsewhere. By 22nd April 1941, Mr Nancekievill notes that '62 teachers have done duty in this School since the opening'.

On 19th November 1941 there is an entry reading, 'Attended the birching of Hunter and Heath at the Police Station.' Mr Browning, the headmaster of the Croydon school from where some of the evacuees had come, was also present so perhaps it was evacuees rather than local lads who were being punished!

The school was inspected in February 1944 by HMI Arnold Platts. He writes:

'The building is perhaps the best of its kind in the county and much hard work has been carried out to put it to good use, whilst the land for gardening has been put into production. Under an enterprising, painstaking and kindly Headmaster the school has not only been established but has in the national emergency made a definite contribution to educational progress in a rural area and has played a prominent and successful part in the evacuation scheme.'

On 16th April 1945 the school re-opened after the Easter holiday with the new name of Great Torrington Modern Secondary School. On 8th and 9th May the school was closed 'for Celebration of Victory over the Germans' and reopened on 10th with a 'Special opening Service for Victory.' Then the following entries are about the results of football matches against local teams!

Mr Nancekievill's final entry is on 29th April 1946. The next entry is on 27th February 1950 when, in rather smaller, less legible handwriting the entry reads, 'Commenced duties as Headmaster of this school A. Hinchley.' Understandably, the entries are more light-hearted featuring agricultural shows, sports and open days, concerts of singing and drama, netball and athletics matches, social clubs to be held on Wednesday afternoons (Young Farmers, Dramatic, Explorers, Handyman, Sketching and Craft). There are trips to London, social evenings for past pupils, foreign visitors and the production on 20th June 1951 of the first school magazine, the *Territonian*.

Jim Bastin took over as headmaster on 12th January 1956. There were 309 pupils (128 girls and 181 boys). February was very cold and Mr Bastin wrote, 'The frozen state of the roads led to very poor attendance: 116 on Wednesday, 151 on Thursday and 198 on Friday (out of 310 now on roll)'. On 3rd May the first mention of May Fair is made and the school is closed for the day. On 8th May the entry reads, 'Two hundred and twenty five children with twelve members of the staff went to Barnstaple today to see Her Majesty the Queen.'

By September the pupil numbers had risen to 352 and in the following years they rose steadily reaching a peak of 478 in 1971. In September 1970, when there were 463 pupils, Mr Bastin wrote, 'This is the largest number on roll since I came here in 1956 and is very near the limit of what can decently be accommodated.' School houses changed to Barton, Leigh, Cleave and Coombe. The school was used as a centre for the 11+ exam. Those who passed the exam went on to grammar school in Bideford (boys) and Barnstaple (girls). 6th May 1960, the day following May Fair, the school was closed for Princess Margaret's wedding. On 24th July 1962 some 500 parents and friends attended Open Day and the school swimming pool was formally opened.

In January 1963 there was severe weather, attendance was poor, most parts of the building were very cold and the lavatories were frozen so the school had to be closed for over a week. Night temperatures were recorded as low as 10 degrees F (-12 degrees C). On 17th January, Mr Bastin wrote:

'School reopened. Lavatories have to be flushed by hand but pans are kept unfrozen by use of agricultural salt every evening and warm water in the morning.'

On 5th February he wrote,

'It has been snowing almost continuously for the past two days. Night temperatures have seldom been above freezing point during the past month and during the same period day temperature has reached 40 degrees F (5 degrees C) on only one or two occasions. The swimming pool has been frozen firm enough for skating for the past three weeks. The bus children were sent home again early this afternoon owing to the snow fall.'

The last of the ice finally disappeared from the swimming pool on 2nd March. There were school trips to the Devon County Show, Longleat and further afield to Paris and every two years small parties of children – and Mr Bastin – went on a cruise.

In April 1969 Mr Harry Colwill, geography teacher, resigned through ill health. Mr Bastin wrote,

'He was the last member of the original staff of this school listed on the first page of this book.'

On 1st September 1972 Don Howard became headmaster. He had a special governors' meeting to discuss plans for new extensions and conversions and a new block called 'West House' was built and opened on 29th November 1973. In January of that year parents' evenings were held to explain to parents of 4th year pupils about the raising of the school leaving age. On 21st March over 30 trees were planted as part of 'Plant a Tree' year with governors and Mr Bastin attending the planting.

In May there was a special governors' meeting to discuss the structure of the re-organised comprehensive school and in June and July internal interviews were held for posts in the comprehensive school dating from September 1974.

In April 1974 the NAS union began a work to rule and overtime ban – North Devon Branch official action. All committees, staff and parents meetings were cancelled. The rest of the entries for the summer term of 1974 involved a fire drill – 'successful 4 minutes – too long, but no "panic" – too many doors and windows open'; May Fair, with the official lunch held in school; a trip to Lundy; a visit by the Army for a

GREAT TORRINGTON REORGANISATION

Dear Mr. Mowll,

The Governors have asked me to give their recommendations for designations of posts of responsibility in the comprehensive school. The list, of course, refers to those posts to be filled internally. All staff listed are at present on the staff of Great Torrington C. S. School.

		Scale
Deputy Head	Mr. Bateman	(Group 9)
Head of Lower School	Mr. D. Woodcock	5
Head of Upper School	Mr. D. Wilson	5
Head of Sciences	Mr. C. Morgan	5
Head of Communications	Mr. B. Nash	5
Year Tutor	Mrs. M. Copp	3
Year Tutor and P.E.(1)	Mr. R. Peacock	4
Year Tutor and Careers	Mr. M. Vanderpant	3
Physics Department	Mr. J. W. Rees	3
Modern Languages Department	Mrs. A. Patrick	3
Remedial Department	Mr. F. Griffiths	3
Music Department	Mr. A. J. Kent	3
Needlecraft Department	Mrs. L. L. Escott	2
Moral Education Department	Mr. J. Burgess	2
Home Economics Department	Miss J. Secker	2
Crafts (Metalwork) Department	Mr. D. A. Giles	2
Crafts (Woodwork/Plastics) Department	Mr. F. Hamling	2

The following Scale 1 posts have also been recommended for designation:

Miss Francis – Geography

Mr. Garisch – Biology

Mr. Quinton – Technical Drawing and General Subjects

Mrs. Triggs – English

Mrs. Woodcock – Art

I would welcome an early opportunity to discuss with you the vacancies to be nationally advertised at the appropriate time and the probable resulting Bonus staffing.

Yours sincerely,

Reorganisation

display on the school field; a French trip; a meeting of heads in the new North Devon and East Devon Areas; a cadet camp in which Messrs Howard, Rees and Griffiths took part; a week of visits by new intake pupils in July. The final entry in the Log Book on Thursday 18th July 1974, the last day of term, ends with a special dinner at Beaford House in the evening to say farewell to two members of staff who were leaving. The following September the school reopened as a comprehensive school.

Subsequent headteachers of the school:

David Nainby April 1984 – July 1998
Dianne Nicholson January 1999 – July 2010
Tracey Amos September 2010 –

The earliest known school in Torrington was founded in the chantry chapel of St James at the castle probably in the 15th century. Mention of 'La Scolehouse' can be found in 1485. Risdon (d.1640) tells us in his 'Survey' regarding Torrington castle that 'there remaineth only a chapel with the scite now converted into a School House'. By the 1770s the scholars were being taught by the Rev. George Wickey in the Town Hall as the building at Castle Hill had fallen into disrepair and was finally taken down in 1780. However, it appears the building was reconstructed and Rev. Wickey continued teaching in the school with his fellow clergy until his death in 1817. This school became a National School (i.e. connected to the Church of England) before 1833.[6]

In March 1671 John Lovering gave £100 for the endowment of a school for the children of Weare Giffard, Torrington and Huntshaw. The school was at Weare Giffard but Torrington children had the right to attend it. This is why the road leading from New Street opposite the church to Weare Giffard is called School Lane. By the 1820s no Torrington children had attended the school for some time.

The first Dennys Rolle (1614-38), Lord of the Manor, is said to have founded the Blue Coat School and a Charity Report tells us that in 1709 another

'Dennys Rolle of Moortown, Torrington, placed in the hands of the trustees £220 for the endowment of a school in Well Street, Torrington, for the children of Great Torrington, to pay for a schoolmaster, and also to pay for "such coats or caps as were worn in Charity Schools of that nature".'[7]

In the 1830s, provision for education of the poor in Torrington consisted of the National School with about 100 boys and the Blue Coat School with about 25 boys. In 1834 John Lord Rolle (1750-1842), who owned the site of the National School, extended the building, adding an upper storey and extending the downstairs room westward for the accommodation of girls which doubled the size of the school. The inscription on the upper storey of this reconstructed Castle School (more recently known as the Eric Palmer Centre) reads:

'This building was erected by the Right Hon. John Lord Rolle of Stevenstone in this County as a School House for the Education of the Poor Children of this Parish in the Principles of the Established Church, Anno Domini 1834.'

In 1850 this National School was amalgamated with the Blue Coat School.[8]

Some Nonconformists, unhappy that education was only provided by the Anglicans, decided to set up their own school on a site belonging to the Hunters Inn (now the Cavalier) between Well Street and Calf Street which opened in July 1835. It was designed for 150 boys and 150 girls but there were never enough scholars to pay more than a total of twelve shillings a week (they paid 3d, 4d and 6d each per week). They were at a disadvantage in having to obtain a master or mistress from the British and Foreign School Society in London and to pay for them (£2 10s a month). The schoolmaster's pronunciation wasn't understood by the Torrington pupils who, as a result, became hard to discipline. The school was in debt by October 1836 and had to close in the summer of 1838. In 1873 the British School was sold and the money used towards a new Board School in Whites Lane. From 1838-73 there were only the Church Schools as public elementary schools, two until 1850 and then only the one. The only other school in Torrington in this period was a so-called 'Ragged School' at the east end of Well Street which only lasted for a short period. After 1850 a good private school was opened in South Street by Samuel Doidge which lasted for over 40 years.[9]

Pat Wilks, who was a child in Torrington during the 1930s, attended a small private school – St George's – at number 18 Potacre Street, a large, three storey house on the corner of Calf Street. Until recently, it was said that the children's coat pegs could still be seen in the hall. Their school playing field was down Gas Lane. Brian Vincent, whose family owned the glove factory, also went there. Another pupil at the same time was Rosemary Sutcliff, the popular children's author. The headmistress was Miss Flo Davies, who Pat says was a good teacher who would put up with no non-sense, and she was assisted by a Miss Jones, who taught the infants, and a young curate, Rev. Jones, who taught them basic Latin. Once a week the pupils went by train to Bideford to the Stella Maris convent where they were taught French ('also pretty basic') by the nuns who refused to speak any English at all. Miss Davies was a staunch Royalist, so the school celebrated Oak Apple Days, Empire Days and Saints' Days, particularly St George's Day. She was also a pillar of the Anglican church so there was plenty of religious training, too. Pat says, 'Possibly the thing I most remember was the respect for our elders which was certainly encouraged. By and large, it was a happy start to life's schooling.'

With thanks to :
Dave Kelly
Tilly and John Kimber
Dianne Nicholson
Jean Shorters
Judith Sutton
Pat Wilks

58   What is that Derelict Factory down in the river valley below Torrington?

The dilapidated industrial building standing forlornly by the River Torridge is the remains of a milk factory that had been there since 1874. It closed in 1993, mainly as a result of milk quotas which had been introduced a decade earlier, and 134 people lost their jobs. For many years it had been one of the town's main employers.

The pioneering Torridge Vale dairy was founded by Robert Sandford, a local greengrocer and entrepreneur, on the site of the old Rolle Canal stores near Taddiport Bridge. The coming of the railway to Torrington in 1872 had seen the end of the canal as a means of transporting goods.

The steam-driven cream separator invented in around 1880 was replacing the work of individual dairy maids and men in the production of butter, extracting cream from considerable quantities of milk daily (200 gallons of milk were being dealt with in an hour). The separated cream was either potted into little Barum Ware jars and sold as rich Devonshire cream or converted into butter. 'Thus was created what was hoped would be a profitable enterprise, and the development of an important local industry specially adapted to the peculiar requirements of the district.'[1]

The factory was surrounded by gardens producing flowers, fruit and vegetables grown for the local markets by the Sandford family. 'Sandfords Gardens' off Mill Street is a reminder of those days. The factory became a dairy depot and added other products including poultry and eggs to the list of items supplied to customers. Milk from Torrington could reach London by train in the same day. Local man, Owen Warne, told me his mother (who was a Sandford) attended Barnstaple Grammar School and on her way to school she would push a handcart carrying pots of clotted cream down to the station, where porters would help to load them onto the train. The cream travelled free of charge from Torrington to Barnstaple because it was travelling with a passenger, so transport only had to be paid from Barnstaple onwards. The cream would be on sale in London later the same day.

Robert Sandford had hoped that local farmers would co-operate with him financially in order to increase the size of the business but his offer of shares met with no response. This was unlike many dairies which started as small co-operatives. He ran the business single-handed for half a century, carrying on a steady trade but not enlarging the business or providing further development. In 1922 he was joined in partnership by William Stacey of Sutcombe. On the death of Robert Sandford in 1924 his nephew, Thomas, who had spent eight years as a trainee at Torridge Vale (1898-1906) before leaving to study dairying at the British Dairy Institute at Reading and then working for United Dairies for 18 years, returned to Torrington and joined Mr Stacey as joint managing director. The business prospered, buildings and machinery were enlarged and the volume of output increased. By 1931 milk was being collected from about 50 farms peaking at 1,850 gallons per day together with cream delivered by or collected from farmers.

In 1932 the dairy became associated with Cow & Gate Ltd and the trading name changed to Torridge Vale Dairies (Devon) Ltd under the same joint managing directors. Stimulated by conditions during the Second World War and encouraged by government policy to enlarge the output of home-grown food, and also to build up an export trade, the factory developed far beyond what its founder could have expected.

The main products processed at Torridge Vale Dairies were butter, cream, spray and roller dried milk and the cooling and dispatch of milk for the liquid market, as and when required. Milk production with a ready and guaranteed market was

Torridge Vale Dairy 1946   Photo courtesy of Bill Brook

increasing and the dairy was growing at considerable speed. By 1939 the peak intake had increased to 10,500 gallons per day (though workers' wages hadn't increased accordingly and they went on strike carrying placards declaring 'Support the men who MAKE cream but can never afford to BUY it') and by 1952 it had risen to 60,000 gallons per day collected from 2,600 farms and sometimes an additional 30,000 gallons per day of 'accommodation milk' was also processed.

By the late 1940s a new larger factory building was completed equipped with modern dairy machinery with much more powerful engines and five new large boilers to produce the steam required. It had one of the largest milk drying process machines in the world, new methods of purification of river water and the first reinforced concrete chimney in the country which rose to a height of 175 feet (nearly 54 metres).

In 1959 the United Dairies merged with Cow & Gate to form Unigate Ltd. Thomas Sandford, one of the six directors of the new company, died in 1961. Like William Stacey, he was a well-known and respected member of the community. He helped establish the Artificial Insemination Centre up at Hatchmoor which helped improve dairy and beef cattle and contributed to the prosperity of the farming community. In 1965 the trading name was changed to Unigate Creameries Ltd and again in 1969 to Unigate Foods Ltd.

The Milk Marketing Board purchased a large share of Unigate's interests, including the Torrington factory, in August 1979. In line with other creameries under MMB control, the dairy became Dairy Crest Foods, Torrington. The last milk churns were used at this time and all deliveries in future were to be by bulk-tanker. A major rebuilding programme was undertaken under the direction of the creamery

Milk reception bank 1960s   Photo courtesy of Bill Brook

manager, Bryan Bence. This included a new separating and butter making area and cold storage to match the extensive manufacturing potential. £5.3 million was invested to enable the whole process to be achieved on a continuous enclosed production line. From the intake of liquid milk to the final packaging, the routing of the products and the cleaning of equipment was all controlled by computer. Operators sat at a keyboard of a 'space-age micro processor which can check more than 600 individual items in only two seconds.'[2] It was one of the most modern milk processing plants in the country producing butter, milk-based dessert and skimmed milk powder. In the 1980s the factory employed 230 production staff and 100 drivers. At the opening of the redeveloped factory in May 1983, employees were praised by Sir Stephen Roberts, chairman of the Milk Marketing Board, for overcoming difficult conditions during the period of redevelopment and responding well to a massive re-training programme and increased levels of production. At this time 950 north Devon farmers supplied the creamery and the chairman of MMB stressed the importance of the west country to the nation's milk industry. 'Between them Devon and Cornwall supply over 11% of all the milk produced in England and Wales', he said, and the fact that the MMB felt it right to invest in modernising and enlarging creameries such as Torrington showed their confidence in the industry's future, especially in the West Country.

According to Graham Martin of the finance department, the demise of the Torrington milk factory started on 2nd April 1984, the day the Common Market decided to bring in milk quotas. From then on unlimited milk production could not continue and a brake was going to be put on to reduce the butter and powder mountains. Up until that date any surplus production that could not be sold to normal markets was sold to the Common Market and, in effect, the taxpayers were paying

Roller powder room

Photo courtesy
of Bill Brook

for this subsidy. The agriculture minister, Peter Walker, had previously encouraged the industry to keep producing in order to reduce our imports of dairy products. On the day this announcement was made the Torrington factory was nearing completion of a £19 million project to build a new spray drier and associated plant to meet industry needs. They were told to stop the building work but it was too advanced and it made more sense to complete it. (One of the workers at the dairy described this new drier made by Danish firm Anhydro as 'a monster'. He also told me that the old drier, made for Cow & Gate, had been used during the Second World War for making soap flakes!).

Quotas meant that milk production was going to be capped to a lower level than 1984 production and farmers were not going to be able to expand their businesses unless they purchased quota from a farmer who had given up milk production. Milk prices are never very good for farmers and with the expansion route closed for them many farmers gave up milk production and so the amount of milk produced in the British Isles started to reduce. Consequently, in the next ten years there was a situation where too many milk factories were chasing a reducing supply of raw material. Milk factories were becoming less efficient and so several rounds of closures occurred within all dairy companies. Torrington hung on longer than most because of its size and the large milk field around it.

Torrington was one of the largest factories in the country and during the 1960s and half the 1970s was able to take in any surplus milk at any time during the year. However, in around 1975 Unigate had decided to extend a sister factory at Chard in Somerset and Express Dairies had decided to build a new factory at North Tawton. Both these events had a significant effect on Torrington. It would no longer receive anywhere near the amount of surplus milk. Today the factory at North Tawton remains making Cheddar cheese and the Chard factory, although still open, does not handle any milk. If these events had not happened, the factory would probably have remained open a little longer but, such was the rationalisation within the industry, it would still have closed.

The management at Torrington, seeing the future of the industry under quotas, tried desperately to bring new 'added value' products to the site. A UHT cream dessert was tried first and then Clover. The latter was very successful but, eventually, because the site was so far away from the main markets and because Dairy Crest needed to make savings to protect its future with the demise of the Milk Marketing Board, Clover production was transferred to a site in the Midlands. Clotted cream had been an important and prize-winning product for Torrington but, unfortunately, under the sale agreement of the site by Unigate in 1979 as Dairy Crest, Torrington, they were not allowed to produce clotted cream for five years. After that time it was not really feasible to start up again.

The factory closed for production on 30th March 1993 with the majority of employees leaving by the end of May. The company set up a 'Job Shop' and all the employees were given advice on pensions etc. and several were found jobs. Graham Martin stayed on in charge to ensure that the factory was properly shut down and during this time some plant was transferred to other factories and a two day sale was held on site to get rid of most of the other items. Mr Martin finally left on 19th February 1994.

'The milk will be transported to creameries outside the area, but it doesn't seem quite natural to have no dairy in the middle of all those dairy farms.'[3] Unemployment in the town rose sharply and families who had several members working at the dairy faced hard times.

Dairy Crest did not want to remain in charge of the empty site and a condition of any sale was that the buyer would have to buy the whole site except for the transport depot which remained for a while and now belongs to M & D Transport. The site was sold for a reduced sum and Graham Martin thought it would remain unsold for a long time but, to his surprise, Dartington Crystal took over the site on the day he left. They were closing their site in Bideford and initially wanted to build alongside their main building in Torrington but the decision was made to see if they could rent somewhere and so they took over the factory but only used two of the buildings. The factory is a very large area to try and keep secure and it proved difficult for the new owners who only used part of it and didn't want to spend vast sums of money on security fencing and so on. The new owners did sell off two buildings and rented out another.

In 1998, a co-operative of 50 local farmers under the name of Torridge Vale Ltd took over part of the building. They wanted to set up a small operation to manufacture all their own milk to retain more profit for themselves. A very good brand was created called 'Definitely Devon'. They wanted to produce more added value products like clotted cream and soft cheese but it proved much more difficult than anticipated. The operation really struggled and a joint venture with Robert Wiseman Dairies helped for a while but the building of the new Wiseman dairy at Bridgwater meant the manufacturing site at Torrington had to close with the loss of over 100 jobs, although some were given work at the Wiseman Okehampton dairy. Torridge Vale Ltd now only uses the site as a base to operate the collection of their farmers' milk for sale to any dairy company, currently Milk Link and previously Arla and Robert Wiseman, amongst others.

Derelict site of old creamery   Photo courtesy Mike Southon and the North Devon Journal

What had once been a thriving hub of activity and a major employer in the town has been for many years now a blot on the beautiful North Devon landscape. Practically every window in the factory is broken, people living nearby reported youngsters breaking in and drinking and were afraid there would be an accident. The building is riddled with asbestos and rats and, tragically, has been the site of two suicides.

In recent years various plans have been drawn up for the dairy site (some at great expense) including the relocation of Dartington Crystal, workshops or housing, or a combination of both, but nothing has been decided. Machinery has been stripped from the building with a noise like a giant moving furniture but a lot of debris is still lying around. A company based in Newton Abbot, Kingscourt Homes Ltd, bought the site in 2009 with plans to redevelop it but the company has now gone into receivership. Torridge District Council planning officers had a meeting in 2010 with HSBC who have taken over the site and secured it. No-one seems to know what

Milkman in town square   Photo courtesy John and Tilly Kimber

will happen next. Over the years local people have had their own ideas, of varying practicality, about possible uses for the site: converting the building into a water mill to supply energy for the town; building environmentally friendly affordable housing; converting what had been a nice Art Deco building into flats with garages on the ground floor (because of the danger of flooding); using it again for industrial purposes to create jobs for local people; letting the area revert to a natural valley.

With thanks to:
Graham Martin (in particular)
Gordon and Greta Bright
Bill Brook

59   Where was the Gazebo, now at Rosemoor, originally situated?

The 18th century gazebo was in the garden of Palmer House, New Street, which was built by John Palmer, brother-in-law of Sir Joshua Reynolds and it appears in some of his paintings. (See 'Which are the Notable Buildings in the town?). A letter in the *Sunday Times* of June 1929 from a certain E. E. Rudd states:

'Sir – There is a gazebo in the grounds of Palmer House in this town with a fine view to the north. It is of historical interest, for Sir Joshua Reynolds and Dr Johnson have sat in it together.'

The gazebo was built possibly at the same time as Palmer House (1752) and was re-erected at Rosemoor in 1999.

In 1897 the Palmers sold Palmer House and, following the subdivision of the Palmer estate during the 20th century, the gazebo ended up marooned at the intersection of four boundary walls. Inaccessible to the public and with no particular owner, the Grade II listed building gradually deteriorated and, at one time, a local man kept his horse in it! It fell into such a dilapidated condition that by the 1990s it featured prominently on the English Heritage Buildings At Risk register and the Devon Historic Buildings Trust set out to save the building. The roof tiles were disintegrating and the cob walls were failing as a result but most of the basic structure was there and the timbers were reusable. A local teacher, Ken Evans-Loude, paid for scaffolding to keep the crumbling structure standing until it was decided what to do with it.

As it was in an inaccessible location, it was decided to dismantle the gazebo and move it to a site where the general public could enjoy this unique building. RHS Garden Rosemoor is a mile and a half out of town and the RHS agreed to receive the gazebo at Rosemoor and take over its stewardship.

In a project that took over three years and cost over £100,000, the Devon Historic Buildings Trust, aided by various grants and bequests, painstakingly took the gazebo apart and rebuilt it, using the original components. As the original site had no vehicular access, all of the original structure was removed by wheelbarrow. It took

Gazebo at
Rosemoor

Photo by author

twelve weeks of painstaking work for contractors J. E. Stacey & Co. Ltd of Holsworthy to carefully measure, dismantle, catalogue and transport the remains of the gazebo, piece by piece to Rosemoor. Faithfully following the original 18th century construction, a lower storey of cob and natural stone walling was formed. An oak framed first floor structure was then added and topped off with a framed timber roof. Altogether, the Palmer Gazebo took five months to rebuild. It was reopened on 23rd September 1999 by Eric Dancer, Lord Lieutenant of Devon, Sir Simon Hornby, President of the RHS, Roger Bowen, Chairman of Devon Historic Buildings Trust and Christopher Bailes, Curator RHS Garden Rosemoor.

The gazebo is a two-storey structure of rendered stone rubble and a slate-hung first floor. It has a hipped slate roof with lead rolls to the hips and a small ball finial and wrought-iron weather vane at the apex. It is an octagonal building with a flight of stone steps at the rear to a first floor room which is entered through a panelled door and restored wooden porch. Inside is a small stone fireplace with slate hearth flanked by china cupboards. There is panelling below the bay window and a moulded dado rail.

Some local people felt that the amount of money spent on restoring the gazebo was excessive for what is, essentially, a folly and others regret that it has moved out of Torrington into the parish of St Giles-in-the-Wood. However, it is a fascinating little building with interesting historical associations and sits easily in the Bicentenary Arboretum at Rosemoor commanding attractive views over the gardens and the

Gazebo behind Palmer House   Photo courtesy of Dave Kelly

slopes of the Torridge valley beyond. To the north the skyline is dominated by the town of Torrington with the spire of the parish church clearly visible. The gazebo's original home, Palmer House, is situated opposite the western entrance to the church.

With thanks to:
John and Tilly Kimber

60 What happens at Torrington Together?

Torrington Together is like a verbal version of *The Crier*, the community news-paper. All the voluntary organisations in the town and district get together to network. They meet twice a year at Torridge Vale Social Club.

It began in 2005 after members of voluntary groups found that their events clashed with other happenings in the town. Community stalwarts Dr Harry Cramp and Dr Jean Tyler were the inspiration behind the initiative. They chaired meetings for the first few years but now that duty is carried out by the Town Mayor. The meetings have a simple structure: current Cavalier Chairman, Chris Stacey, reads the Minutes from the previous meeting and then two or three representatives of voluntary organisations have five minutes each to outline the purpose and activities of their particular organisation. Timings are strictly adhered to. Questions are asked from the floor after each speech.

Up to 50 representatives regularly attend and provide positive input. It is amazing just how much voluntary organised activity there is in and around Torrington that supports young and old, fit and infirm. In a South West survey, it was found that Torrington has the greatest number of volunteers per head of population in the whole of the region. If Prime Minister, David Cameron, wants to see his 'Big Society' in action, he ought to come to this town.

After half an hour or so, members enjoy refreshments provided by Sue Parish and network with each other. During that time representatives ask the Chairperson for a three minute slot after refreshments to announce forthcoming events or to request help on particular issues. A representative from *The Crier* is always present to ensure that accurate publicity for activities is posted in their monthly magazine. Town and District Councillors also attend to give an update on any project that needs political will or muscle, such as development of the Eric Palmer Centre or the Blue Coat infant school building in Whites Lane. The police are present as well and provide data on issues of the day that affect the town.

Sometimes the meeting can go on for nearly three hours and members always leave with a tremendously good feeling about the town they inhabit.

With thanks to:
Bob Brewer
Jean Tyler

61   Has there been much New Building recently in Torrington?

Originally, most of the population lived close to the town centre in houses lining the main streets – South Street, Well Street and Mill Street – with 'scattered residential development along New Street but little on Calf Street, being mainly barns, linhays and gardens.'[1]

The second half of the 19th century was a period of great development in Torrington and throughout the country. The town acquired two markets and a school and the Town Hall was rebuilt in 1861 though several features from the earlier hall, including the panelled chamber, were retained. The waterworks and reservoir at Blackerton were constructed in 1871 and the gasworks in Gas Lane supplied the town with power and light. The cemetery on the outskirts of town was laid out in 1855 with shrubs and trees, two mortuary chapels and a lodge. The Baptist chapel had been built in 1829, the Methodist chapel in 1832 and the Howe Congregational church was built in 1857 replacing a much earlier chapel.

The first new housing development was Pathfields off the road to South Molton built by Larry Alexander in the mid-1960s. The area was originally a triangular field with a path running through it from Donnacroft to what is now Burwood, hence the name. Outside Larry's office in Calf Street, where Dafforn & Son used to be, was a board advertising the properties at Pathfields: '3 bedrooms £3,000, 2 bedrooms £2,000.'[2] Warren Close between New Street and Warren Lane was built by Staceys in the 1960s on a field where games used to be played at May Fair. The first properties in Dartington Fields up at the eastern end of town were built for Swedish glass blowers at the Dartington Glass factory which opened in 1967. The houses at Greenbank, on the other side of the main road from Dartington Fields, were built in 1968/69. Castle Hill Gardens between Castle Street and New Road was built in the mid-1970s on fields around the Gush and Dent ironcraft works which used to be where the Castle Gardens Surgery is now. The building of Burwood started in 1975. The *North Devon Journal* stated, 'Cornish developers announce plans to build 190 houses at Burwood.'

More recent developments have been Kingsmead, near the senior school between Calvesford Road and Hatchmoor Road, which was started in 1996 and took about two years to build. The first people moved in on 28 February 1997 – Catherine and Roger Payne – and it so happened that they had also been the first to move into Castle Hill Gardens in 1974. Hopton Place, the development behind Dartington Crystal to the north of the town, was built in 2006 and Torrington Gate, up by the Cottage Hospital, in 2007. This last development was delayed for six months because a nest of slow worms was discovered and builders waited until they had grown and dispersed! People need somewhere to live but health and education services aren't necessarily able to expand at the same time and the small narrow streets struggle to cope with increased traffic and parking, especially when one of the main car parks has been built on.

Generally, the amount of new building in Torrington has been restricted by the commons which surround the town on three sides. Sometimes this has led to houses being squashed into rather unsuitable spaces in the town.

A builder bought a plot of land behind the Torrington Arms in New Street in 2003 and applied to build on it. He originally wished to build two houses but claims the District Council urged him to build more so he applied to build four, then eight and finally six houses. There was understandably a lot of opposition from residents of Louise Terrace, which faces the plot across a narrow lane, and other home-owners living near the piece of land. The Town Council recommended refusal of the application on the grounds of over-intensive development, highway considerations (there is a difficult narrow exit into the main road and no room to turn a vehicle) and sewage considerations. Meanwhile, the District Council recommended approval on condition that the builder made an 'education contribution' as a condition of any development. I can never understand the morality of allowing unsuitable building to take place as long as payment is made by the developer for some other project in the locality but this seems to be common practice these days. However, as yet, nothing has been built on this piece of land.

Tolleys built a row of houses in the garden of 18 Potacre Street, presumably hoping to demolish the high wall that is only a few metres in front of the buildings, but the wall is listed so they haven't been able to take it down. The houses must be very dark inside.

Owners of large properties in the area of Warren Lane have sold off parts of their gardens and houses, sometimes large, have been built which have no garden to speak of. Small houses have also been built in the gardens of smaller properties, for instance in Town Park and up at Dartington Fields. Other houses have been jammed into cramped spaces which have no vehicular access so exacerbating the parking situation in the town. New Street car park was the only place where HGVs could

Above: New houses behind old wall

Photo by the author

Below: Torrington Gate

Photo by the author

turn and provided parking for residents in the terraced houses along the main road. A Lidl supermarket has been built here and a small car park with rather restricted turning space has been provided in one corner of the site.

At the same time as there has been quite a lot of new development in Torrington, older premises have lain empty and are becoming increasingly derelict, which is sad to see. These include the dairy down in the Torridge valley, the old glove factory in Whites Lane, the old Blue Coat infants' school also in Whites Lane and, for some years, the Eric Palmer Centre at Barley Grove. After being purchased in 2009 and partially renovated, this building has now been adapted for use as a fitness centre (March 2012).

With thanks to:
Chris Allin
Ken Egan
Mary Hayes
Geoff Huxtable
Derek and Margaret Jewell
Dave Kelly
Dulcie Leate
Mike Machin
Daphne Metherell
Caroline Norvill
Catherine Payne
Danny Ryan
Judith and Nigel Sutton
Margaret Trounson
Rob Ware

62   When was the Rotary Club of Torrington established?

A Rotary Club was set up in Torrington in the late 1960s. Four senior members of commerce and industry had been approved by the Rotary organisation to form a club helped by a newcomer to the town with Rotary experience and with advice from the Extension Officer from Okehampton. It took a couple of years to establish the club and the first President was Lt Col. John Pearson in 1970. In the 1970s there was lots of industry in Torrington and there was a wide range of people amongst the first men to be invited to join the club. Many of those skills have now been lost in the town. The Rotary Club provided an environment in which businessmen were able to network. There wasn't much fund-raising done in the early days. At first they used to meet for lunch upstairs in the Green Lantern and then moved across the square to the Black Horse. In 2010, aware that the nature of people's working lives had changed, the club decided to meet on Tuesday evenings at 6.30 rather than at lunch time.

With its motto of 'Service above Self' the club has achieved a lot in helping different sections of the community. This has included taking elderly people to events at the Plough arts centre, to Christmas lunch at one of the local schools each year and to Toc-H in Bideford. In the mid-1960s Dr Bickford, a local GP, opened the centre named after him as somewhere for retired men to be able to go and chat during the day rather than hanging about under the Town Hall. The lease on the property in South Street was held by J. B Reed and Rotary bought the freehold for £4,500 in 1976 and the centre continues to be self-funding with revenue from the two flats upstairs. The club's first project was to provide a TV set for the cottage hospital. When new public toilets were built in South Street car park there was no disabled provision so Rotary paid for that. When VAT was first introduced, Rotary held a public meeting about how it would all work. They take part in National Rotary projects such as providing free blood pressure testing to raise awareness of health issues.

The Rotary Club has worked with young people in schools organising the Youth Speaks public speaking competition, holding mock job interviews for every pupil in year 11, running leadership courses and sponsoring teenagers on work experience abroad. A music and arts festival was run for 13 years involving schools over a wide area of North Devon and Cornwall which was sponsored by Rotary.

The local club has raised a lot of money through a variety of activities including banger racing, wine and wisdom evenings, Sunday lunches and fairs.

Rotary is an international organisation and the Torrington club has supported many projects world-wide. For many years one of the members has collected unwanted spectacles which are sent to help people with poor sight in the third world. In his opinion, two of the club's best international projects involved helping a doctor in Jamaica and providing funding for Latvian farmers to come over to Britain:

In the 1980s one of the first members of the Torrington club, Jimmy Martin, decided to visit every Torrington in the world. He came upon one in Jamaica which was little more than 'two houses and a shippen' and met a doctor there who was struggling for bedding and medicines for sick people. Jimmy felt that his Rotary club should do something to help and they sent out a load of sheets and pillowcases by boat, in a crate 'like a small bungalow' made by George Copp, and some unused drugs.

After the break-up of the USSR, land that had been taken from farmers in the Balkan states at the end of the Second World War and made into collective farms was given back but people no longer knew how to till the land. Two lads came over to the UK to learn about western farming methods. Two years later a few members of the Torrington club raised money, together with other Rotary groups, to bring 12 farmers over to the UK for six weeks.

Other international projects in recent years have included the following:
- purchasing about 40 Shelter Boxes;
- collecting in town in response to the Pakistan floods which raised over £640 plus an immediate payment of £250 from club funds and a further £420 received from an anonymous donor;
- a collection in aid of victims of the Japan earthquake which raised £1,100;
- continued long-term support of the doctor at Little John's House in Romania + donation of £500;

- supporting the Rotary Club of Cwmbran Vale Christmas pudding appeal to raise money for the Adopt A Minefield charity;
- donating £250 to support the Rotary Club of Barnstaple appeal to cover   transportation costs of a large quantity of donated surplus medical equipment to Malindi Hospital in Kenya;
- continued support of Practical Action - £250 to their Water Aid programme in   Kenya;
- continued work in the eradication of polio – 1,000 crocus bulbs were planted in Rack Park garden in recognition of Rotary International's world-wide campaign and the Ruby Giant 'purple' crocuses planted there represent the dye colour dabbed on children's little fingers to indicate they've been immunised against polio;
- hosting teams from Australia, Thailand, Brazil and the Caribbean, together with the Rotary Clubs of Bideford Bridge and Barnstaple, in the Group Study Exchange;
- helping the district raise money to build a school in Sri Lanka following the tsunami;
- providing clean water and equipment for a school in Uganda.

Torrington Rotary opened its doors to women in the early years of this century. Despite the misgivings of some of the older members, they have proved to be very hard-working and effective members of the club. This year's President is a woman for the first time (2011).

Rotary is not all work and no play. Members relax by playing skittles against other clubs and there is an annual inter-club sports evening involving darts, pool, table tennis, shove ha'penny and cribbage.

With thanks to:
Bob Brewer
John Kimber
Rick Smale

63   **Does Torrington have any contact with other towns of the same name?**

Torrington, Connecticut was first settled in 1735 and given permission to organise a government and incorporate as a town in 1740. The fast moving waters of the Naugatuck River were used as water power for early 19th century industries – a woollen mill and two brass mills – and in 1849 the railway connected Torrington with other population centres which stimulated further industrial growth. The town's growing industrial plants attracted English, Irish and German immigrants throughout the 19th and early 20th centuries and between 1880 and 1920 Torrington's population exploded from 3,000 to 22,000 as immigration from southern and eastern Europe increased. Torrington was chartered as a city in 1923. In 1955 a huge flood destroyed much of the downtown area and property in the region when two hurricanes caused local rivers to overflow. Torrington is the birthplace of John Brown, the abolitionist, in 1805. The population in 2010 was 36,383.

The earliest contact between Torrington, Connecticut and Great Torrington (as I shall call our town in this section for the sake of clarity) appears to be in 1883 when the Mayor of Great Torrington, William Ashplant, received a letter from the editor of the *Torrington Register*, one of the daily papers of the American Torrington, requesting details about the Devonshire town. These were supplied and the newspaper adopted the borough arms as a trademark at the head of the newspaper.[1]

In 1897 the rector of Trinity Church in Torrington, Connecticut wrote to the Town Clerk, George Doe, asking for a stone from the parish church of Great Torrington which they wanted to incorporate into the new Trinity Church which was being built. With the consent of the vicar of Great Torrington, the Rev. Frank Emlyn-Jones, this was done and a photo of the piece of stone mounted on a slab of Sienna marble with an inscription and placed in the tower vestibule of the new American church was received. This project was paid for by a parishioner, John Davey, a Devonshire man who had been confirmed in the parish church by the Bishop of Exeter. In 1899 he came to England and visited Great Torrington after an absence of 50 years.[2]

In September 1920 a deputation from Torrington, Connecticut bringing greetings from the Warden and Burgesses of the town to the 'mother' town in Devon were welcomed at the Town Hall by the Mayor, William Luxton, and other townspeople. In 1933 courtesies were exchanged again when Mrs Walter Bayntun Starky, wife of the Great Torrington Mayor, visited the American town.[3]

If Torrington, Connecticut can be called the 'daughter' town, Torrington, Wyoming is the 'grand-daughter' town founded by William G. Curtis in 1889 and named by him after his home town in Connecticut. He was the first postmaster, running the post office from his homestead, and served twice as Mayor after the incorporation of the town. By 1908 Torrington had a national bank, three general stores, two hotels and a pharmacy. The town is situated in the fertile valley of the North Platte River and was originally a watering and coaling station for the Chicago, Burlington and Quincy Railroad. Agriculture was the major occupation – sugar beet, beans, potatoes, cattle and sheep – and the Holly Sugar Company which opened in 1926 has remained the major employer in Torrington ever since. Again, a stone from our ancient parish church was sent to Wyoming to be built into the new All Saints' Church there. In 1940 the population was 2,400 which by 1946 had increased to over 4,500. By 2000 it was 5,776 (and refers to itself as a 'city' on its website!). Torrington is on the Oregon Trail.

In 1994 I visited Torrington, Wyoming during a family holiday to the USA. We thought it would be interesting to meet someone from the town and, as we all had connections with Great Torrington School, it seemed logical to try and make contact with their senior school, assuming there was one. I wrote a letter addressed to 'The Principal, Torrington High School' and received a reply from John Binning who wrote, 'Dear Brewers, We are looking forward to your visit. . .'

We found the town to be of a similar size to Great Torrington but located on a plain surrounded by mountains. Its streets were built on a grid system with, seemingly, a church at each intersection and there were pleasant tree-lined streets of attractive houses. The main street was very 'wild west'!

We met John Binning and his wife, Anne, who showed us around their school and we were very impressed with its facilities which included a special room for the school silver band to practise in and a football stadium complete with stand which Bob, my husband, thought was 'awesome'. The school was very proud of its sporting achievements and an honours board listing pupils who had won awards in a variety of sports covered a complete wall of the reception area. Bob, as deputy head of Great Torrington School, had hoped to initiate a contact between our school and theirs but John, who struck us as being rather inward-looking, showed no interest in this idea so nothing came of it. Bob was very disappointed. However, John and Anne were friendly to us and introduced us to a couple of friends and colleagues whom we met for a drink in the Trail Lodge bar one evening and who invited us to breakfast on the morning we were leaving Torrington. We also met a member of the local fire service who told us to call in at the fire station where he gave us various tokens connected to his work to bring back as a greeting to the firemen in our town, which we duly did. I don't know whether any connection was ever forged between the two fire services.

Torrington, New South Wales in Australia was named after its English counterpart in Devon. It is on the Northern Tablelands of the New England district of NSW, at an altitude of 1,200 metres, surrounded by a landscape of spectacular granite rock formations, streams and waterfalls and although there is often snow in winter the summers are delightfully cool in comparison to the surrounding lower areas. The inhabitants feel more Queensland oriented as they are only 30 miles from the border and four hours drive from the state capital, Brisbane, while Sydney, NSW's capital, is a good nine hours drive south.

Torrington Wyoming   Photo courtesy of Bob Brewer

The discovery of the very rich Torrington tin lode in 1881 created much excitement but in a very short time the small prospectors had lost control to overseas mining companies. In the 1920s 500 men were employed at the mines but the industry virtually shut down after the Second World War. Tin mining continued in a small way in the area until the early 1980s and there are still remains of about 360 old mines.Many gem 'fossickers' continue to visit to hunt for topaz, beryl, emerald, quartz and other minerals.Like our town, Torrington NSW is surrounded by common land on which the residents run cattle to keep the roadside verges eaten down to reduce fire hazard. At the end of the 20th century employment centred around shearing, apiary – producing NSW's 'top honey'[4] - the operation of earth-moving machinery and rural employment on the surrounding sheep grazing properties. The population in 1999 was 112.

In 2001 Bob and I went to Australia and we visited Torrington. We turned off the main road just before Deepwater and drove, partly along a dirt road, to the village which was a collection of rather run-down homesteads dotted about in the middle of nowhere. We were made very welcome by Lyn and Ollie Pocock, proprietors of the Tablelands Bar and Grill where we stayed the night. Their son, Steve, took us for a drive into the bush and showed us old mining places, fossicking holes, a rock called 'The Mystery Face' and up to 'Thunderbolt's Lookout' with its wonderful 360 degree view. When we got back, a group of local people had come to the hotel to meet us. We gave them a photo, plaque and map we'd brought as greetings from our Mayor, Roy Foster, and a copy of my book 'Torrington Burning'. Lyn gave us some things in return and the others drifted off and returned with their own gifts which ranged from a handful of gems and home-made Christmas decorations to old photos of Torrington people from a century ago when it was a thriving mining town with 4,000 inhabitants (in 2001 there were 72). We met the Spanish owner of the caravan park and the second oldest inhabitant who was 83 and Bob was challenged to a game of pool by Steve. We were getting pretty hungry and, eventually, Steve disappeared into the kitchen and prepared a scrumptious meal of soup, Nile perch and prawns with vegetables.

Torrington NSW has had a struggle to survive. The saw mill closed in the 1960s. The post office and general store closed in 1997 so the nearest shops are in Emmaville, 15 miles to the west, or Deepwater, 15 miles to the east on the New England Highway. For some years there have not been enough children in the village to keep the school open so they attend school in Emmaville where the vicar, doctor and cottage hospital are also based. The Tableland Bar and Grill closed permanently in October 2003. The population is now (2011) about 85 souls who lead an isolated existence. People who go to Torrington NSW are those who wish to get away from it all.

One of the main characters in Sebastian Faulks's novel, 'Human Traces', comes from Torrington in Lincolnshire. Looking at a present-day map, there are two small hamlets on the edge of Gleasby Moor north of Wragby just off the A157 called East and West Torrington. As far as I am aware, our town has had no contact with these places.

Torrington, NSW

Photo courtesy of Bob Brewer

64   What else is there to see in Torrington?

Old police station:

Peel House, number 7 New Street and Peel Cottage on the edge of the churchyard were the former police station before the present one was built up at Pathfields. The houses next door with the angled front doors were police houses. There was a lock-up round at the back. If you wanted to report something at the police office, you went round the side into the churchyard where there was a stable door with a counter behind it. Dave Kelly remembers 'Trigger', Bill White, Sergeant Ball and Sergeant Street (Michael's father) and said in those days you stood to attention when you saw a policeman. He and Roy Beer, who lived opposite as a boy, remember that the fire siren used to be outside the old police station in New Street.

Old fire station:

The fire station used to be at Barley Grove. There were two sheds, one behind the Newmarket pub and the other by the car park. Ladders were kept in the market hall hung up on the wall and these were removed when the pannier market was refurbished.

The 'football house':

Keep a look out for this house at 21 New Street. Whenever England are taking part in an international football tournament like the World Cup its owners paint the house in the red and white flag of St George.

Graffiti wall:

There is a graffiti wall in the children's playground and skateboard park in Calf Street where young local artists can display their talent.

Old fire station and engine 1929   Photo courtesy of Elaine Weeks

A very old house:

Number 33 South Street is believed to have been here during the Civil War in the 1640s. It was possibly the last house in the street at that time as the neighbouring three-storey house is of a much later date. The present owner moved into the house in 1940 when his mother was headmistress of the Blue Coat School. It was difficult to find a house in Torrington as many of them were being used as billets for members of the regiments who were stationed in the town during the Second World War. There was possibly a small dame school in the house before the Board School in Whites Lane and the Blue Coat School at Barley Grove were started. It is also believed that the property was a telephone exchange at one time: there was a telegraph pole in the back garden which would have brought lines into the house and an alcove indoors where the switchboard could have been. There is also a trapdoor in the floor which leads out to the double BT concrete covers in the street outside. As the owner says, the house would have been the information centre of Torrington with the telephonists able to listen in to local telephone conversations. A brass plate was found in the house bearing the name of a dentist, Mr Willetts, who lived and worked there at one time. There is a system of bells in each room for summoning servants in days gone by.

With thanks to:
Roy Beer
Graham Blair-Williams
Dave Kelly
Grahame Rutherford

Above: The 'football house'   Photo taken by the author

Below: Graffiti wall   Photo taken by the author

Lazarus Press
DEVON

Creedy Publishing
Torrington

Appendix

Present and former shops in Torrington based on a list compiled by Margaret Trounson, Wendy Wigley and Roy Beer
(starting with the most recent and going back in time)

SOUTH STREET
Number:
1 Private house; Tor Books, antiquarian and second-hand books; Rising Sun inn.
2 Private house; 1980s/90s bakers, early 1980s Jolly's; pre-WW2-1960s Squires butchers.
3 Private house; Fashion Fabrics material shop owned by Mia Rothwell and, before her, Roger and Pat Hiscock. May have been a bank at one time.
4 Private house; David Wright accountant; wool shop run by Vera Hutchings in 1980s and then Joan Long; saddler.
5 Easyfixx computer repairs; 2007 Wolfman Tattooz; 2006 tool shop; 1990s chiropodist and osteopath; second-hand shop selling ornaments etc.
7 Crawford's newsagent; 2007 Jeneca Beads; 2004 Body Rock clothing; 1992 Torridge Gallery pictures and framing service; 1990 Special Occasions cards, soft toys and gift wrap; 1970s New Gallery local crafts; The Fisherman's Retreat fishing tackle; Sandford's fruit and vegetables; clothes shop; cosmetics.
8 Private house; 1990s Hardings solicitors; 1980s Wyre's engraver and jeweller; 1960s/70s Windsor's sweet shop; Couch sweets.
Heywood House – 2007 antiquarian books; council office; Hannaford and Ward auctioneer.
9 2007 Silverity jewellers; Love Lea's; Elizabeth Harris's Torrington Jewellers; H & E Pointon watchmaker, jeweller and silversmith; G. S. Wright watchmaker and jeweller; Miss Chubb's sweet shop.
10 Newmarket pub.
11 Love Lea's – shabby chic; 2006 Lets Go travel agent; Dewfresh fruit and veg.
11a (logically 13 but numbered 11a – for good luck?) The Soap Kitchen; Kimber's antiques; late 1990s Bear's Antiques; 1980s Knit-n-Purl wool shop; Lorette's ladies and gents fashions; 1970s Susan fashions; Jennings drapers.
12 and 12a HQ hairdressers / **12a** Designers Florists
 2003 Scammell Adamson estate agents / florist
 1990s Garden Craft flowers
 Badcock's florist
 Ken Sluman's TV and electricals
 1939-1967 Boots the chemist.
14 2012 empty; 2011 Panamart; 2007 Stones Solicitors; 1990s Burd Pearse solicitors; Nationwide building society; Land Society (which became the Nationwide); 1950s/60s Boase and Cruwys solicitors. Morgue at the back so could have been a funeral parlour.
15-17 R & S Ware butchers; 1990s The Freezer Centre; Ernie Lawrence ironmongers; Nancekivell's cottage and ironmongers.
15a 1980s Craft Affair.
16 Taffs fish and chip shop (established 1958); Gabe Lee cabinet maker.

18 Captain Jack's restaurant; West of England pub; Charles Doe linen draper, undertaker and wine merchant.

19 Kebab and pizza (takeaway and eat in); café serving all-day breakfast etc; mid-1990s Pop-In snack bar.

20 Whiskers pet centre; Swallows Tea Shoppe; Plucknett's electricals; Castle Hill studio and china shop.

21 River Reads fishing and second-hand book shop; 1960s Ken Colwill's shoe shop.

22 Co-op supermarket; Somerfield; Gateway; Brian Ford; 1967/69 Wooldridge grocers; Hammett's; 1930s Jack White's grocers; 1920s World Stores; sweet shop.

23 Bickford Centre (for the over 60s); possibly an antique shop here in the 1970s; Frank Musson bicycle shop; 1920s Dyer Hartnoll butchers; Stanley Popham.

24 Xanadu greengrocers; cosmetics etc.

25 Empty; Cosmi-Cuts cards, gifts, toiletries, pots and pans, etc; fruit and vegetables; antiques; Thomas Andrews photographer.

26 Empty; Roo Jaxx clothes; Crush clothes; 1990s Namaste jewellery, essential oils, crystals, incense, crafts etc; Dawn's clothes shop; Horace Sleep (Industrial) Ltd work and leisure wear; 1980s Lorette's ladies and gents fashions; Castle Studios photographer, Ron Newbold.

27 Greenfingers florist; 1970s Way Ahead hairdressers; Wynn Olley hairdressers; 1950s coffee shop owned by the Gent sisters.

28 Landmark Trust building let out as holiday accommodation; 1960s Social Security office; Food Office during the Second World War (rifle range at the back).

29 Maya Indian Cuisine; c1956-2006 P. Frank Singh and Sons clothing, bedding and linen; pre mid-1950s Boase and Cruwys solicitors (cottage at the back where Mr and Mrs Slade lived who cleaned for solicitors).

31 Kiz Angell's ROC (Redeeming Our Communities); Linda Bayliss antiques; The Taste Buds restaurant; Jenkins tea rooms and bakers shop.

37 Browns delicatessen and restaurant; Top of the Town restaurant; Brock's shoe shop; dress shop possibly run by a Miss Beale; Ron Juniper's lawnmower repair shop; 1920s/30s Miss Veale's drapers.

42 Furse House – private house; Singh's clothes shop and general drapers.

46 (owned by Singh family) Londis; Nijjars supermarket. Next door – Instant Images, Embroidery clothes and school uniforms; CAT computer shop; Singh's shoe shop; insurance agent. In the 1960s both shops were the Co-op. Other side of Londis and behind down an alley – P & M Motors.

48 Private house; clockmaker's.

HIGH STREET

Number:

1 Lloyds pharmacy; Peter Turton pharmacist and photographic chemist; 1950s/60s Pringles chemist; 1908 Sidney Buckle chemist.

2 Ian's hairdressing; Frays newsagent and stationers; Hedley Bowden gents outfitters.

3 M & V Ferry hardware and DIY; Pow furnishings; Sing or other furnishings; gas shop.

4 Green Lantern bakers and café; Bowden's outfitters; 1908 Seth Diamond drapers; 1880-1908 James A. Bray; up to 1860s the Bell Inn.

5 NatWest bank; National Provincial bank.

Town Lands office next to Town Hall; public toilets.

7 Post Office; Chapman grocers; J. Lyle grocer; J. J. Handford chemist.

9 Obsessions hairdresser; Sarah Lou hairdresser; 1990s Whiskers pet shop; Torrington Sports including off licence, confectionery, tobacco and fishing permits; G. Nock confectioner and tobacconist; Mrs Tickle's sweet shop.

8 & 10 Squires Electrical and RM Electrical Services/Slice of Life salad and sandwich bar; Squires Electrical; Sparks' seeds, fruit and vegetables/a café, possibly Miss Beer's tea rooms.

11 Fresh 'n' Fruity greengrocers; Chris Heath's garage (closed when Tavern Mews built in 1970s/80s); Nick Rowe's garage (Hillman cars); Eddie Tickle's Central Garage.

12 Barclays bank; butchers.

13 Spar; Sussex gas showroom; Neales dress shop; Webbers drapers; Hoopers general drapers, tea and grocery.

14 Torrington Jewellers (Elizabeth Harris); 2004 HQ hairdressers; office stationery.

15 Black Horse.

16 The Mole and the Haggis bookshop; 14/16 Heywood and Hodge ammunition dealers and ironmongers.

17 Webbers estate agents (previously with Bristol and West branch); 1960s antique shop; Copper Kettle café; Frisby's shoe shop; 1950s Squires record shop; 1920s R. J. Tippett confectioner and fruiterer (sign revealed when Webbers refurbished the outside); India and China Tea Company provision merchants.

FORE STREET
Number:

1 Empty; HSBC bank; Midland bank; Turrall stationery; Mr Beck's chemist.

2 Lloyds TSB bank; Bill Bowden tailor (gents outfitters) above.

3 Toyzone; Ron Martin's Toy Box; Serendipity crafts and quality gifts; Direct – Hotpoint centre; SWEB; Mr Luxton's bakers.

4 Butchers – Steve Gladwin, Farm Fresh, Reddaway, John Watkins.

5 Red Cross shop; Nick Harman's restaurant.

6 Sorting office; Post Office; 1850 Bartlett and Fowlers printing office.

7 Globe hotel.

8 Studio C (opened July 2011); empty for years; Martins newsagent; Hargreaves newsagent; Dywells newsagent and café; Shorts paper shop.

8a Chapters hair salon; 1999 Westcountry Pasties; 1993 Choices gift shop; 1980s Kathy's Fashions.

9 Plough arts centre; drill hall.

10 A & J opticians; Great Torrington cards and balloons; P & L Trading – new and used household and gardening items; Eastmonds ironmongers.

13 Bond Oxborough estate agents; Peter Adams estate agents; Dyers jewellers and watchmakers; 1991 Reflections fashion and leisure; 1990 Westward financial services; Davies drapers.

15 John Patt fruit and vegetables; Milburn's dress shop; Metherall's dress shop and drapers; Mountjoy and Baker dress shop.

POTACRE STREET
Number:

2 Nationwide building society; Portman building society; Regency West of England building society; part of Downing's drapers.

4 The Garage in the Square – motor, marine, agricultural.

6 Sandford's bakers; Warnes greengrocers; Blatchford saddler; rag and bone.

8 Private house; Rebecca's restaurant; Les Weeks Castle Drinks (home-made lemonade).

10a Forget-Me-Not tearoom and gallery 'coming soon' (April 2012); Taylor's tearoom gallery (closed in 2012); Cherry's tea rooms; Jack Stevens hairdresser; 1990 Just Juniors baby and childrenswear; Mrs Babbington's shop.

12 SPRA (Society for the Protection and Rehoming of Animals) charity shop; health food shop; 1980s/90s Bacchus Wines; Potacre Street Studio local crafts; Mr Ashley's and Mr Davis's gents outfitters at different times.

16 used to be the Black Swan pub.

CORNMARKET STREET

Number:

2 Torrington Framing; 2011 Jeneca Beads; Cowling estate agents; Partners estate Agents; 1990s Trilby's hairdressers; 1980s Sue Searle 'And Pigs Can Fly' art and crafts; c1935-45 possibly Ralph Reddaway milliner.

4 Part of Kenwyn stove company; 1960s Gem cleaners; music shop; Mr Penberthy pianos.

5 Empty; Slice of Life/Second Nature beauty clinic; Mendham's hairdresser.

6 Kenwyn stove company; card shop; 1980s Pandora's Box; Gates estate agents; Mrs Squires sweets.

7 Jayne Poole photographer; Bert Malton turf accountants; Plucknett's radios; MrSquire's radios; Mr Old's grocers ('the best ham in town').

9 Empty; café; 1990s Choices gift shop; 1980s The Brass and Gift Shop; Mrs Babbington's toys and gifts. It was a stationers and turned into a barracks during WW2.

9a 1998 Computers and Things.

12 Tanya's holistic beauty and nails; 1999 Occasions party accessories; 1993 R & G Autos – car spares and accessories; Rowe clocks.

20/22 Volunteer Bureau; Hospice shop; Mrs Long's wool shop; 1960s Slade greengrocer/Pophams bakers; Stapleton's fruit and vegetables.

24 Private house; The House of the Setting Sun gift shop and café; Setting Sun pub.

CASTLE STREET

Number:

1 Tattersalls letting agency; 1980s Robinson Cooke estate agents; Alford's boots and shoes.

18 R. Gist & Son funeral directors and monumental masons.

PANNIER MARKET

Up left hand side:

1 & 3 Crafty Needles wools, materials and accessories; Brown's butchers.

5 Fish 'n' Chip (creative, restore, re-invent).

7 Times Past.

9 Sheena's sweet shop; 2006 What a load of old cobblers – watch and shoe repairs, key cutting; 2004 River Reads – angling pastimes.

11 Odds & Sods second-hand furniture, antiques, collectables.

13 Market café.

Market hall at the top where local produce, cards, books, fish, household items and lots more are sold on Thursday, Friday and Saturday.

Up right hand side:

2 CAT (Computers At Torrington); Dragonfly crafts; 2006 As crafty as you like – craft items for making cards, scrapbooks etc; 2000 Lamplight lighting of all kinds; Bromley's bakers.

4 & 6 Fiddlesticks Trading Co.

8 Socks.

10 Red Cross shop.

12 Second-Hand Toys – swap shop.

14 The Gallery – an arts and crafts co-operative; 2006 Helen Bailes ceramics and crafts; 2004 As crafty as you like.

WELL STREET
Number:

2 Paul Donner optician; Downing's drapers.

2a Yau's House Chinese take-away; Loi's House Chinese take-away; part of Downings.

3 Joanna Ford books, antiques and collectables; Ralph Mitchell's wet fish shop; 1990s Town and Country Financial Services – Mike Scone; Mrs Eady's fish and chips.

4 Jack and Molly's Trading Company; charity shops including Faith, Hope and Charity and Well Spring; Carousel Crafts; Copp's printers.

5 Hospice shop; 2004 Torrington Family Project; 1990s Torridge bathroom, heating and tile centre; Crocus 'n' Toads teenage drop-in centre; 1980s the freezer centre; Yeo's china and furnishings.

7 L. A. Wash 'n' Dry launderette; 1980s Trilby's hair stylists; George Yeo's ironmongers and toys.

30 Private house; Jade designer clothes and knitwear, handmade pottery and antique jewellery.

31 Bissett's shoes.

33 Kia Ora fish and chips take-away and café; Mrs Thacker's café; Jury's café (with the first jukebox in town?).

On the north side of the street the Old Inn Mews marks the site where there was once an old pub of that name. Next door there used to be a babywear factory – Robec's – run by a Mr and Mrs Beck where lots of local women worked. A bookie operated from one of the cottages with steps up to the front door next to the Admiral Vernon (previously the New Inn and now a private house). After a couple of cottages there was a garage, Hammond's re-spraying which had been Heard's garage where buses were parked, now Elizabeth Court. There was an old thatched cottage where Percy Reed had his barber shop, next to number 24, a double-fronted house, and then the Cavalier pub (previously called the Hunters Inn).

On the south side of Well Street, from Kia Ora to the end and around the corner (where Cavalier Court is now) used to be Heard's garage. Then it became Les Smale & Son motorcycles and cycles. Now (April 2012) along that stretch are:

Well Street Clinic – Chiropody, Osteopathy, Reflexology,Sports Massage.

Chef Lin – Chinese meals to take away.

Basil's off-licence, DVD rental and confectionery and Vision On video rental.

Lower Well Street (on the other side of New Road) –

42 Third door along on the left was a Co-op.

69 Tayberry Cottage – all foods and tobacco. (Is this Alice Reed's?)

74 1940s-60s Popham's bakers.

NEW ROAD

On western side of the street –

New Road Garage – sales, service and repairs.

McColls general store; BJ's; 1990s Tuck Shop videos.

Sing & Gist carpets, furniture, beds, curtains.
On eastern side of the street –
Barley Grove service station – BP, previously Shell.
Torbridge vet group; Bunter Curtis tuck shop.

HALSDON ROAD / WHITES LANE
6 Halsdon Terrace – dental practice; 1980s/90sTarka Country Hotel; Norman and Sue Marsh's vegetarian hotel; Council Office.
5 Halsdon Terrace – 1980s Oliver's wholefoods; Just Juniors baby and childrenswear.
The house to the left of the school – 1950s/60s June Leate's sweet shop.
Next door to Leate's sweet shop – 1930s Miss Mountjoy's tuck shop.
The house to the right of the school – Roy Leate's electrical shop called H. H. Burrows.

MILL STREET
5 Private house; Potter's shop.
29 Sandfords Gardens on corner with Mill Street – Private house for disabled; Derek and Margaret Bidgway's general store.
130 Private house; fish and chip shop.

NEW STREET
By Church Gate – empty to let; Instant Images embroidery and school uniform; Ooh La La fascinators, hats, basques etc; Crawford's newsagent; Bowden printers above; Jack Hutchings newsagent; Ernie Rew bookie and Clean Windows.
Church Walk – 1990s The Toy Box.
Number:
4 (corner of School Lane) Private house; 1940s/50s Mr Plucknett's radio and electrical shop.
6 Dafforn undertaker; café for teenagers which didn't get off the ground; 1990s Young's newsagents; Creighton's newsagent and convenience store.
12 Private house; Tracey's restaurant; Cobbledick's animal feed; egg packing; petrol pump.
Tapscott's glove factory was next door, set back from the road.
26 Bruce Edyvean's monumental stone mason.
29 Private house; 1990s S. Kingston quality fruit shop; Patt's greengrocers; John Creighton's paper shop; after WW1 Mr Langloyd's paper shop.
32 Mr Slade's sweet shop.
44 Mr Kelly's fish shop.
50 The Soup Kitchen; late 1990s Westcountry Pasties; 1960s-1990s Darch's butchers; Mr Kelly's meat shop.
56 Private house; Slade's general store.
58 Private house; Dave Ward's glass and glazing; Marshall's yard (home of the station bus?).
72 Private house; undertakers; cabinet and coffin maker and home maintenance.
74 Private house; Mr Len Short hairdresser.
Baptist church was British restaurant during the war.
85 Private house; Pett's butchers; late 1930s/40s Mrs Copp's sweet shop.
85a Private house; 1980s-90s Allen's Stores; Mrs Fisher's stores; Glad Hutchins general store; post WW2 Bert Watkins butcher.

116 Ron Sussex and Sons plumbing and heating engineers (access in Stonemans Lane); 1940s Whiteman's cake shop; Miss Silliphant's bakers.
125 Private house; 1950s Mrs Bowden's general store.
In public car park next to Lidl – Torrington Motors; Halsdon Machinery; during WW2 Pope's garage.
179 Private house; 1890s grocery and sweet shop with advertisements for Fry's Cocoa and Quaker Oats outside.
Next to number **184** was Torrington Animal Supplies.
196 Private house; Weeks butchers in garage.
199 Private house; Flossy Newcombe's sweet shop.
203 1936 Clarence Blight made and sold early wireless sets (Radio Normandy).

TOWN PARK
15 or 17 Mr and Mrs P. Avery's general store.

CALF STREET
Number:
Doe Court; Sid Roberts's garage (also ambulance kept here); Les Smale's garage.
7 Private house; Torrington Angling Supplies.
11 Private house; Mrs Potter's sweet shop.
12 Private house; Cardew blacksmith.
35 Private house; hairdressers; Miss Taylor's groceries.
57 Private house; cabinet maker.
77 'Charcoal' Nicholls fish and chip shop ('he knew how to burn his fish and chips!').
94 Happydays convenience store; Eight till Late; 1990s Masons late shop; Spar; Centra food market; Gilbert's started by Ernie Gilbert in the 1950s; Mr Darch's shippen and dairy.
At entrance to Torrington Gate, Morton garage; Goose Green garage; Herbie Baker garage and sweet shop.

With thanks also to:
John and Jackie Davis

Notes

1   Where is Torrington?
1.'A Jerusalem in England', *Western Morning News*, 9 January 1964 referring to an article entitled 'Torrington' by Rev. G. Frankling Owen in the *Western Daily Standard* (published in Plymouth 1869-70). 'Torrington certainly is a "surprise find" for any tourists who have never heard of or seen this English Jerusalem.'

2   Is the town called Torrington or Great Torrington?
1.'Tun' (later spelt 'ton') means farm, therefore Toritun (Torrington) is farm (or estate) on the Torridge. (Alexander and Hooper – 'The History of Great Torrington' p.5)
2.Tristram Risdon – 'Survey of Devon'.
3.Rev. Frederick Colby – 'The History of Great Torrington'.

3   How old is the town?
1.Leonard Jackson – 'Roads and Bridges of the Torridge Valley'.
2.There is local folklore about King Hubba the Dane being killed in a battle at 'Bloody Corner' in Northam. Nick Arnold, a children's author from Appledore who writes the 'Horrible Science' books, has discovered that a real Viking called Ubbi Ragnarsson was killed in a battle in a fortress named Cynuit in 878. He has a theory that this battle was fought, not in Northam, but at Kenwith on the Beaford road outside Torrington. The name Cynuit can be linked to the nearby settlement called Kingscott. He is writing a paper on the battle and intends to publish a short version of it on the Appledore Book Festival website and may turn his research into a book for children. (*North Devon Journal*, 18 September 2008).
3.'Domesday Book' edited by John Morris.
4.W. G. Hoskins – 'Devon' p.59.
5.Alexander and Hooper – 'The History of Great Torrington' p.16.
6.John Leland – The Itinerary of John Leland the Antiquary 1534 – 1543 in 'Early Tours in Devon and Cornwall' edited by R. Pearse Chope (also quoted in Alexander and Hooper p.25).

4   What is the Population of Torrington?
1.Calculated by John Wardman – 'The Forgotten Battle'.
2.Wardman p.62.

5   Where was the Medieval Castle situated?
1.R. A. Higham and S. Goddard – 'Proceedings of the Devon Archaeological Society', vol. 45 (1987), Department of History and Archaeology, Exeter University (from the archive of the Great Torrington Bowling Club).
2.Higham and Goddard.

7   What happens at May Fair?
1.*North Devon Journal*, 8 May 1924 – 'Revival of May-Fair'.
2.*North Devon Journal*, 8 May 1939 – 'Torrington Forges Forward'
3.From a typescript, source unknown, in Torrington library archive box file.

8   What are those Strip Fields across the valley?
1.Alexander and Hooper p.74.
2.Bill Horner, Devon County Council assistant archaeologist, *North Devon Journal*, 9 July 1998.

10   Did Torrington ever have a Livestock Market?
1.Tristram Risdon – 'Survey of Devon' p.272 quoted in Alexander and Hooper p.168.
2.John Wardman- 'The Forgotten Battle' p.65.
3.G. M. Doe – Trans. Dev. Assoc. lxxi, p.54 quoted in Alexander and Hooper p.114.

4.G. M. Doe – 'Sticks and Stones' and L. R. Jackson – 'Roads and Bridges of the Torridge Valley' p.13.
5.G. M. Doe – 'Some Torrington Sticks and Stones'.
6.Alexander and Hooper p.113.

11   When was the Battle of Torrington?
1.1645 according to the Julian Calendar (see full explanation in Notes for 'How old is the parish church?').
2.John Wardman – 'The Forgotten Battle: Torrington 1646'
3.R. W. Cotton – 'Barnstaple during the Great Civil War' p.481.
4.Alexander and Hooper – 'The History of Great Torrington' p.85.
5.P. Q. Karkeek – paper on 'Fairfax in the West' read at the Ashburton meeting of the Devonshire Association in 1876, quoted in Alexander and Hooper p.90-92.

13   How far do the Commons extend and for how long have they existed?
1.Www.torringtoncommon.co.uk.
2.Risdon – 'Survey of Devon'.
3.Collingham – 'Torrington Common: A guide to life on the Common 2001-2002'.
4.Alexander and Hooper – 'A History of Great Torrington' p.80.
5.Barber – 'A Sketchbook of Torrington Commons' p.14/15.
6.Barber p.16.
7.Barber p.6.
8.Barber p.25.
9.Barber p.26.
10.Barber p.30.
11.Barber p.31.
12.Barber p.32.
13.Barber p.22.

14   Who are the Torrington Cavaliers?
1.Bob Brewer – 'Built to Burn: The Great Torrington Cavaliers 1970-2010'.
2.Judy Barber – 'A Sketchbook of Torrington Commons' pp.14 and 34.
3.Barber p.36.

15   Where was the Old Workhouse?
1.Trans. Dev. Assoc. lxx, p.228 G. M. Doe quoted in Alexander and Hooper p.131.

16   Which are the Oldest Streets in the town?
1.John Wardman – 'The Forgotten Battle' p.62 and Alexander and Hooper – 'The History of Great Torrington' p.207/8.
2.Wardman p.62/3 from Folios 7,92,93,99; A Survey of the Towns Lands.
3.Wardman p.63.
4.George M. Doe – 'Old Torrington Landmarks'.
5.Leonard Jackson – 'Roads and Bridges of the Torridge Valley'.
6.Westcote – 'View of Devonshire'.
7.Alexander and Hooper pp.207-210.
8.Jackson.
9.Peter Christie – 'North Devon History' – article in *Bideford Gazette*, 5 February 1982 – 'When was New Road new?'
10.*Devon and Exeter Gazette*, 7 December 1928 and Doe – 'Old Torrington Landmarks'
11.Jackson – 'Roads and Bridges ...'
12.Alexander and Hooper p.155.
13.Cherry and Pevsner – 'The Buildings of England: Devon'

14. Judy Barber – 'Little Torrington and Taddiport' p.158.
15. Alexander and Hooper p.58.
16. Jackson – 'Roads and Bridges'
17. Rosemary Anne Lauder – 'Market Towns of North Devon'.

18   What Industries were there in Torrington in the past?
1. Alexander and Hooper – 'The History of Great Torrington' p.168.
2. John Leland – 'Early Tours in Devon and Cornwall' quoted in Alexander and Hooper p.168.
3. Tristram Risdon p.272 quoted in Alexander and Hooper p.168.
4. Eman Bowen – 'Map of Devonshire Hundreds' c1750 quoted in Alexander and Hooper p.169.
5. Lewis's 'Topographical Dictionary of England' 1833 quoted in Alexander and Hooper p.170.
6. George M. Doe in a paper read at Barnstaple, 1938.
7. Tristram Risdon quoted in Alexander and Hooper p.173.
8. Alexander and Hooper p.174.
9. Alexander and Hooper p.175.
10. Alison Grant – 'North Devon Pottery' p.95 (Edward Gaskell *publishers* 2005)

19   What Industries are there in Torrington?
1. Mike Lamprey – Mayor of Torrington (1998/99).
2. *North Devon Journal*, 25 November 2010 – 'Residents complain about "putrid" smell'.

20   Where does the River Torridge rise?
1. Rosemary Anne Lauder – 'A Tale of Two Rivers' p.47.
2. Leonard R. Jackson – 'Roads and Bridges of the Torridge Valley' p.61.
3. Jackson p.56.
4. Jackson p.56.
5. Jackson p.55.
6. Judy Barber – 'A Sketchbook of the Commons' p.12.
7. Jackson.

23   How long has there been a Community Hospital in Torrington?
1. Endowed Charities (County of Devon) Parish of Great Torrington, 1919, pp.56 ff quoted in Alexander and Hooper p.78).

24   Is Taddiport part of Torrington?
1. Alexander and Hooper – 'The History of Great Torrington' p.23.
2. Judy Barber – 'Little Torrington and Taddiport' p.10.
3. Alexander and Hooper p.75.
4. Barber p.67.
5. Barber p.9.
6. Barber p.9.
7. Barber p.10.
8. Rosemary Anne Lauder – 'A Tale of Two Rivers' p.32.
9. Barber p.152/3.
10. Barry D. Hughes – 'Rolle Canal and The North Devon Limestone Trade' p.59 Edward Gaskell *publishers* 2006.
11. Hughes p.59
12. Sue Scrutton – 'Lord Rolle's Canal' p.38.
13. Barber p.23.

25   How old is the Pannier Market?
1. Moira Brewer – 'Torrington Burning' p.19-20.

26　When was there a Railway Service to Torrington?
1.Rod Garner – 'The Torrington and Marland Light Railway', p.7.
2.John Nicholas – 'Lines to Torrington' p.30.
3.Nicholas pp.31 and 39.
4.Nicholas p.39.
5.Garner p.68.
6.Nicholas p.79.
7.Nicholas pp.79 and 88.
8.Nicholas p.88.
9.Nicholas p.88/89.
10.Nicholas p.89.
11.Nicholas p.89.
12.Nicholas p.106.

27　Why is the glass factory called Dartington Crystal?
1.Robert Marshall – 'Made in Devon' article in 'Devon Life', Vol. 7 1971 April pp.26-28.
2.Linda and Stuart Smithson – 'Dartington Glass: The First Twenty Years 1967-1987. Incorporating Wedgewood Crystal 1983-1987. The Art of Frank Thrower' (Published by L. and S. Smithson, Torrington, 2007).

28　Where was Sydney House?
1.www.great-torrington.com/to-do-and-see/secret-garden.html

29　How many Churches are there in Torrington?
1.Alexander and Hooper – 'The History of Great Torrington' pp.163 and 164.
2.Alexander and Hooper p.164.
3.'A Short History of the Baptist Churches in North Devon', 1885, p.32.
4.Alexander and Hooper p.167.
5.Alexander and Hooper p.161.
6.www.bidefordcatholicchurches.org.uk/torringtoninfo.htm

30　How old is the Parish Church?
1.The Julian calendar was formerly in use in many European countries and their colonies rather than the Gregorian calendar currently in use in most countries. For a period of 170 years (1582-1752) both dating systems were in concurrent use in different parts of Western Europe and its colonies. The Julian calendar had drifted by 11 days from the solar calendar (due to its excess of leap years) so dates differ between the systems. The start of the Julian year was not always 1st January and was altered at different times in different countries. From the 12th century to 1752 the civil or legal year in England began on 25th March (Lady Day) so, for example, the execution of Charles I was recorded at the time in Parliament as happening on 30th January 1648 while in modern English language texts this date is usually recorded as 30th January 1649. Thus the Battle of Torrington was recorded at the time as February 1645 while today we generally refer to it as having taken place in February 1646.
2.Tristram Risdon - 'Survey of Devon' p.272.
3.*White's Devonshire Directory* of 1850.
4.Risdon p.273.
5.'Devon and Cornwall Notes and Queries', i, p.126 quoted in Alexander and Hooper p.57.
6.Alexander and Hooper – 'The History of Great Torrington' p.29.
7.George M. Doe – 'Old Torrington Landmarks'.
8.33 metres.
9.Cherry and Pevsner – 'The Buildings of England: Devon'.
10.'Church Guide' website – www.great-torrington.org.uk/guide.htm
11.The preceding paragraphs are taken from the 'Church Guide' website.

12.*The Crier*, December 2008/January 2009 – 'St Michael's Church Tower Development'.
13.Dr F. T. Colby, Trans. Dev. Assoc., 1889, 'Torrington Worthies' quoted in Alexander and Hooper p.50.
14.*North Devon Journal*, 15 April 2010 – 'Vicar's goodbye after 30 years'.
15 *North Devon Journal*, 25 August 2011 – 'New rector will arrive next month'.

31   What Shops are there in Torrington?

1.*North Devon Journal*, 26 May 2011 – 'Good citizen award for traders.'
2.Torrington Fairtrade Guide 2011.
3.*North Devon Journal*, 21 January 2010 – 'Tatt's Life' by Anne Tattersall.
4.*North Devon Journal*, 3 March 2011 – 'Lease of café famous for its 45p cup of tea is up for sale.'
5.*North Devon Journal*, 1 December 2011 – 'Town bank to close' by Will Topps.
6.Items from Peter Christie's 'Looking Back' column in the *North Devon Journal* (1951-59).
7.*North Devon Gazette*, 27 July 2011 – 'Shop filled with French goods.'

33   How long has Torrington been twinned with Roscoff?

1.The *Observer*, 21 December 2008 – 'Tradition of French onion farmers in UK under threat' by Elizabeth Day.
2.The *Guardian*, 2 December 2011 – 'Small-town Tory council dumps continental "twins"' by Luke Harding.

34   Who were the Rolles?

1.Rosemary Anne Lauder – 'Vanished Houses of North Devon' p.6.

35   How many Pubs are there in Torrington?

1.Terry Finnamore – 'Petticoats to Pitchforks' p.31-32.

36   Where is Mill Street?

1.Alexander and Hooper – 'The History of Great Torrington' p.164.

38   What is that empty building that looks rather like a chapel in Whites Lane?

1.Devon Life, October 1990 – 'Keeping the upper hand' by Margaret Waddingham.
2.Industries of North Devon, author unknown, written in 1880s.

39   Where is Rosemoor?

1.*The Garden Magazine*, May 2010 – 'RHS Garden Rosemoor' by Jim Gardiner.
2.Gardiner.

40   What happened in Torrington during the Second World War?

1.Peter Christie – – Suffering on the Crimean Battlefields' - 'Even More North Devon History p.77. Edward Gaskell *publishers*
2.John Nicholas – 'Lines to Torrington' p.72.
3.Terry Finnamore – 'Petticoats to Pitchforks' Edward Gaskell *publishers* p.14.
4.Terry Finnamore p.35.
5.Terry Finnamore p.39.
6.Terry Finnamore p.58.

41   What Sports are played in Torrington?

1.Information from Wikipedia.
2.*North Devon Journal*, 16 February 2012 – 'Torrington swimming pool set to reopen.'
3.*North Devon Gazette*, 18 April 2012 – '24-hour swim relay helps struggling club.'
4.Judy Barber – 'A Sketchbook of Torrington Commons' p.30.

42   Is the Bowling Club really as old as the date on its clubhouse?
1.P. Q. Karkeek – 'Fairfax in the West' read at the Ashburton meeting of the Devonshire Association in 1876.
2.Battle of Torrington, 1645 or 1646? See explanation of Julian calendar in use at the time in Notes for 'How old is the parish church?'
3.Alexander and Hooper p.141.
4.Higham and Goddard, Department of History and Archaeology, Exeter University.

43   Which are the Notable Buildings in the town?
1.W. G. Hoskins – 'Devon'.
2.Cherry and Pevsner – 'The Buildings of England: DEVON'.
3.Cherry and Pevsner.
4.'Retirement Time' by 'The Viper':

I feel the time has come at last
For me to pack my bags
And snake off to retirement
And to think up some new gags.

I've packed my fangs and shedded skins
And polished up my scales
And to Towcester I will slither now
As I take my final bow.

I send you all my kind regards
My love and admiration
And I know that you will all stay strong
Throughout the whole duration.

And so I leave the Town Hall Trust
With a chuckle and a smile
And I hope that I've amused you all
Three years? That's quite a while!

I think I've done all that I can
And sense some mild applause
And who knows? One day I might come back
To support another cause.

5.Rosemary Sutcliff – 'Blue Remembered Hills' p.83.
6.Rosemary Sutcliff – 'Blue Remembered Hills' p.84.
7.Great Torrington Free Town Guide 2008.
8.Alexander and Hooper – 'The History of Great Torrington' p.152/153.
9.Cherry and Pevsner.
10.'Time and Chance' by Averil Mackenzie-Grieve who lived at Castle Hill as a child.
11.*The Crier* December 2011/January 2012 – 'Vicarage Turkey Oak Tree' by Chris Foster.
12.A. E. Richardson and C. Lovell-Gill – 'Regional Architecture of the West of England.'
13.Alexander and Hooper pp.50,51 and 151.
14.Judy Barber – 'Little Torrington and Taddiport: The Memories of a Devon Parish' p.65.
15.Sophie Lund – 'Salvage Operation' – article about Cross in House and Garden, October 1998.

51 What goes on at the Plough?
1.*North Devon Journal Herald*, 20 August 1914.
2.*North Devon Journal Herald*.
3.*North Devon Gazette*, 28 December 2011 – 'Cash windfall for Plough'.
4.www.plough-arts.org/mural.php

52 What is the long cobble-covered hump in the churchyard?
1.*North Devon Journal*, 22 February 1996 – 'Torrington fights the Civil War again' by Rob Baker.
2.*The Crier*, February 2012 – 'Heritage Museum' by Val Morris.
3.*North Devon Journal*, 27 January 2011 – 'Remembering victims of the Civil War'.

53 When was the Torrington Canal in operation and where was it?
1.Sue Scrutton – 'Lord Rolle's Canal' p.5.
2.Barry D. Hughes – 'Rolle Canal and the North Devon Limestone Trade' p.39.
3.Scrutton p.14.
4.Hughes p.57.
5.Hughes p.57.
6.Scrutton p.61.

55 How long has the Library been at Castle Hill?
1.*The Bideford and North Devon Weekly Gazette*, 24th August 1937.
2.Devon Libraries 'Welcome' leaflet (Devon County Council).

57 How many Schools are there in Torrington?
1.www.bluecoat.childrencentre.org/
2.*North Devon Journal*, 28 July 2011 – 'Children's centre wins praise in Ofsted report'.
3.*North Devon Journal*, 1 December 2005 – 'Outdoor activities help pupils learn' by Adam Wilshaw.
4.www.great-torrington-junior.co.uk/
5.www.greattorrington.devon.sch.uk/
6.Alexander and Hooper – 'The History of Great Torrington' p.149-150.
7.Alexander and Hooper p.149.
8.Alexander and Hooper p.151.
9.Alexander and Hooper p.153-154.

58.What is that Derelict Factory down in the river valley below Torrington?
1.Alexander and Hooper – 'The History of Great Torrington' p.177.
2.*Bideford and North Devon Gazette*, 13 May 1983 – 'Computer-controlled butter-making at Torrington plant'.
3.*Guardian*, 28 November 1992 – 'Families face jobs void as dairy town is milked by economy.'

61 Has there been much New Building recently in Torrington?
1.John Wardman – 'The Forgotten Battle' p.63 from a survey of the Towns Lands.
2.As told to me by Dave Kelly.

63 Does Torrington have any contact with other towns of the same name?
1.Alexander and Hooper – 'The History of Great Torrington' p.202.
2.Alexander and Hooper p.202.
3.Alexander and Hooper -.203.
4.Letter from Beverley and Malcolm Bower of Torrington NSW to the Mayor, Mayoress, Councillors and people of Great Torrington, Devon, 17 December 1999.

Bibliography

Alexander, J. J. and Hooper , W. R. – 'The History of Great Torrington in the County of Devon' (Advance Studio, Sutton, Surrey, 1948)

'A Short History of the Baptist Churches in North Devon', 1885

Barber, Judy – 'A Sketchbook of Torrington Commons' (Published by The Commons Conservators, Torrington, Devon, 1993)

Barber, Judy – 'Little Torrington and Taddiport: Memories of a Devon Parish' (Published by the Little Torrington Parish Council, 2005)

Barber, Judy – 'The Plough: Past and Present' (1994)

Bower, Beverley and Malcolm – Letter from Torrington, NSW to the Mayor, Mayoress, Councillors and people of Great Torrington, Devon – 17 December 1999

Brewer, Bob – 'Built to Burn: The Great Torrington Cavaliers 1970-2010' (Creedy Publishing, 2010)

Brewer, Moira – 'Torrington Burning' (Creedy Publishing, 1996)

Cherry, Bridget and Pevsner, Niklaus – 'The Buildings of England: Devon', Second Edition, (Penguin, 1989)

Christie, Peter – 'A North Devon Chronology' from 'The Heritage Album: 175 years in North Devon (1824-1999)' reproduced courtesy of the *North Devon Journal*

Christie, Peter – 'Even More North Devon History' - 'Suffering on the Crimean Battlefields' (Edward Gaskell *publishers*, 1998)

Christie, Peter – 'Looking Back' (1951-59) in the *North Devon Journal*

Christie, Peter – 'North Devon History' (Edward Gaskell *publishers*, 1995)

Colby, Rev. Frederick T. – 'The History of Great Torrington' (read at Torrington, July 1875). Reports of the Devonshire Association, Vol. 7, 1875

Collingham, Michael – 'Torrington Common: A guide to life on the Common 2001-2002'

Cotton, R. W. – 'Barnstaple during the Great Civil War' (London, 1889)

Cresswell, Beatrix F. – 'Some Notes on the History of the Parish Church of Saint Michael, Great Torrington' (Exeter: Southwoods [Exeter] Ltd, 1929)

Devon Circular Walks, Great Torrington Area (1) Torrington Commons

Devon Libraries 'Welcome' leaflet (Devon County Council)

Devon Life, October 1990 – 'Keeping the upper hand' by Margaret Waddingham

Doe, George M. – 'Devon and Cornwall Notes and Queries' Vol. XIX (1936-37)

Doe, George M. – 'Old Torrington Landmarks' (Bideford Gazette Ltd, 1931)

Doe, George M. – 'Some Torrington Sticks and Stones' (Bideford Gazette Ltd, 1928)

Finnamore, Terry – 'Petticoats to Pitchforks' (Edward Gaskell *publishers*, Bideford 2004)

Gardiner, Jim – 'RHS Garden Rosemoor' article in 'The Garden', May 2010

Garner, Rod – 'The Torrington and Marland Light Railway' (Kestrel Railway Books and Rod Garner, 2006)

Gazebo at Rosemoor – information panels in gazebo

Gough, Terry – 'The Tarka Trail' – Exploring the old rail routes by cycle and foot (Railway Heritage from the Nostalgia Collection, 1998)

Grant, Alison – 'North Devon Pottery' (Edward Gaskell *publishers* 2005)

Great Torrington and District Community Development Trust leaflet

Great Torrington and District Community Development Trust Ltd First Annual Report – 'Parting the Clouds', 1 April 1996 – 31 March 1997

Great Torrington Commons Conservators – 'Torrington Common Tree Trail'

Great Torrington Free Town Guides – 1994, 1997, 2004, 2008

Great Torrington Town Traders Guide (2011)

Great Torrington Union Workhouse, from the 1871 census

Great Torrington School Log Book

Higham, R. A. and Goddard, S. – 'Proceedings of the Devon Archaeological Society', vol. 45 (1987) (from the archive of the Great Torrington Bowling Club)

Hoskins, W. G. - 'Devon' (Collins, 1954)

House and Garden, October 1998 – 'Salvage Operation' by Sophie Lund

Hughes, Barry D. – 'Rolle Canal and The North Devon Limestone Trade (Edward Gaskell *publishers*, 2006)

Industries of North Devon – Vaughan's Glove Factory – author unknown

Jackson, Leonard R. - 'Roads and Bridges of the Torridge Valley'

Jenkinson, Tim and Taylor, Patrick – 'The Toll-houses of North Devon' (Polystar Press,

Ipswich, 2010)

Karkeek, P. Q. – 'Fairfax in the West' read at the Ashburton meeting of the Devonshire Association in 1876.

Keble Martin, Rev. W. – 'Flora of Devon' (1939)

Kelly's Directories 1866, 1873 and 1935

Lampard-Vachell, B. G. – 'Wild Birds of Torrington and District' (1944)

Landmark Trust Spring 1997 Newsletter – article by David Alexander

Lauder, Rosemary Anne – 'A Tale of Two Rivers' (Maslands, Tiverton, 1986)

Lauder, Rosemary Anne – 'Market Towns of North Devon' (Halsgrove, 1983)

Lauder, Rosemary Anne – 'Vanished Houses of North Devon' (Self-published, 1981)

Leland, John – 'The Itinerary of John Leland the Antiquary 1534-43' in 'Early Tours in Devon and Cornwall' edited by R. Pearse Chope (first published in 1918). Reprinted with a new introduction by Alan Gibson (David and Charles, Newton Abbot, 1967)

Lysons – 'History of Devonshire', 1822

Marshall, Robert – 'Made in Devon' article in 'Devon Life', Vol. 7 1971 April pp.26, 27, 28

Miller, Shan – 'Taddiport: Leper Colony' pamphlet

Morris, John: general editor – 'Domesday Book: 9 Devon' edited by Caroline and Frank Thorn (Phillimore, Chichester, 1985)

Nicholas, John – 'Lines to Torrington' (Oxford Publishing Co. 1984)

Nicholson, Jay – film of Vaughan's Glove Factory, 2002

Pigot's Directories 1822-23 and 1830

Richardson, A. E. and Lovell-Gill, C. – 'Regional Architecture of the West of England'

Risdon, Tristram – 'Survey of Devon', c1632 (printed 1714/full version 1811)

Robb, Graham – 'The Discovery of France' (Picador, 2007)

Sainsbury, Peter – 'The Transition from Tradition to Technology: A history of the Dairy Industry in Devon' (1991)

Sampson, Mike – 'An outline history of the modern day fair' in History and Archives of the May Fair

Scott, Sir Walter – 'Marmion' (Canto VI, section XXX)

Scoular, Sheila – pamphlet 'Discover Great Torrington, North Devon – The English Jerusalem'

Scrutton, Susan – 'Lord Rolle's Canal' (Jamaica Press, Hartland, 2006)

Scrutton, Susan and Cramp, Harry – 'Sydney House' (published by Great Torrington Town Council, MMII)

Smithson, Linda and Stuart – 'Dartington Glass: The First Twenty Years 1967-1987. Incorporating Wedgewood Crystal 1983-1987. The Art of Frank Thrower' (Published by L. and S. Smithson, Torrington, 2007)

Sutcliff, Rosemary – 'Blue Remembered Hills: A Recollection' (Oxford University Press, 1984)

'The TARKA TRAIL – An introduction to the 180 mile recreational route' pamphlet (Tarka Country Tourism Association)

Torrington and District Historical Society leaflet – 'Historyngton' – August 2009

Torrington Fairtrade Guide 2011

Torrington – Roscoff Twinning Association file

Vincent, Harold – 'Is the fabric glove trade to die out? A Wail from the West'

Wardman, John – 'The Forgotten Battle: Torrington 1646' (Fire & Steel 350 Ltd, 1996)

Westcote, Thomas – 'A View of Devonshire' c1625-1630 (published at Exeter, 1845)

White's Devonshire Directory 1850

NEWSPAPERS:

Bideford and North Devon Gazette:
13 May 1983 – 'Computer-controlled butter-making at Torrington plant'

Bideford and North Devon Weekly Gazette:
24 August 1937 – opening of library in market hall

The Crier – News and Community Diary for the Torrington Area:
December 2008/January 2009 – 'St Michael's Church Tower Development'
May 2009 – 'The History of Torrington May Fair'
December 2011/January 2012 – 'Abbeyfield in Torrington'
December 2011/January 2012 – 'Vicarage Turkey Oak Tree' by Chris Foster
February 2012 – 'Heritage Museum' by Val Morris

Devon and Exeter Gazette:
7 December 1928 – opening of Rolle Bridge, 1928

Gazette and Advertiser:
12 December 1996 – 'Thanks a million!'
3 November 1999 – 'Market opening makes history'

Guardian:
28 November 1992 – 'Families face jobs void as dairy town is milked by economy'
2 December 2011 – 'Small-town Tory council dumps continental "twins"' by Luke Harding
October 2011 – 'Independent Bookshops Directory'

North Devon Gazette:
27 July 2011 – 'Shop filled with French Goods'
13 July 2011 – 'New walks promoted on the Tarka Trail'
28 December 2011 – 'Cash windfall for Plough'
18 April 2012 – '24-hour swim relay helps struggling club'

North Devon Journal (Herald):
20 August 1914 – departure of the Yeomanry from the drill hall
8 May 1924 – 'Revival of May-Fair'
8 May 1939, 'Torrington Forges Forward'
8 June 1995 – 'Developers set for talks over pannier market' by Rob Baker
22 February 1996 – 'Torrington fights the Civil War again' by Rob Baker
18 December 1997 – 'Optimism over new market' by Stuart Austen
4 June 1998 – 'IT centre to be named for town's unsung inventor' by Stuart Austen
9 July 1998 – article about the Taddiport leper strips by Bill Horner, Devon County Council assistant archaeologist
15 October 1998 – 'Creamery bid co-op gives work start date' by Stuart Austen
4 November 1999 – 'New-look market draws the crowds' by Brian Price
2 May 2002 – 'Service to recall inferno horror of Sydney House' by Emma Pearcy
8 April 2004 – 'Anger over new homes plan for narrow street' by Emma Pearcy
18 August 2005 – 'Residents rage at third building bid' by Adam Wilshaw
13 October 2005 – 'Contentious plan for terrace held up again' by Adam Wilshaw
1 December 2005 – 'Outdoor activities help pupils learn' by Adam Wilshaw
15 June 2006 – 'Sandford's still hot at baking' by Jane Steeples
11 January 2007 – 'Car makes cracking entry' by Laura Churchill
18 September 2008 – Hubba the Dane
7 May 2009 – 'Torridge Vale club celebrates 60th anniversary' by Laura Churchill
25 June 2009 – 'Dairy workers celebrate'
17 September 2009 – article by Ksmith
11 March 2010 – 'Stay local to do shopping'
15 April 2010 – 'Vicar's goodbye after 30 years'
10 June 2010 – 'Owner of ex-creamery site is bust' by Laura Churchill
25 November 2010 – 'Residents complain about "putrid" smell'
27 January 2011 – 'Remembering victims of the Civil War'
17 February 2011 – 'Torrington one of UK top 5 towns' by Eleanor Joslin
17 February 2011 – 'Shoppers say "more choice please"' by Eleanor Joslin
3 March 2011 – 'Lease of café famous for its 45p cup of tea is up for sale'
3 March 2011 – 'Streets are lit up for 10th Taddiport festival'
3 March 2011 – 'Molly follows in family footsteps to be May Queen' by Laura Churchill
26 May 2011 – 'Good citizen award for traders'
14 July 2011 – 'School cuts three teachers'
14 July 2011 – 'Secondary school gets academy OK'
28 July 2011 – 'Children's centre wins praise in Ofsted report'
25 August 2011 – 'New rector will arrive next month'
1 December 2011 – 'New hope for homeless museum'
16 February 2012 – 'Torrington swimming pool set to reopen'

Observer:
21 December 2008 – 'Tradition of French onion farmers in UK under threat' by Elizabeth Day

Western Morning News:
30 December 1936 – 'Windy Cross Restored'
9 January 1964 – 'Torrington' by Rev. G. Frankling Owen
23 September 2010 – 'Crystal is a glass act for others to follow'

WEBSITES:
www.abbeyfieldsouthwest.org.uk
www.carehome.co.uk
www.bbc.co.uk/ww2peopleswar/stories
www.bidefordcatholicchurches.org.uk/torringtoninfo.htm
www.bluecoat.childrencentre.org
www.britishlistedbuildings.co.uk/en-487087-gazebo-at-rosemoor
www.dartingtoncrystal.co.uk
www.dhtb.org.uk/Gazebo.html
www.explorenorthdevon.org
www.gardens-guide.com/gardenpages/_0092.htm
www.great-torrington.com/history/index.html
www.great-torrington.com/to-do-and-see/secret-garden.html
www.great-torring-junior.co.uk
www.great-torrington.org.uk/guide.htm
www.great-torringtoncrier.co.uk
www.greattorrington.devon.sch.uk
www.greattorrington-townhall.org/Town Hall at Risk.htm
www.hatchmoor.co.uk
www.plough-arts.org/mural.php
www.rhs.org.uk/rosemoor
www.tarkavalleyrailway.co.uk
www.theploughartscentre.org.uk
www.therollecanal.co.uk
www.thisisplymouth.co.uk/news/Torrington-Cottage-Hospital-celebrates-centenary
www.torringtonbaptist.org/history/
www.torringtoncommon.co.uk
www.torringtonplayers.com
www.torringtonsilverband.co.uk
www.torrington-1646.co.uk
www.workhouses.org.uk/Torrington
Wikipedia: Torrington, Connecticut; Torrington, Wyoming; Torrington NSW

INDEX

Cockwill, Maurice 46, 139, 159, 179, 182
Cockwill, Nigel 177
coffee tavern 134, 148
Colby, Rev. Frederic 119
Collier, Robert 147
Collingham, Michael 46
Colwill, Harry 244
Common Lake 41, 43, 44, 45, 55
Commons 8, 17, 22, 36, 39, 40-47, 50, 54-57, 61, 66, 90, 96-97, 151, 155-158, 170, 175, 178-179, 181-183, 203, 228-229, 235, 239, 258
Community Development Trust 93, 193, 210, 232-234, 285
Community Hospital 8, 82, 84
Congregational Union 117
Congregationalists 112, 117
Conservative Club 107, 110, 151, 182, 193
Conservators 39, 41, 42, 43, 45, 46, 179, 235
Copp, George 261
Copp, Gwendoline 24
Copp, Janet 25
Copp, John 25
Cordwainers' Chamber 188
Corner House 189, 190, 191
Cornmarket 20, 21, 53, 56, 150, 174, 188
Cornmarket Street 20, 21, 56, 150, 174, 188
Corps of Drums 141, 215
Cory Manor 69
Cosmi-Cuts 131, 132
Cottage Hospital 83, 84, 145, 190, 257, 260
Cotton, Reubin 140
Countess of Richmond and Derby, Lady Margaret 14, 15, 119
Countryside Commission 80
County Library 231
Covety's Well 43
Cow & Gate 248, 249, 250
Cow and Gate 99
Crafty Needles 92
Cramp, Abigail 23
Cramp, Annette 23
Cramp, Dr Harry 43, 94, 112, 140, 189, 256
Cramp, Jennifer 23
Crediton 13, 33, 51, 127, 174, 176
Crockers Court 91
Cromwell 34, 117, 125
Cross House (or 'Cross') 113, 136, 171, 189, 195, 204-205, 208-209, 213
Cross Parks 96
Croxford, Larry 140
Cullen, Leigh 239
Culver House 201

D
D'Alberti, Lisa 128, 167, 175
Dairy Crest 67, 91, 201, 211, 249, 251, 252
Daisy Cottage 89
Dancer, Eric 254

Daniel, Ken and Irene 59
Darch, Doreen 23
Darch family 200
Darch's butchers 136, 276
Darkham Wood 64, 72, 229
Dartington Crystal 8, 67, 68, 102, 103, 105, 106, 107, 141, 160, 252-253, 257
Dartington Fields 103, 134, 257, 258
Dartington Glass 67, 103, 106, 164, 257
Dartington Hall 102, 104
Dartington Hall Trust 102
Dartmoor 11, 71, 80, 161, 170, 172, 181
Dave Ward's electrical shop 136
Davey, Roger 163, 164, 179, 182
Davie, John Chapman 117
Davies, Evan 117
Davies, Miss 190, 191, 247
Davis, Dave 141
DCBA 184, 185
de Groot, Caroline 224
de Merton, Richard, 18
de Toriton 13, 17
de Toriton, William 17
de Tracy, Henry 17
Deane, Elizabeth (niece of Joshua Reynolds), 191
Deane, Luke 65-66, 91
Dedalls Lane 204
Definitely Devon 252
Denys Yonge Trust 192, 204
Designers florist and giftware 135
Devon County Council 52, 56-57, 66, 72, 80, 108, 155, 192-193, 210, 237
Devon Dowsers 35, 224
Devon Historic Buildings Trust 254
Devonshire kerseys 61
Devonshire Regiment of the North Devon Yeomanry 221
Dewslade 42
Dick Baker's Hill 86
Dick Hill's Lane 212
Dippermill 71
Dixon, Philip 7, 45, 66, 123
Doe, Catherine 124
Doe, George 202, 208, 209, 263
Doe, George M. 31, 278
Doe, Misses 134, 173
Doidge, Samuel 194, 196, 247
Domesday 13, 85
Donnacroft 176, 177, 257
Donner, Paul optician 135
Doolan, Ronald 111
Down, John 7, 26, 31, 32, 171, 175, 180
Downing's drapers 135, 271, 273
Downs, Joanna 23
Downs, Kimberly 23
Drake, Geoffrey 111
Drew 113, 116, 203, 209, 235
Drew, Richard 113

X

Notes

Notes

Notes